The Complete Guide to

MID-ATLANTIC GARDENING

Techniques for Growing Landscape & Garden Plants in Rhode Island, Delaware, Maryland, New Jersey, Pennsylvania, eastern Massachusetts, Connecticut, southeastern & northwestern New York

by Lynn Steiner

Creative Publishing
international

MINNEAPOLIS, MINNESOTA
www.creativepub.com

Creative Publishing international

Copyright © 2012
Creative Publishing international, Inc.
400 First Avenue North, Suite 300
Minneapolis, Minnesota 55401
1-800-328-0590
www.creativepub.com

Printed in China

10 9 8 7 6 5 4 3 2 1

Library of Congress Cataloging-in-Publication Data

Steiner, Lynn M., 1958-
 The complete guide to Mid-Atlantic gardening : techniques for growing
landscape & garden plants in Rhode Island, Delaware, Maryland,
New Jersey, Pennsylvania, eastern Massachusetts, Connecticut,
southeastern & northwestern New York / [author, Lynn Steiner].
     p. cm. -- (Complete guide)
 At head of title: Branded by Black & Decker.
 Summary: "Provides a practical approach to gardening for
the novice to intermediate gardener. Includes plant species
descriptions, time-saving techniques and regional information for
the Mid-Atlantic states"--Provided by publisher.
 Includes index.
 ISBN 978-1-58923-651-6 (soft cover)
 1. Gardening--Middle Atlantic States. I. Title. II. Series: Complete
guide (Creative Publishing International)
 SB453.2.M527S74 2012
 635.0974--dc23
                        2011036952

The Complete Guide to Mid-Atlantic Gardening
Created by: The Editors of Creative Publishing international, Inc., in cooperation with Black & Decker.
Black & Decker® is a trademark of The Black & Decker Corporation and is used under license.

President/CEO: Ken Fund
Group Publisher: Bryan Trandem

Home Improvement Group

Associate Publisher: Mark Johanson
Managing Editor: Tracy Stanley
Editor: Jordan Wiklund

Creative Director: Michele Lanci
Art Direction/Design: Brad Springer, James Kegley, Kim Winscher,
    Brenda Canales

Lead Photographer: Corean Kormarec
Set Builder: James Parmeter
Production Managers: Laura Hokkanen, Linda Halls

Author: Lynn Steiner
Page Layout Artist: Mighty Media
Shop Help: Mary Archer
Proofreader: Samantha Johnson

NOTICE TO READERS

For safety, use caution, care, and good judgment when following the procedures described in this book. The publisher and Black & Decker cannot assume responsibility for any damage to property or injury to persons as a result of misuse of the information provided.

The techniques shown in this book are general techniques for various applications. In some instances, additional techniques not shown in this book may be required. Always follow manufacturers' instructions included with products, since deviating from the directions may void warranties. The projects in this book vary widely as to skill levels required: some may not be appropriate for all do-it-yourselfers, and some may require professional help.

Consult your local building department for information on building permits, codes, and other laws as they apply to your project.

CONTENTS

THE COMPLETE GUIDE TO MID-ATLANTIC GARDENING

CONTENTS *Continued*

About this Book

Just like North America is made up of many different types of people, it is also made up of many different plant-growing regions. And just as you can often tell where a person comes from by the way they dress, speak, or act, you can often tell where a plant comes from by the way it looks and how it grows. This book is all about celebrating the region where you live and enjoying the unique gardening opportunities it has to offer.

You'll find many benefits to be reaped from tending a home garden. Not only will you add beauty to your landscape and neighborhood, you will increase the value of your property and improve your quality of life.

Gardening allows you to mix relaxation with beneficial outdoor activity while providing an outlet to relieve stress. When you add vegetables and herbs to your garden, you will also reap the additional health benefits you get from growing your own food.

In addition to providing you with a place to relax and spend time with friends and family, your garden can also help preserve part of your region's plant heritage. When populated with regional plants, your gardens will provide food and habitat for native fauna, especially beneficial insects and birds and butterflies. Native pollinating insects rely on regional plants for food and nectar, and gardens are becoming more and more important in this process as natural plant habitats are lost.

This book is intended for anyone who wants to take a more regional approach to his or her gardening. Maybe you've just purchased your first house and you are looking to spruce it up. Maybe you're finally ready to make the commitment to growing your own food and want to know how to get started. Maybe you're looking to install your first perennial border. Or maybe you've inherited an overgrown landscape and need to know how to get it back in shape.

Whether you garden a tiny city lot or a sprawling country estate, you'll find this book is just what you need to get started and to sharpen your skills. The pages are packed with practical information and hundreds of step-by-step photos to take you through the basic techniques involved in all major aspects of gardening. The information is designed to help you become a responsible and sustainable gardener so you can complement your natural surroundings. Priority is put on choosing the right plant for the right place so you can reduce or eliminate your need for chemical fertilizers, pesticides, and watering, as well as on choosing plants that are beneficial to native pollinating insects and birds.

A Garden of Your Own

The Mid-Atlantic was once dominated by stately, shaded forests, ranging from the dense shade of maples and basswoods to the more open shade provided by oaks. The towering Appalachian Mountains give way to rolling hills and rounded summits, and then to miles of jagged coastline. Scattered throughout was a mosaic of plant communities, including wetlands, open sunny grasslands, and partially-shaded barrens. All of these habitats provide inspiration for gardeners in this area to celebrate their plant heritage and create special places of their own—places where they feel comfortable, surrounded by plants reflecting their heritage and the people who have come before them.

Gardeners in the Mid-Atlantic have all four seasons to contend with. Each year, the welcome new growth of spring glides into lush summer gardens filled with a brash show of color. Fall brings a more diffused, but just as showy, color palette—one last gasp before the subtlety of winter returns. Gardening heightens our awareness of these seasons and allows us to experience them in all their glory in our own yards.

This region's unique climate, geography, and natural features make it a special place to tend a plot of land.

    The climate of this region provides enough natural moisture, sunlight, and summer warmth to support many types of plants. Soils range from clay to loam to sand, and are generally fertile enough to successfully grow a wide variety of plants without a lot of input.

    But this region also provides many challenges for gardeners. Harsh winter temperatures and late spring frosts or early fall cold snaps can occur unexpectedly and be devastating. This region can also receive long dry spells and periods of torrential, unending rain, both of which can be stressful for plants. By acknowledging these challenges and choosing plants that tolerate, and even thrive, in these conditions, you will be on your way toward a successful garden.

    This book will help you sort through the many plants available and choose the ones that are best suited to your landscape, your growing conditions, and your lifestyle. Plants included in this book were chosen based on their suitability for the climate of the Mid-Atlantic, their availability at local garden centers, and their low maintenance. Many of them are native plants that have evolved in the same growing conditions, and most are resistant to insect and disease problems and adapted to natural rainfall amounts. Many also provide important pollen and food sources for native insects and birds.

Native pollinating insects rely on regional plants for food and nectar sources, and gardens become more and more important for this as more and more natural areas are lost. Here a bee and a swallowtail butterfly both enjoy purple conflowers.

Because your gardens will be filled with plants that are well-adapted to the climate, soil, and temperatures found here, they will be easy to maintain.

Winters can be long in this region, but that doesn't mean they have to be boring. Use shrubs and trees with interesting bark and colorful, persistent fruits, perennials with showy seed heads and foliage, and ornamental grasses to make your landscape attractive year round.

This region boasts beautiful fall color, thanks to the maples and other trees that do well here.

It's important to have fun in your garden. There are no hard-and-fast rules in gardening. Experiment to learn what works best for you and your lifestyle.

The long growing season provides ample opportunity for food gardeners to grow a wide array of vegetables and herbs.

Many beautiful flowering shrubs do well in this region, such as the arrowwood viburnum.

THE BASICS

GETTING OFF TO A STRONG START

Anyone can garden. It may only be a few containers on the deck of your high rise or it may be a large country estate with room for perennial borders, vegetables, and fruit trees. No matter what size your garden is, there are a few basic principles you need to understand to manage it successfully.

This chapter explains some of the basic terminology so you will be able to "talk the talk" when buying plants. You'll get a thorough understanding of the limitations of your climate and your site and learn how to work with what you have. Then you'll learn how to prepare your garden site before you move on to the excitement of choosing which plants to grow and where to grow them.

Once you have mastered the basics, you will be on your way to creating a beautiful garden that enhances your property as well as brings you joy as you tend to it. This border includes easy-to-grow plants such as astilbe, sedum, and cosmos.

"Vinca" is a common name for this showy garden annual (*Catharanthus roseus*), top, as well as for an unrelated perennial groundcover (*Vinca minor*), bottom, that can become invasive in certain situations. A good reason why you can't always rely on common names.

'Goldsturm' is a common cultivar of black-eyed Susan (*Rudbeckia fulgida*). It is good for gardeners to know cultivar names, since this is how many plants are labeled at garden centers.

TALKING THE TALK

One of the most confusing things for new gardeners is understanding the lingo. You may feel like you need to learn a whole new language before you can successfully shop for a plant! Here are a few terms that will be helpful to know as you walk the aisles of a garden center or peruse the pages of a seed catalog. You will also find more terminology defined in specific chapters throughout this book.

Common names are given to plants by the people who use them. Although they are fun and popular, they can be confusing because they often differ in different areas of the country and several plants may share the same common name.

A better name to learn is the **botanical name**, which consists of two parts: genus and species. This name is Latin, which can make for some interesting pronunciations, but each plant has only one correct botanical name and if you use this name, you can be assured of which plant you are getting.

The first part of the two-part botanical name is the **genus**. It indicates a group of plants with similar characteristics, usually flowering and fruiting parts. It is followed by the **species**, which more specifically describes the individual plant. The genus name is capitalized and is followed by the lowercased species name. The two words are usually set in italics or underlined, as compared to the common name which is not.

A **cultivar** ("cultivated variety") is a plant set apart because it has one or more traits that distinguish it from the species. It does not occur naturally but rather is maintained by cultivation. A cultivar name should be placed in single quotes and placed behind the species name or before the common name, but it is not always found this way. Sometimes it is used alone and sometimes it is used as a common, name. And sometimes it is indicated by a "cv." in front of it.

A **hybrid** is a plant that originated from a cross between two species. It is set off by a small "×" before the species name. Hybrids are plants that have been manipulated to have the best qualities of each parent. You can have a cultivar of a hybrid.

Other names gardeners may run across include **patent** and **trademark** names. These are similar to common names but they are patented by the breeder and cannot be used for any other plants. These names are indicated by the symbols ™ or ® and they are not set in single quotes.

Annuals complete their life cycle in one growing season, usually starting out as seeds in spring and dying when a frost hits or they have set seeds and completed their "mission" on this earth. They may reseed, but generally annuals are replanted every year. Examples of annuals include petunias, marigolds, lettuces, and carrots.

Perennials live for more than one growing season, if all goes well, that is! These plants have root systems that survive winters. This term is generally used to describe herbaceous plants, but technically it applies to woody plants as well. Herbaceous perennials have a shorter blooming period than annuals, but they live from year to year. Examples of perennials include hostas, delphiniums, and daylilies, as well as asparagus and sage.

Biennials require two growing seasons to complete their life cycle. Typically they grow leaves the first year and then produce flowers the second season. Examples of biennials include foxglove, hollyhock, and sweet William. They are typically sold as second-year plants that will bloom the year you buy them and are often grouped with annuals.

Herbaceous plants are those that have soft, succulent, nonwoody stems. Annuals, perennials, bulbs, and grasses are herbaceous. They are in contrast to **woody plants**, which have bark or some other hard tissue that persists from year to year. Woody plants include trees, shrubs, and vines, which all grow in diameter from year to year.

Hardy is a relative term. It is generally used to describe plants that can withstand prolonged temperatures at or below freezing without being killed or severely damaged. But in northern areas, hardy can be used to describe plants that survive temperatures below zero or even colder.

Half-hardy plants can tolerate long periods of cold weather, but they may be damaged or killed by frost. They often die to the ground in a freeze but then grow back.

Tender plants are typically tropical plants that are grown as houseplants or annuals in northern climates. They cannot tolerate temperatures below freezing.

Plants can be **evergreen** or **deciduous**. Deciduous plants lose all their leaves at one point, usually in fall, and get a new set, usually in spring. Evergreen plants have leaves that stay green and grow throughout the year. They are typically thought of as needled conifers such as spruces and pines, but there are also "broad-leaved" evergreen plants such as rhododendrons. Some herbaceous plants also remain evergreen throughout the year. All evergreens have their leaves replaced, it's just not all at once like deciduous plants so it is less noticeable.

Dioecious and **monoecious** are terms used to describe where a plant's reproductive parts are found. Plants that have male and female flowers on separate plants are dioecious. Plants that have both flower types on the same plant are monoecious. This is mainly important if you are growing plants that you either want to produce fruits or you don't want to produce fruits. If you want fruits on dioecious plants (i.e. hollies) you need to make sure you plant both male and female plants. If you don't want fruits (i.e. gingko) you want to make sure you only plant a male species.

THE NAME GAME

These are all names for the same plant:

- **Common names:** Red maple, rock maple, scarlet maple, soft maple, swamp maple, water maple
- **Species:** *Acer rubrum*
- **Cultivar:** 'Franksred'
- **Trademark name:** Red Sunset™

Red Sunset™ maple

"Variegated" is a term used to describe plants with leaves that are edged, spotted, or blotched with one or more colors, typically white or yellowish but also shades of red and purple. *Yucca filamentosa* 'Color Guard' is shown here.

ZONING IN

A very important aspect of successful gardening is understanding your climate and the limitations it puts on your gardening endeavors. The United States Department of Agriculture has developed a plant hardiness zone system that you should use as a starting point for plant selection. It is based on average minimum temperatures in an area. The lower the number of the hardiness zone, the more severe the winter climate.

Within your landscape you will most likely have "microclimates;" areas that are more protected or more exposed. For example, the area along a south-facing building may be protected enough to support plants rated one or even two hardiness zones warmer (higher number) than your overall ranking. And an open, exposed area on the north side of your house may be a zone colder (lower number).

If you will be growing tender annuals and vegetables, you will also want to be aware of your first and last frost dates, which in turn determine the length of your growing season. These dates will help you determine when to sow seeds and plant tender plants outside in spring as well as how late in the season you can plant perennials and woody plants. But don't rely solely on the calendar. Frosts can come earlier in autumn or later in spring.

The area along the south side of a building often warms up quite a bit earlier in spring than other areas, so it is a good place to experiment with tender shrubs and other plants that might not normally be hardy in your area.

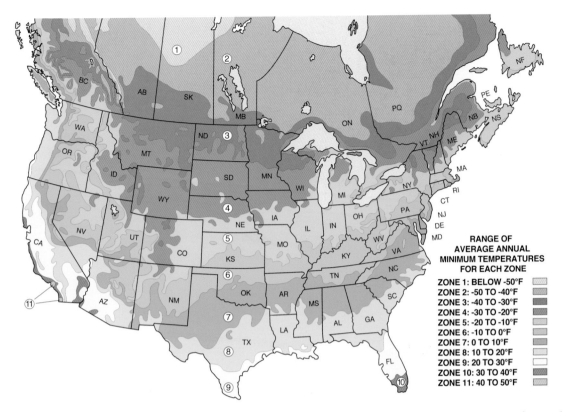

Identify your hardiness zone and use it as a starting point for your plant choices, but do not live and die by your hardiness zone. There are many factors that come into play when it comes to plant survival. Wind, humidity, rainfall amounts, and elevation—as well as age of planting and location in your yard—will affect a plant's ability to survive.

FIRST AND LAST FROST DATES

Here are some average last and first frost dates for selected cities in the Mid-Atlantic region. Use it as a basis to plan your seed starting and planting. Your state university extension service's website is a good place to get more accurate information for your specific area. They usually have frost dates listed with information on vegetable planting.

CITY	LAST FROST DATE	FIRST FROST DATE
Washington, D.C.	April 16	October 21
Philadelphia, PA	April 17	October 25
New York, NY	April 18	October 20
Newark, NJ	April 18	October 20
Hartford, CT	April 26	October 9
Pittsburgh, PA	April 29	October 17
Baltimore, MD	April 30	October 15
Boston, MA	May 1	October 11
Buffalo, NY	May 4	October 10
Providence, RI	May 6	October 3
Scranton, PA	May 14	September 29

GOING UNDERGROUND

Nothing is as crucial to gardening success as having good soil. Unfortunately, a lot of people want to skip this less-glamorous step and move right on to the planting part. Fight the urge. The time and effort you put into making your soil the best it can be will really pay off in the long run in terms of healthier plants, more abundant harvests, and less overall maintenance.

SOIL TEXTURE

Soils typically have four components—sand, silt, clay, and organic matter. The proportions of these ingredients largely determine the soil texture, which in turn determines other soil properties such as fertility, porosity, and water retention. Heavier soils hold more moisture; sandy soils drain faster.

Sand and silt are the chief sources of minerals required by plants, such as potassium, calcium, and phosphorous. Silt particles are smaller and yield their minerals more readily than sand, making silt soils more fertile than sandy soils. Clay particles are the finest in size and a heavy clay soil has reduced pore spaces between the particles. These smaller spaces make it difficult for water, air, and plant roots to penetrate effectively.

Clay soils generally create the greatest problem for gardeners. They tend to stay cold and wet in spring, delaying planting and reducing seed germination. Heavy soils have poor drainage, which can lead to plants drowning due to lack of oxygen. Plants grown in poorly drained soils develop shallow roots and often the crowns will rot over winter. The best thing you can do to improve heavy soils is to add abundant organic matter. You can also use raised beds (see chapter 3).

Organic matter, also known as humus, is decomposing plant or animal material. It is an important component of soils and must not be overlooked. Organic matter determines a soil's capacity to produce nitrogen, supports the community of soil microorganisms crucial to plant life, and retains bacterial byproducts such as water and carbon dioxide. It also creates a moist, slightly acidic environment critical for the transfer of minerals from soil particles to plants.

A good place to start in understanding your soil is to have it tested by a soil-testing laboratory; check with your local university extension office for labs in your area. A soil test will provide you with information on existing soil texture, pH, and fertility, along with recommendations on what to add to improve it.

Soil Test Report

Sample No.
008
Nitrogen (N)
(ppm)
20

Soil Texture
Sandy Loam

Phosphorus (P)
(ppm)
15

Soil pH
6.8

Potassium (K)
(ppm)
125

Nitrogen (N)
Phosphorus (P)
Potassium (K)
Soil PH

Very Low   Low   Medium   High   Very High

3   4   5   6   7   8   9
Acid   Optimum   Alkaline

Recommendations for Home Lawn: Apply according to the instructions on the fertilizer bag or container. Since meeting the exact amount required for each nutrient will not be possible in most cases, it is more important to apply the amount of nitrogen required and compromise some for phosphate and potash. Grass clippings left on the lawn is a sound practice.

For Vegetable and Flower Gardens: Manure, compost or other forms of organic matter may be added. These amendments provide a good source of trace nutrients and improve soil granulation. Three to five bushels of manure or compost per 100 sq. ft. are recommended.

SOIL FERTILITY

Plants require fifteen or so nutrients for growth and survival. The big three—nitrogen, phosphorous, and potassium—are required in substantial quantities and their presence is used to generally define soil fertility.

Nitrogen ensures normal vegetative growth and a healthy green color. Deficiencies result in stunted plants with a yellowish green color. Excess nitrogen causes rank vegetative growth, often at the expense of flowering and a healthy root system. Nitrogen leaches out of soil easily, and as plants grow and remove nitrogen, more needs to be added to the soil. Phosphorus, important to flowering, fruiting and root development, is more stable in soils than nitrogen and doesn't have to be added unless soil tests indicate a deficiency. Potassium is essential for healthy development of roots and stems. It may need to be added to soils where plants are grown continuously.

Micronutrients necessary for healthy plants include magnesium, manganese, calcium, zinc, copper, iron, sulfur, cobalt, sodium, boron, and iodine. Since they are used in small quantities, most soils have enough for normal plant growth. Deficiencies do occur, however.

If your soil test indicates you are significantly lacking in any of these nutrients, you will want to amend your soil before planting. Your test results should tell you what to add to correct the deficiency.

Good garden soil that is loose, friable, and rich in organic matter is the foundation for successful gardening. Take the necessary time to get it right before planting.

Iron chlorosis, a yellowing of foliage between the leaf veins caused by lack of available iron in the soil, can be a problem in alkaline soils.

SOIL pH

Soil acidity and alkalinity are measured in terms of pH on a scale from 1 to 14. A 7 on the scale indicates the soil is neutral in pH. Lower than 7, the soil is increasingly acidic; higher than 7, it is increasingly alkaline. Soil pH is important because it affects the availability of nutrients necessary for plant growth. Most nutrients are most soluble at a pH between 6 and 7. That is why most plants grow best in "slightly acidic soil."

Most plants tolerate a range of soil pH, but some survive only within a narrow window. It is important to know what these plants these are and to change the soil pH before planting them, if possible. It is possible to change soil pH after planting, but it's not as easy. You can raise soil pH by adding agricultural lime, calcium, or wood ashes (in moderation). To get the desired slightly acidic soil many plants require, lower the soil pH by adding pine-needle or oak-leaf mulch, organic matter, ground oak leaves, or sulfur (in moderation). Here again, your soil test results will provide you with specific amounts of each to add.

THE RIBBON TEST

One way to get a basic idea of your soil texture is to perform a simple ribbon test.

1 Take a handful of soil and dampen it with water until it is moldable, almost like moist putty.

2 Roll the soil into a ball, as if working with cookie dough.

3 Using your thumb and forefinger, gently press the soil until the ball begins to roll out of your closed hand. The ribbon will begin to form, and will eventually break under its own weight. If the soil crumbles and doesn't form a ribbon at all, you have sandy soil.

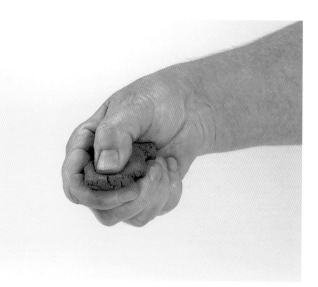

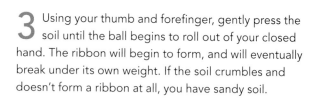

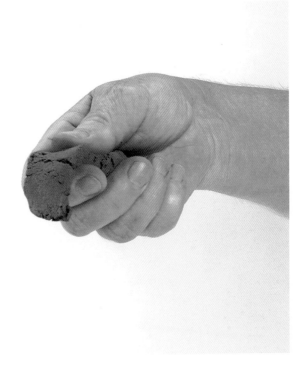

4 If a ribbon more than one inch long forms before it breaks, you have silty soil.

5 If a ribbon 1–2 inches long forms before it breaks, you have clay soil.

6 If a ribbon greater than 2 inches forms before it breaks, you have very heavy and poorly drained soil. It will not be suitable for a garden without some major amendments.

EACH GARDEN HAS ITS OWN SOIL CONDITIONS

Your soil type may be completely different from your neighbor's; gardens close in proximity often have vastly different soil types, with different colors and textures from the outset.

It is difficult to add too much organic matter such as compost, especially if it is partly decomposed. A good goal is to add a layer to established gardens every spring.

IMPROVING YOUR SOIL

A big part of successful gardening is choosing plants that are well suited to your existing soil texture, pH, and moisture conditions. However, if your soil is deficient or has been drastically changed by construction or other factors, do all you can to improve it before planting.

Adding organic matter is the key to improving soil texture, fertility, and pH. Organic matter increases the aeration of clay soils and improves the moisture and nutrient retention of sandy soils. It adds valuable nutrients at a slow and steady pace, and it has a buffering effect on soil pH, helping to keep it in a desirable range.

The best source of organic matter for gardeners is compost. (For information on how to make compost, see chapter 7.) Other good sources of organic matter are composted manure and chopped straw and hay. Avoid using peat-based products as soil amendments. Not only are they expensive and not very effective, but the process of extracting peat from bogs is environmentally harmful to these natural habitats.

As with other amendments, the easiest time to add organic matter is before planting a bed. Loosen the soil with a spade or digging fork to a depth of at least 10 to 12 inches—more if possible. Spread a layer of compost or composted manure 2 to 4 inches deep over the entire bed. Use a fork to mix it thoroughly into your soil. If your soil is very heavy (high in clay), add 2 inches of sharp builder's sand along with the compost or manure. Sand alone will only make matters worse, but when it is added with organic matter to heavy soil, it does help loosen the soil.

CREATING A NEW GARDEN

Gardens fall into two basic categories: beds and borders. Freestanding island beds are intended to be viewed from all sides, so the tallest plants usually go in the middle and the smaller ones around the edges. However, don't be afraid to plant some taller "see through" plants around the outside. Beds are often in some sort of relaxed circular shape, but they can be square or rectangular. They can also be attached to a patio or found along a driveway or sidewalk.

Borders are designed to be viewed mainly from one side. They can have straight or curved edges and they can even turn corners. They are most effective when they have some sort of backdrop to set the plants off. This can come in the form of a fence, wall, or a row of taller, darker plants. Borders can be made up of all the same class of plant (i.e. perennial border, shrub border) or they can be mixed borders, containing perennials, annuals, bulbs, grasses, shrubs, roses, and small trees. Some people even include vegetables and herbs in mixed borders. Because of the diversity of their plants, mixed borders tend to look better year-round than gardens made up of only one plant type.

PROTECTING LARGE TREES

Be careful when preparing a new garden under a large tree. Disturb the soil as little as possible because digging can damage the tree's active surface roots. If you will be installing a garden right under a tree's canopy, it is best to dig an individual planting hole for each plant and add organic matter to the hole as needed, rather than till or dig up the entire area.

These free-standing symmetrical garden beds in the front yard contribute to this home's formal feel.

CREATING A NEW GARDEN BED

Chances are there is already something growing where you want to install your new garden. And chances are it's not desirable vegetation. As tempting as it is, do not just jump right in and start planting, figuring it will be easy to just pull the weeds as you go. Proper site preparation is the key to success. Take the time to get rid of existing vegetation and improve the soil before you start putting plants in the ground. This preparation will pay significant dividends.

1 USE A GARDEN HOSE to outline your new garden.

Use a sun-warmed garden hose to lay out your proposed garden, following the topography of the site. Most gardens look best with gentle curves rather than straight lines.

2 REMOVE EXISTING VEGETATION.

There are several ways to get rid of existing vegetation. Which way you choose depends on how much time you have and how you feel about using herbicides.

OPTION 1 The most natural way to create a new garden bed is to dig it up manually. Just be sure to get rid of all the existing plant roots. Even tiny pieces of tough perennial-weed roots can grow into big bad weeds in no time. A major disadvantage with this method is that you lose substantial amounts of topsoil. To avoid this, if you have the time, you can simply turn the sod over and allow it to decay on site. This will take at least one growing season.

Option 1: Turn sod over

OPTION 2 You can also smother the existing vegetation with about 6 inches of organic mulch such as straw, shredded bark, or compost. Mow closely in spring, cover with a thick layer of newspaper (ten sheets or so) and the organic mulch, and let it stand all summer. Replenish the mulch in fall, and by the next spring your garden should be ready for planting. This method works best on lawn areas rather than areas with lots of deep-rooted perennial weeds.

Option 2: Smother vegetation

OPTION 3 If you don't have a year to prepare the soil or the manual method doesn't appeal to you, you can use a nonselective glycophosphate-based herbicide such as Roundup, which kills tops and roots of herbaceous plants. If you follow directions exactly, aim carefully, and use only when necessary, these products should kill unwanted plants without causing undue harm to the environment. Allow at least 2 weeks for all the vegetation to die after spraying. Tough perennial weeds may require a second application.

Option 3: Spray with herbicide

3 TURN IN SOIL AMENDMENTS to a depth of 6 to 10 inches.

Once the existing vegetation is dead or removed, turn the soil by hand or with a tiller, and add soil amendments. Do not use a tiller without killing all existing vegetation first—it may look like you've created a bare planting area, but all you've done is ground the roots into smaller pieces that will sprout into more plants than you started with. Even after multiple tillings spaced weeks apart, you'll be haunted by these root pieces.

4 EDGE THE GARDEN.

Install edging to keep lawn grasses from invading your garden. The best option is to install a barrier of some type. When it comes to barriers, it's worth paying more for a quality material. Metal edging buried 4 inches or more into the soil effectively keeps turf from sneaking in. If you go with black plastic edging, use contractor grade to avoid having to replace it in a few years.

5 COVER THE NEW GARDEN WITH MULCH.

Mulching your new garden will not only help keep the weeds from settling in, it will also help maintain soil moisture and prevent the soil from washing away until you can get the plants established. Cover the entire prepared garden bed with 2 to 3 inches of an organic mulch such as shredded bark, pine bark nuggets, cocoa bean hulls, and shredded leaves. Avoid using grass clippings; they tend to mat down and become smelly. For information on how much mulch to buy, see chapter 7.

THE SHADY SIDE OF GARDENING

Sunlight is one of the basic requirements for plant survival, but some plants require less than others. Obviously your gardening life will be easier if you choose plants that will thrive in the available sunlight. If possible, observe your proposed garden site at various times of the growing season to determine your available sunlight and then choose plants appropriate for the amount of light your garden gets. Keep in mind that if your garden is large, you may have multiple sunlight levels within the space.

In most cases, shade levels are out of the gardener's control. However, corrective actions like removing a few large tree limbs can bring a heavily shaded area into partial shade, thereby greatly expanding your plant choices. You can also plant shade trees that will eventually increase the amount of shade you have if you wish to plant shade-loving plants in the future.

To some gardeners, shade is a place where grass won't grow and flower choices are limited to impatiens and hostas. Not true! Unless you are growing food crops (vegetables, herbs, fruits), shade is not always a bad thing. First of all, where would you rather be on a hot, sunny summer afternoon? Pulling weeds in a sunny border or taking respite under the canopy of large shade trees? And lower light levels mean fewer weeds—another definite advantage to shade gardening. Best of all, a shade garden or a planting of groundcovers means you can give up the impossible struggle to grow lawn in shady areas.

Dappled shade is produced under open-canopied trees, where there is a moving pattern of sunlight and shade throughout most of the day. Many shade- and sun-loving plants will do fine in this type of light.

The degrees of sunlight and shade change with the growing season. "Full sun" is found in areas with no overhead obstructions where plants will receive six hours or more of direct sun. "Light shade" areas receive bright to full sun for all but a few hours each day. There may be a partial canopy of trees overhead, but they do not shade the area for very long. Areas with bright light or sun for about half the day are called "partial shade" or "medium shade." Most shade plants will do fine in light or partial shade, especially if the sun is morning sun. "Full shade" (also called "dense shade") areas are shaded for most of the day, often under a full canopy of trees, and are suitable for only the most shade-tolerant plants.

Although shade gardens can be formal, the natural growth habits of most shade plants lend them to a more informal setting. Rather than concentrate on individual plants, think in terms of large groupings, allowing flowers and groundcovers to spread and to form natural drifts whenever possible.

DESIGN CONSIDERATIONS FOR A SHADE GARDEN

⊛ When it comes to laying out a shade garden, simplicity, rather than ostentation, is the key. Textures, shapes, and shades of green play important roles—usually more important than flowers.

⊛ Create points of interest to contrast with the sea of summer green by using embellishments such as sculptures, bird baths, or containers of shade-tolerant annuals.

⊛ Take a cue from nature and design your shade garden in layers, with trees as the ceiling, shrubs and small trees creating walls of structure, and groundcovers and perennials forming the carpet.

Bare-root **Container-grown** **Balled-and-burlapped**

Woody plants are available for sale as bare-root, container-grown, or balled-and-burlapped specimens. Bare-root plants (left) are the most economical, but they must be planted during the dormant season, before growth begins. Container-grown plants (center) can be planted anytime during the growing season, as long as you can provide ample water. Balled-and-burlapped specimens (right) are the most expensive way to go, but they are usually larger in size and will fill out a garden quicker.

BUYING PLANTS

Selecting plants for your garden is definitely one of the most fun aspects of gardening. But you should also be practical in your approach. It's a little like furnishing a house: some plants will serve a function and some will be more for accent, but they should all tie together so the end result is a well-designed, functioning "room."

Most annuals and vegetables are sold in cell packs of six to nine plants. Perennials are usually sold in individual pots, which can range in size from 4 inches up to 2 gallons or more. Obviously the larger the container, the larger the root system and the quicker you will get to your desired effect. Many times a perennial in a larger container can be divided into several smaller plants, providing you with more plants for your dollar.

If you can afford it, potted plants are the best way to go with perennials and woody plants. Container plants become established quickly and give you a better looking garden sooner. Your best success will come from plants with a well-established root system. For perennials and ornamental grasses, go with a container size of at least 4 inches; larger if your budget allows. Shrubs and trees should obviously be in containers proportionate to their size.

If cost is a concern or if you are planting a lot of one species such as a hedge or a groundcover, consider using bare-root plants or plugs if you can find them. Plugs are small, cone-shaped pots, usually about 2 inches in diameter and about 5 inches long. They are often sold in six- or nine-packs like annuals. Plugs usually establish themselves rather quickly and do just as well as container plants in the long run. Shrubs and even some trees are available bare-root (without soil) in spring.

STARTING PLANTS FROM SEEDS

Starting your own seeds opens the door to a wide range of species you won't find at local nurseries. It can also save you money. Instead of buying three small pots of your favorite annual, you can buy a pack of seeds for about one-third of the price and get more plants than you can find room for. If properly stored in cool, dry conditions (the refrigerator works fine), many seeds will last 2 years or even more, stretching your investment even farther.

Seeds that germinate and grow quickly can be sown directly outdoors. But many annuals and vegetables require a longer period of time to reach flowering or fruiting and need to be started indoors. Indoor seed starting is a rewarding endeavor, but it does require some specific equipment and space.

Adequate light is crucial to success. Winter sun is usually not strong enough to produce healthy seedlings. You'll need to provide artificial light in the form of an inexpensive shop-light fixture holding two 40-watt fluorescent tubes. Suspend the fixture over a bench or table, making sure you can raise and lower the lights as needed as the plants grow.

You'll also need containers, seed-starting medium, and, of course, seeds. Seeds should be ordered or purchased in late winter. Some seeds need to be sown by mid-January to have garden-sized blooming plants by mid-May. On the other hand, seeds sown too early result in leggy (tall and weak-stemmed) plants that don't transplant well. Your seed packet will list how many weeks to start the seeds before your last frost date.

ORDERING BY MAIL

Mail-order shopping is convenient and provides you with a larger selection of plants. Here are some tips for success:

- Order from a reputable nursery that has a refund or replacement process.
- With perennial plants, order from a nursery with the same climate as you have.
- Order early for a better selection.
- Specify a shipping date so plants don't arrive before you are ready to plant them.
- Unpack plants as soon as they arrive and examine them carefully for any problems.
- Plant as soon as possible after receiving plants. This exception is bare-root plants, which should be soaked in a bucket of water at least an hour before planting.

Make sure any plant you bring home from the nursery has a plant tag in it. This tag provides valuable information you will need for planting. Some gardeners also like to place the tag near their newly planted plant so they can differentiate it from weeds.

STARTING SEEDS INDOORS

1 FILL CONTAINERS to within about a half inch of the top with soilless mix and place in a tray of water to saturate the soil. You want to be sure to use a purchased lightweight, soilless mix that is sterilized and free of disease organisms rather than garden soil, which is usually too heavy, poorly drained, and can contain harmful fungi or bacteria.

**2 CAREFULLY SOW THE SEEDS** on the surface and cover with the appropriate amount of medium.

3 PUT THE CONTAINER IN A PLASTIC BAG
and seal it to maintain humidity. Place the
containers in a warm spot out of direct sunlight. The top
of a refrigerator or freezer works well. Check daily for
germination. You may need to open the bag for a little
while to prevent excessive moisture buildup, which can
lead to damping off.

4 REMOVE THE PLASTIC BAG when the seedlings
first start showing up and place the container under
fluorescent lights, leaving about 1 inch between the tops
of the plants and the light. Adjust the light as needed to
keep it 1 to 3 inches above the seedlings as they grow.

5 WHEN SEEDLINGS HAVE ONE OR TWO SETS
OF LEAVES, use a small, pointed scissors to thin out
excess seedlings. Avoid pulling the unwanted seedlings
because it can uproot nearby seedlings.

6 TRANSPLANT SEEDLINGS into individual pots
when they have two sets of leaves, gently prying
seedlings out of the soil and separating the roots, if
necessary. Place pots back under lights.

GETTING PLANTS IN THE GROUND

In most areas of the country, the best time to put plants in the ground is spring. This gives them ample time to become established before they have to endure their first winter in the ground. Container-grown summer- and fall-blooming flowers and most woody plants can be planted in spring or fall—actually all season long if you are diligent about watering when needed. You may also need to provide shelter from the sun for a few weeks.

Before putting plants in the ground, place container plants in your prepared garden to see the big picture. You may find that you didn't quite buy enough plants to cover your allotted gardening area, in which case you may want to space them farther apart. You may find that you have too many of some plants and need to divide them into other areas of your garden. Some plants have extensive root systems and don't like to be moved once they are established. Careful thought should be given to placing these plants since they don't respond well to transplanting. And always consider the mature height and spread size of trees or shrubs when planting and make sure they won't grow too close to a building, sidewalk, other plants, or up into overhead wires. The new planting may look a bit sparse at first, but it is better than having to uproot mature plants that have overgrown their spots.

Potted plants need to be carefully removed from their containers. If grown in a loose soilless mix, shake off the excess and plant them like bare-root plants. If roots are circling, disentangle them to encourage outward growth. If the root ball is dense, use a sharp knife to cut through some of the roots. Cutting may sound harsh, but the roots must be free to move into the surrounding soil.

Make sure the plants are well-watered in their containers right up until the time they go into the ground. Try to avoid stepping in your garden as much as possible when planting. Start planting in the middle and work outwards. Pull away the mulch and dig a planting hole as deep as the plant's nursery container.

Give your newly planted garden a good soaking right after installation, regardless of the soil moisture levels. You may also want to stick the plant tags next to the plants to help you remember what you planted and differentiate them from weeds.

Your new transplants will require plenty of sprinkling in their first growing season if rainfall is inadequate. Keep soil adequately moist until new perennial plants have a full year of growth. One to two inches of water every three days for the first month is a good measure. If autumn is dry, continue watering until the first hard frost. Once fully established—after three to four years—most woody plants and herbaceous perennials should only require supplemental watering during dry spells.

If you've prepared your soil properly and amended it as needed, newly planted gardens don't need fertilizer. You run the risk of burning the roots and you will also encourage weeds. And there is a very good chance a granular fertilizer will wash away before the tiny plant roots have a chance to take it up.

PLANTS TO AVOID

A walk through the nursery or a look through a nursery catalog may leave you feeling overwhelmed by the list of plants you can include in your gardens. Here are a few tips on how to whittle the list down and avoid planting things that will only cause you more grief down the road.

Avoid including prolific seeders and/or aggressive spreaders, especially in small gardens. While these traits may be appealing when you are just starting out and want to cover a lot of ground quickly, these plants can turn into weeds you'll fight for years to come. It's better to cover bare ground with mulch and add plants as you can afford to or as your existing plants become large enough to divide.

If you really want to raise more aggressive plants, there are some maintenance techniques you can use to keep these plants under control. With a little education you can learn the seedling stages of these plants and be ready to weed some of them out or transplant them as soon as they reach a suitable size. You may also want to deadhead (cut off the mature blossoms) some of the more prolific seeders before they get a chance to set seed. Aggressive plants can be kept in check by digging out some of the encroaching stems and roots each spring or by planting them in large nursery containers sunk into the ground.

Most importantly, avoid any invasive plants that can escape to nearby areas and become pests by crowding out native species, destroying their indigent ecosystems. After land clearing, the invasion of exotic plants is the second greatest threat to our natural areas. This list of potentially invasive exotic plants includes such familiar landscape plants as bugleweed (*Ajuga reptans*), baby's breath (*Gypsophila paniculata*), spotted deadnettle (*Lamium maculatum*), Amur maple (*Acer ginnala*), Norway maple (*Acer platanoides*), tree of heaven (*Ailanthus altissima*), barberries (*Berberis* species), Siberian peashrub (*Caragana arborescens*), burning bush (*Euonymus alatus*), common privet (*Ligustrum vulgare*), and European mountain ash (*Sorbus aucuparia*). For an up-to-date list of invasive plants in your region, refer to the Invasive Plant Atlas of the Unites States at www. invasiveplantatlas.org.

Even though they are pretty, some landscape plants such as purple loosestrife can escape from gardens and establish themselves in natural habitats, causing great harm to native plants and animals.

THE PLANNING STAGE

CREATING YOUR IDEAL GARDEN

For most new gardeners, it is best to start small with an eye on the future. In this chapter you'll learn how to prioritize your needs and how to make the best of your existing site conditions. You'll get some ideas on how to personalize your garden as well as make it attractive and welcoming to anyone else who may visit it.

Start by asking yourself a few questions. Do you want a colorful garden full of flowers? Is growing your own food a priority? Are you looking for a place to relax and enjoy the outdoors? Are you interested in making gardening a hobby, or do you want the lowest possible maintenance? There is no such thing as a no-maintenance garden, but there are many things you can do to greatly reduce the amount of time you have to spend tending your garden.

Are you ready to take the plunge into an exciting new hobby with a goal of planting an exquisite garden filled with year-round beauty? Or do you prefer gardening with minimal care? Whichever it is, gardening is a versatile endeavor and there is a practice of gardening to fit the demands of everyone.

No matter where you live, you can surround yourself with a beautiful garden. Giving a little thought to what you want before you start choosing plants will help bring you down the path to success.

MAKE IT YOUR OWN

Before you get too far along in your planning process, give some thought to a style for your garden. Are you looking for a neat, trim, formal garden or do you prefer a more relaxed, natural-looking garden? Is it important to you that your garden blends into the rest of the neighborhood or do you want to create a spot solely for your own enjoyment? As tempting as it is to go out and start buying plants that appeal to you, the results will be much more pleasing if you think about the overall character of your garden beforehand.

Get ideas from magazines, books, and websites, as well as from public gardens in your area and gardens down the street. Keep in mind the style of your house, but don't be afraid. Any style will work if done correctly and the right plants are chosen. More important is to keep plants in scale with the home, especially trees. Smaller homes call for smaller plants and larger homes need larger plants to balance them.

Give regional consideration to your garden style. It is usually best to stick with plants and a style that is suitable for your area. Not only will it look better, it will also be easier to maintain. A sure way to give your garden a true sense of place and make it look like it belongs in your area is to use plants that are native to your region.

Garden design is a series of choices. Start by understanding your site and what you have to work with and knowing the basic intention of the garden, and work from there to create your own little piece of paradise. Remember that gardening is not just about the end result. It's also about the process, which should be enjoyable as well as provide you with fresh air and exercise.

USING NATIVE PLANTS

Native plants are those species that grew naturally in an area before the greatest influx of European settlement, about the mid-1800s in most areas of North America. Native plants tend to lend themselves to less formal gardens, but many of them can also be used in formal settings as well.

There are many benefits to using native plants. For many gardeners, the initial attraction comes from native plants' reputation of being lower maintenance than a manicured lawn and exotic shrubs. For the most part this is true—provided native plants are given landscape situations that match their cultural requirements. Because they have evolved and adapted to their surroundings, native plants tend to be tolerant of tough conditions such as drought and poor soil and are better adapted to local climatic conditions and better able to resist any negative effects of insects and diseases.

The less tangible—but possibly more important—side of using native plants, is the connection you make with nature. Gardening with natives instills an understanding of our natural world—its cycles, changes, and history. By observing native plants throughout the year, a gardener gains insight into seasonal rhythms and life cycles. You will see an increase in birds, butterflies, and pollinating insects, making your garden a livelier place.

To find out what plants were native in your area, check out your state's Department of Natural Resources website, which often includes a list of native plants or links where you can find them. Your Agricultural Extension office can be helpful as well.

Native plants and natural gardens tend to be more informal and loosely structured, but they can also work fine in smaller, more formal settings with the right plant selection and planting techniques.

TAKING STOCK

Even if you're the type of person who doesn't like to plan everything on paper, you should have some organized approach to your garden. Start with a rough sketch of your property. Identify everything that is on the site, including your home and garage, existing trees and shrubs, driveways, sidewalks, outbuildings, doors, windows, faucets, downspouts, air conditioners, and existing plants and gardens. Pay special attention to overhead wires that can get in the way of trees. And keep in mind city maintenance of roads and sidewalks, especially if they will be salted in winter.

Give thought to where the natural traffic patterns are or will be. No matter how beautiful it is, if a garden is placed where the kids' shortcut to the playground is, it will be doomed. And make sure you know where your property lines are. You don't want to invest hundreds of dollars in a large shade tree only to find you planted it on your neighbor's property. Locate above and below-ground utilities. Here again, you don't want to invest in a large tree or shrub that's going to grow into telephone or electric wires only to have to be pruned drastically or even cut down in its prime. And don't forget to look beyond your own property. Most city and suburban gardeners inherit views from their neighbors, and they aren't always pretty and require some sort of screening. All of these things will help you decide where to place your gardens and what type of gardens you should plant.

STARTING FROM SCRATCH

If you are building a new home, you have the luxury of starting with a clean slate. You can decide where you want your large shade trees and just how much lawn you need. Instead of getting rid of lawn to create a garden, you can simply edge your garden areas and cover them with mulch until you can get around to planting.

Unfortunately, budget constrictions are often a major consideration and all too often the landscape gets put low on the priority list after house details are met. Try to at least give some thought to what you would like to see on your property so you have a working plan that you can develop as time and finances allow. And as tempting as it is, try to avoid planting fast-growing, weak-wooded trees that will often outgrow their space and become a storm hazard after a few years. It is much better to invest in fewer, slower-growing trees that will last several lifetimes and not become major maintenance issues.

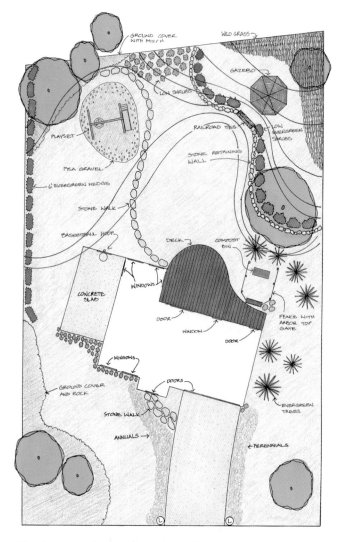

You may want to develop a site map, sort of a "bird's eye view" of your property to help you get a better perspective of what you have to work with. Start by focusing on the broad picture, and then narrow things down into specific areas, or "rooms," in your landscape. Think about the purpose of each room and how best to garden it so you can achieve your goals.

UPDATING AN EXISTING GARDEN

Many people move into an established landscape and have to work within certain parameters already established by the previous homeowner, such as large shade trees, hedges, patios, and fences. If you share their taste and have similar needs, you can pick up where they left off. If you have different goals, you'll need to decide what to keep and what to eventually change.

Trees and shrubs can be valuable assets or formidable obstacles. If they are quality, healthy specimens, you'll probably want to do what you can to incorporate them into your garden plans. However, if they are fast-growing, weak-wooded species, it may be better to have them removed before they get any bigger or come crashing down on your home in a wind storm.

The best gardens look as if they belong on the site and evolved there naturally. Keep this in mind as you look at the overall size of your property and the contours of the land. Think of your garden as part of an outdoor room and keep the purpose of that room in mind. Use trees and shrubs to provide structure and "walls" and groundcovers and paving materials for the "flooring." Fill in with showy perennials and annuals and accent the setting with benches, birdbaths, and other adornments.

DEALING WITH ROAD SALT

Road salt damages plants by interfering with water uptake, which can leads to browning and even death of some plants. If your soil is heavy and your garden is near a road that is salted in winter, you will want to look for plants that can tolerate the conditions. It may also be a good idea to stick with herbaceous plants that go dormant in winter rather than shrubs which are more easily damaged. If your soil is sandy and drains well, the road salt should flush through your soil before your plants start growing in spring.

New homes seldom offer rich, blossoming gardens, prompting contractors to install basic shrubbery and plant life. Here, transplanted shrubs sit on a bed of surrounding mulch, while rosebuds add a splash of color to an expansive lawn and lot. This lawn is ideal for front yard customization with duel rows of garden beds, or the beginning of what will someday be a beautiful wooded lot.

Herbaceous plants are usually a welcome sight, unless they are an aggressive or invasive species. Here again, it's better to remove these problem plants completely before you start any new gardens. If possible, remove these undesirable plants by gently digging them out and covering the bare areas with mulch or planting inexpensive annual plants. Allow nearby plants to fill in, or begin incorporating perennials, grasses, and bulbs that match what you want from your garden. If you have a large area covered with "bad" plants, you'll want to consider one of the techniques for removing existing vegetation described in chapter 1 in the section on creating a new garden.

GARDEN NEEDS CHECKLIST

Gardens can serve a multitude of purposes and solve problems. Here are some things to consider as you plan where to garden and what kind of garden you want. Do you want your garden to:

⊛ Add interest to the front yard
⊛ Provide a place to grow beautiful flowers
⊛ Attract butterflies, birds, and pollinating insects
⊛ Create a boundary
⊛ Hide an unsightly building or foundation
⊛ Provide an accent for a patio or deck
⊛ Create an outdoor room for family activities or entertaining
⊛ Provide fresh vegetables for your family
⊛ Reduce the amount of lawn you have to take care of
⊛ Soften a fence or side of a building

Everyone has functional parts of their landscape, such as garbage bins and alleys, to deal with. A well-designed garden against an attractive screening material goes a long way in making functional areas more attractive.

If you are working with a developed landscape, take note of existing plants and decide what you want to save and what you want to discard. Note which plants seem to be doing well and note their growing conditions. Since many plants are particular about their growing requirements, you'll get clues as to what existing soil and light conditions you have.

ESTABLISHING STRUCTURE

A garden is more than just plants. Most well-designed gardens are complemented by the surrounding hardscape, which consists of elements in your landscape that aren't living. It includes paths, fences, outdoor kitchens, decks, irrigation systems, lighting, patios, fire pits, driveways, arbors, compost bins, and stairways. These structures should be given as much thought as the plants you choose—perhaps even more, since they are permanent and expensive.

Since building hardscapes involves hard work and expense, it is important to get them right. Some things are relatively easy to install and you may want to do them on your own to save money. Outdoor lighting kits make installation a relatively easy task for gardeners with all levels of DIY ability. Drip irrigation systems are within the reach of most do-it-yourselfers. But there are some things it is usually worth paying for to get them done professionally. Brick walkways are very effective in garden design and for getting around, but if incorrectly laid, they can be a detraction and a hazard. Unless you have plumbing experience, have a pro install your underground sprinkler system.

PATHS AND WALKWAYS

Paths and walkways allow access to the inner areas of a garden while reducing the chances for plants to be trampled. Some paths are meant to whisper the way to go; others are meant to shout it. Making a path obvious doesn't mean it has to be boring, however. Bend it around a corner so it disappears for a while, and place plants and stones to break up the sight line of the path edges. Avoid edging the path with rigid rows of plants, stones, or logs, and vary the materials that form the path. Meandering

The hardscape includes functional items such as pathways and benches, as well as accent features such as sculptures and water gardens.

paths look more natural than straight ones. Plant your smaller, more delicate flowers next to paths where they can be seen and enjoyed.

CREATING BOUNDARIES

A good fence or hedge can make a good neighbor if it is in scale with your garden and tall and dense enough to serve its purpose. Evergreen trees or shrubs planted close together will provide you with year-round privacy as well as an attractive backdrop for your garden. You can also use tall perennials and/or grasses if you only need screening during the growing season.

Fences can be made of wood, vinyl, metal, or stone. If you are looking solely for privacy, the first three should work just fine. You can plant vines to soften a metal fence or a row of shrubs in front to screen it. If you are looking for something more decorative, consider a stone wall. They are almost maintenance-free and they give the garden a look of permanence and set off plants nicely.

Decking, fencing, and planter walls are all part of the hardscape of a garden.

INSTALLING HARDSCAPES

BEGINNER	ADVANCED DIYer OR PRO
⊛ Drip irrigation system	⊛ Underground sprinkler system
⊛ Stepping stone pathway	⊛ Brick walkway
⊛ Small garden pond	⊛ Waterfall and large pond
⊛ Wooden deck	⊛ Stone patio
⊛ Simple solar outdoor lighting systems	⊛ Elaborate outdoor lighting systems
⊛ Black plastic garden edging	⊛ Metal garden edging
⊛ Building a simple trellis	⊛ Building and installing a large arbor or pergola
⊛ Installing a metal fence	⊛ Building a rock wall
⊛ Installing a wood retaining wall	⊛ Retaining a hillside with rocks
⊛ Creating spot for your grill	⊛ Outdoor kitchens

Some hardscape projects are easily done by the homeowner. But others, such as rock retaining walls and large ponds, are best left to professionals.

Paths should blend with their surroundings, but they should always be well-set and wide enough for safe use. In this photo, widely spaced stepping stones are interplanted with creeping thyme, a low-growing groundcover that tolerates quite a bit of foot traffic. Other good walkway materials include brick, gravel, wood chips, and even bare soil. Avoid using mulches on sloped pathways. It can easily wash away in heavy downpours.

A dry-stacked stone wall should look like it almost rose right out of the ground. Choose a stone type that is typically found in your region for the most natural look.

Garden ornaments such as pergolas, gazing balls, and benches are a good way for you to personalize your garden.

ACCESSORIZING YOUR GARDEN

Not everything in your hardscape has to be functional. Most gardens benefit from a few accoutrements such as sculpture, fountains, containers, sundials, and gazing balls. Attractive birdhouses and birdbaths will serve double duty as garden ornaments and habitat for birds. Keep in mind, however, that in most cases these items are meant to be accents to the plants. They should compliment the plants and blend in rather than look like they were simply plopped down in the middle of the garden.

1 **PLACE STEPPING STONES** in a desired pathway. Rotating the stones for jaunty angles and asymmetrical lines is an easy way to liven up a backyard path. Stepping stones are available in a wide variety of textures, shapes, and sizes, so take the time to select what's right for your garden. Here, natural stones on turf provide a useful and decorative accent.

2 **ALLOW THE STEPPING STONES TO REMAIN** on the lawn for several days to kill the grass. This provides an outline for excavation and makes turf removal much easier.

PATHWAY VARIETIES

Not all pathways are flat or demand stone. This staircase is made of logs, and is a fine complement to the dense foliage all around. Take care, though—wood is slippery when it is wet. Consider installing a handrail alongside your steps. Use small plants and groundcovers to tie the steps into the path and the rest of the landscape.

3 DIG AROUND THE OUTLINE for each stone and excavate the soil or turf. To allow room for a layer of sand to stabilize the stepping stone, dig each hole 2 inches deeper than the height of the stone. Spread sand in each hole.

4 PLACE STEPPING STONES in sand-filled holes, adding or removing sand until each stepping stone is stable. Sand serves as grout, filling in the small gaps between the hole and the surrounding turf.

MAKING THE MOST OF A SMALL SPACE

Gardening in a small space has its limits, but it need not be limiting. There are actually several advantages. It's much easier to keep up on maintenance, the initial cost is less, and you can pay attention to small details that get lost in larger spaces.

For the most part, small gardens are considered as a whole rather than part of a larger landscape. You can still have small rooms and areas, but everything should tie together and work as one composition. The principles laid out at the beginning of this chapter still apply. Decide what you want to be the main function of your small space (a place for entertaining, play, growing your own food, showcasing as many types of plants as possible) and work from there.

Obviously you won't be able to grow every plant you like, so it's important to start with a plant list and stick with it as much as possible. And also limit your color choices, maybe sticking with two or three main colors for more cohesion. Incorporate various textures within your color palette to increase interest and variety. With fewer plants, every plant will need to serve a purpose and ideally it will offer at least two seasons of interest.

You can use large shade trees, but make sure they are upright and vase-shaped rather than round. Prune them so they provide a nice ceiling but don't have lower branches creating heavy shade. A good alternative is to plant small trees that stay under 45 feet or so. You can also select large shrubs and prune them to small scale.

Since all of your plants will be viewed at close range, it is important they do well where they are planted. Sickly plants will really stand out. They should be removed and replaced with something better suited to the site. Keep up with maintenance and grooming for the same reasons.

BALCONY GARDENING

If you are an apartment dweller with only a balcony to garden outdoors, don't despair. With a few considerations you can turn your balcony into a very attractive and productive small-space garden.

First, you need to think vertically. Do everything you can to encourage plants to grow upward and downward rather than sideways. Install wall shelves and use

Urban gardeners often have to garden within the confines of courtyards, but they can still create a beautiful spot that serves a purpose as well as becomes a showplace for a variety of plants.

There are a few things to keep in mind when gardening in a small space. Dwarf cultivars of shrubs are good choices, as well as limiting your color palette. While this small city backyard garden includes a lot of plants, the color palette is limited to white flowers and plants with interesting foliage characteristics.

trellises against a wall to train plants upward. Vining plants can grow down to cover your balcony edges.

Grow bags hang off the ground and have multiple holes in the front where you can plant annuals or small vegetables such as lettuces and herbs. These bags can be hung on the outside of your balcony railings to gain space. Another way to gain space is to raise your taller plants off the ground and place them on benches or plant stands and use the remaining space beneath them for smaller vegetables, herbs, salad greens, and flowers.

On the practical side, keep in mind the weight your balcony can bear. Large containers full of soil can be quite heavy so you may want to stick with lightweight container materials, such as plastic. Also consider container drainage. You don't want an angry neighbor below you because you've allowed water to drip down onto their balcony. Access to water is another consideration. Consider purchasing a hose that can connect to your kitchen sink and allow you to water plants on your balcony.

THE UPSIDE OF SMALL GARDENS

- You are usually only dealing with one "room" rather than several, making design easier.
- It takes fewer plants to make a dramatic effect.
- Maintenance is easier.
- It's easy to create intimacy and define a space.
- Since you need less, you can afford more interesting plants and higher quality hardscape materials and ornaments.
- If your tastes change as your gardening evolves, it's much easier to rework the space.

As with all small-space gardening, be sure to keep your balcony garden plants healthy and well-groomed. This will not only make them look better, but reduce your chances of insect or disease infestations, which can be devastating to a balcony garden and very difficult to control.

GARDENING UP FRONT

When thinking about a place for your garden, don't overlook the front yard. There's no law that says your front yard has to be planted in turfgrasses and look like every other front yard on the block. This is a great way for space-starved gardeners to find room for all the plants they want to grow. On many properties it is the area best suited to gardening. And it's a great gift to your neighbors and passersby.

However, there are a few things to consider before tearing up your front yard. The front yard probably isn't the best place for your vegetable garden, but you can certainly feel free to integrate a few edibles into any garden. Proper plant selection and good maintenance are vital. Nothing will set your neighbors off faster than if you dig up the front yard one day and let it be taken over by weeds while you wait for plants to fill in.

BOULEVARD GARDENING

There are many reasons to garden on boulevards. From a gardening standpoint, they offer extended opportunities for space-starved urban gardeners. From an

In a front yard dominated by a large shade tree, a garden of shade-loving plants is often a much better alternative to the struggle of trying to grow traditional turfgrasses.

environmental standpoint, they can be very effective at keeping grass clippings out of the street and storm sewers. But boulevards are among the most challenging spots to grow and maintain plants. The soil is usually compacted and low in fertility and often gets bombarded with road salt in winter. They are usually hot, dry and sunny—unpleasant conditions for tending, and often the garden hose doesn't reach that far, creating maintenance issues. Consequently, most boulevards remain covered with poorly grown turfgrasses or weeds.

TIPS FOR BOULEVARD GARDENING

- Good soil drainage is key since you need the water to percolate down rather than run off.
- Keep your soil line slightly below the sidewalk and curb heights to make sure no soil washes away.
- It's usually best to stick with low-growing clumping plants, but wider boulevards can handle shrubs and even small trees.
- Make sure your plants don't block people's ability to see at intersections.
- Stay away from prolific self seeders; even a couple extra plants can make this small space look weedy.

Boulevard strips, or tree lawns as they are sometimes called, are the narrow areas between the sidewalk and the street. As prevalent as they are in urban landscapes, boulevards are often neglected when it comes to gardening. This is unfortunate since they are in plain view of anyone who visits or passes by on the sidewalk.

There's no rule that says a front yard has to be planted in lawn grasses. A neat, well-maintained planting of groundcovers, shrubs, and perennials can be just as effective and usually requires much less maintenance.

A few other things to keep in mind: Any plant growing over a foot in height will probably need to be cut back in fall, and plan on cutting back any remaining plants in spring and raking off the debris. Be aware of any city ordinances that govern boulevards. In most communities, homeowners own the space between the sidewalk and the street but the city has the legal right to enter this utility-filled area. Be aware that the city may need to dig up the boulevard or sidewalk to repair and upgrade utilities and you will be responsible for repairing any damage. Some cities also put height restrictions on boulevard plants.

GOING TO POTS

Whether you do it out of necessity or as an additional way to grow plants, container gardening is limited only by your imagination. It is an option open to anyone who wants an enjoyable and creative way to exercise a green thumb. It can range from a patio surrounded by large terra cotta pots filled with a mixture of perennials, annuals, and even shrubs to a simple pot of herbs on the deck. For space-starved gardeners or those with limited sunlight, it can provide a way to grow several different types of vegetables. And container gardens

ENTRY GARDENS

The entrance to your home should be easy to spot, welcoming, and safe for arriving guests. Here are some tips for a successful entry garden:

◉ Keep it clean of debris; avoid plants that produce fruits or nuts that fall and can become slipping hazards.

◉ Edge the walkway with low-growing plants to make the path feel wider.

◉ Install outdoor lighting.

◉ If you have room, add a bench or small table where people can rest or set packages.

◉ Use brightly colored plants to draw attention to the entry. Guests shouldn't have to wonder where it is.

◉ Make sure your paving material is safe to walk on, even when wet.

◉ Do not use mulch on paths near entryways. It is too easily tracked indoors on shoes.

Plants along a front walkway should be low and mounding so they do not tower over visitors using the front door.

don't just have to sit on the deck or patio. Hanging baskets and wall planters are also options.

One often-overlooked benefit of container gardens is the portability. You can grow showy annuals in a container in the sunlight and then move them into a shady patio or deck garden when you entertain, just as you would move a bouquet of flowers onto your dining room table indoors. The container can be moved back into the sunlight after a few days to continue growing. Along the same lines, a few containers can be used in a perennial border to perk up areas going through a "dry spell" in terms of color. When other things come into bloom the containers can be moved to brighten up other areas.

Container gardens are easy to change out with the seasons. You can start with a pot of spring bulbs, move on to a show of annuals, get through the fall with mums, ornamental kale, and pansies, and then go through the winter with evergreens and showy seedpods and dried flowers.

Remember that houseplants make good container plants as well. Many enjoy "vacationing" outside for the summer where they can soak up the extra humidity. Just make sure to acclimate them gradually and don't put them out until after all danger of spring frost is past and temperatures are consistently in the 50s at night.

Even if you don't have room to plant a full-sized garden, you can get the same effect by grouping containers. This deck grouping includes hot-colored gazania flowers, the bold, tropical leaves of a dark purple canna, and an ornamental grass for textural contrast.

CONTAINER TYPES

Plastic pots are inexpensive and easy to move, but they usually only last one or two gardening seasons.

Plants grow well in **terra cotta pots** but they dry out rapidly and may need daily water checks.

Glazed ceramic pots are good choices if they have several drainage holes.

Wooden containers are inclined to rot. Redwood and cedar are more rot-resistant and can be used without staining or painting. Avoid wood treated with creosote, penta, or other toxic compounds.

TIP: Be sure the container is large enough. Small pots restrict the root area and dry out very quickly. The size and number of plants to be grown will determine the size of the container used.

PRACTICAL ASPECTS
OF CONTAINER GARDENING

Start container gardening by analyzing your available sunlight and choosing plants that will grow well in your conditions. Your planting medium needs to drain readily so the roots don't rot, while retaining enough moisture that you don't need to be watering all the time.

A sterilized soilless mixture is a good choice for most container gardens. Regular garden soil is usually too heavy and there is a high risk it contains soil-borne diseases and weed seeds that will wreak havoc in a container. Common ingredients in soilless mixes are peat moss, ground wood or pine bark, sand, perlite, and vermiculite, and some have a slow-release fertilizer and limestone added to them. If you will be growing perennial plants or vegetables in containers, it is a good idea to add some bagged compost or manure to get a richer, heavier soil.

Your container will require regular fertilization. A good rule of thumb is to use a diluted liquid fertilizer about every 2 weeks. If you applied a slow-release granular

Annuals aren't the only plants that do well in containers. Dwarf shrubs, succulents, and herbs all make interesting container plants.

WINDOW BOXES

Window boxes bring a charming, old-fashioned look to a home. To be successful, they require a slightly different approach than regular containers.

When it comes to plant selection, you need to be aware of the long, narrow shape. A row of annuals all the same height looks boring and unnatural. A better plan is to stagger a mixture of two or three types of plants, generally placing taller plants in back and shorter plants in the middle and front. Allow trailing plants to spill over the front and sides and don't be afraid to include a climbing plant to add additional height. But don't go overboard and completely block the view from inside the house!

Other issues to consider when selecting plants: Unlike most container gardens, window boxes are usually viewed at eye level and from only one side. Because they are right up against the house, air circulation is greatly reduced and the risk of disease problems increases. Due to their location, window boxes can be difficult to water.

Lastly, keep in mind the added weight of the box filled with wet soil and make sure to securely fasten the box to studs inside the house or garage wall.

Create a mini cottage garden by planting a window box with a variety of annuals. This one includes blue salvia, petunia, Dahlberg daisy, and ivy geranium.

fertilizer at planting time, you may not need to do any supplemental fertilizing. It all depends on what you are growing. Many traditional annuals and perennials will be fine with a one-time granular application. Most of the newer annuals and perennials and vegetables in containers will need additional applications. And some plants, such as evergreen shrubs, will require an acid-based fertilizer to do well.

Containers can dry out quickly, especially those in full sun. In hot, dry weather your containers may need to be watered daily. Do not place saucers under containers as you would indoors. You want the water to drain freely. Place containers on bricks or blocks to elevate them and allow free drainage.

There are many choices when it comes to the container to use, ranging from plastic to ceramic to terra cotta to wood. Plant roots need adequate room to grow, so make sure your container is large enough. It must also have adequate drainage holes. After that, let your creative juices flow!

1 **CHOOSE A CONTAINER** with at least one drainage hole in the bottom so excess water can escape. Cover the drainage holes with a few layers of newspaper to prevent the soil from washing out. If your container is large, you may want to consider a layer of pot shards or some other loose material to reduce the amount of potting mix you need to use.

2 **FILL THE CONTAINER** about half full with planting mix. Add a slow-release fertilizer according to package directions, and then add enough additional mix to come within about an inch of the rim.

3 EXPERIMENT WITH THE DESIGN while plants are still in their containers. Place the tallest plant in the center and fill around it with lower-growing plants. Plant trailing plants near the perimeter.

4 STARTING WITH THE MIDDLE PLANTS and working outward, remove the plants from their pots and plant them, keeping the soil level about an inch below the container rim to allow for watering. Water well once all of the plants are set.

FIT TO EAT

GROWING VEGETABLES AND HERBS

Growing your own food is a very rewarding experience. Whether you have a single tomato plant on your deck or a large garden full of vegetables and herbs, food you grow yourself will be fresher and usually better-tasting than what you can buy at the supermarket. Growing your own food crops also allows you to taste many more varieties of vegetables and herbs than can be found at commercial outlets. And, you will be able to enjoy organically-grown foods for a fraction of what they cost at the supermarket.

Your vegetable gardening will only be successful if you choose varieties suitable to your climate, plant them properly, provide the correct growing conditions, and harvest at the right time. This chapter will outline the basics, providing you with enough information to have a simple yet productive garden. With a little experience under your belt, you'll be able to move on to new varieties and growing techniques, as well as some of the more challenging vegetables and herbs.

Growing your own organic vegetables and herbs is easy if you start with the right varieties and provide the proper growing conditions.

PLANNING AND PREPARING YOUR GARDEN

HOW BIG?

The biggest mistake made by beginning vegetable gardeners is starting too big. By midsummer, they are overwhelmed by the tasks at hand and discouragement and guilt set in. Food gardening should be just as much fun as ornamental gardening—even more if you enjoy cooking and eating fresh vegetables and herbs. Start with a single raised bed or a small garden patch that is approximately 12 by 12 feet in dimension. Plan for expansion so you can add beds or increase the size of your garden as your skills improve.

Most vegetable gardens are square or rectangular in shape, but there's no rule that says they have to be.

WHERE?

Most vegetables and herbs require full sun to do well. Place your garden in a spot that receives at least 6 hours of sunlight a day. Remember that buildings, not just trees, provide shade, especially in spring and fall when the sun is lower in the sky. Buildings can also block breezes, hindering wind pollination and increasing the chances of disease due to poor air circulation. On the other hand, exposed sites without a windbreak of some type will probably be too harsh.

The closer you can place the garden to your kitchen door, the more likely you are to tend it and harvest from it. A garden out of sight can quickly become a garden out of control. Keep in mind that you can grow vegetables and herbs in more than one spot, and some of these plants can even be incorporated into your ornamental gardens.

PATHWAYS

Pathways are extremely important in the vegetable garden. They need to be wide enough to allow for foot traffic as well as wheelbarrows and garden carts. What looks like a sufficient path in spring can become overgrown and congested by summer.

Kitchen-door gardens are an especially good place for herbs, where the cook can easily snip a few fresh sprigs as needed.

PRETTY & TASTY

Edible landscaping is an attractive way to increase the amount of space you have to grow food. It could include planting fruit- and nut-bearing trees and shrubs, or tucking in a pepper plant among your flowers, or edging a walkway with herbs.

In addition to having attractive edible flowers or fruits, plants chosen for edible landscaping should have attractive foliage and an interesting and somewhat controllable growth habit. Examples of effective edible landscaping: fruit trees used as ornamentals; fruit-and nut-bearing shrubs; herbs and vegetables in flower gardens; grapes and kiwis as vines; strawberries and creeping thyme as groundcovers.

In this fine example of edible landscaping, tomatoes, parsley, rosemary, and strawberries grow alongside dahlias and other ornamentals. The nasturtium planted in the foreground has edible leaves and flowers and the hops vine overhead will be useful to home brewers.

In addition to being very handy, well-designed raised beds can also become an attractive part of a garden.

Paths can be permanent or temporary and made of inorganic or organic materials, including bare soil. Bricks, concrete, or stone can be used for permanent pathways. Organic path materials include leaves, sawdust, wood chips, grass clippings, and aged straw. Just be sure your covering material is spread thick enough to exclude weeds and is comfortable enough to walk on.

RAISED BEDS

Raised beds are good choices for growing vegetables and herbs, especially where soil conditions or drainage problems make gardening difficult. Raised beds allow you to create a rich, well-drained soil in any area. Raised beds also warm up earlier in spring, allowing for earlier planting. They are easier to tend and weed, as long as they aren't too wide. And, they look nice!

A raised bed can range from a simple mound of soil to an elaborate bed framed with wood, plastic, or concrete blocks. Raised beds created by hilling up soil are inexpensive and it's easy to change their sizes and shapes. The downside is that they have to be built every year, which can be quite a bit of back-breaking work each spring.

Permanent enclosed raised beds cost more up front, but most gardeners find they are worth the investment because they require less maintenance and are easier to tend. Soil in raised beds does not get compacted from foot traffic so the soil tends to stay loose and is better for root growth. You'll find fewer weeds in enclosed raised beds and they are easier to tend because they are up off the ground.

Raised beds should be no wider than 4 feet to allow you to easily reach from one side to the middle without stepping inside. Orient your beds north to south, if possible, to maximize sun exposure. If you are using wood, be sure to use a naturally long-lived wood such as cedar or redwood. Avoid using treated wood where you will be growing food crops. If you are plagued by gophers or moles, you can line the bottom of your bed with wide-mesh hardware cloth to create a barrier. A weed barrier fabric may be laid at the bed base to help control weeds.

WHEN SUN IS IN SHORT SUPPLY

Most vegetables and herbs require at least 6 hours of sunlight to do well. Here are a few plants that will succeed on less than 6 hours a day, though yields and fruit sizes may be smaller.

- Arugula
- Beet
- Broccoli
- Cabbage
- Carrot
- Chervil
- Chinese cabbage
- Chives
- Kale
- Leaf lettuce
- Mint
- Parsley
- Pea
- Radish
- Scallion or green onion
- Spinach
- Swiss chard
- Turnip

BUILDING A SIMPLE RAISED BED

1 CUT THE WOOD and assemble the frame upside down on a flat surface. Drive deck screws through pilot holes at the corners.

2 REINFORCE THE CORNERS by nailing metal corner brace hardware. Use galvanized joist hanger nails to fasten the braces.

3 POSITION THE BED FRAME in your garden location. Bury the bottom at least 2 inches below grade.

4 FILL THE BED with a suitable planting soil and rake smooth. The surface of the soil should be at least an inch or two below the top edges of the frame.

CONTAINER GARDENING

There are several vegetables and herbs that do well in containers. Just make sure your container has good drainage, is heavy enough that it won't topple in the wind, and is large enough to support the root systems of your plants. Lettuces and other greens can get by in 6 inches of soil, but root crops like carrots need at least a foot of soil. Black nursery containers are good practical choices, but you can also use more-attractive ceramic and terra cotta containers.

Just about any vegetable and most herbs can be grown in a container, especially bush-type varieties. But you will have better luck with compact varieties that were specifically bred for container use. Here are some to consider:

- Bean: 'Bush Blue Lake', 'Tender Crop', 'Derby'
- Beet: 'Little Ball', 'Little Egypt', 'Ruby Queen'
- Broccoli: 'Green Comet', 'Dandy Early'
- Cabbage: 'Minicole', 'Fast Ball', 'Flash'
- Carrot: 'Little Finger', 'Thumbelina', 'Baby Spike'
- Cauliflower: 'Early Snowball'
- Cucumber: 'Spacemaster', 'Salad Bush', 'Bush Champion'
- Eggplant: 'Dusky', 'Morden Midget', 'Bambino'
- Kale: any variety
- Lettuce: 'Salad Bowl', 'Buttercrunch', 'Little Gem'
- Melon: 'Minnesota Midget'
- Pea: 'Little Marvel', 'Early Patio', 'Snowbird'
- Pepper: any variety
- Radish: 'Cherry Belle', 'Early Scarlet', 'Sparkler'
- Spinach: any variety
- Summer Squash: 'Scallopini', 'Gold Rush', 'Peter Pan'
- Swiss Chard: any variety
- Tomato: 'Patio', 'Tiny Tim', 'Sweet 100 Patio', 'Burpee's Pixie'
- Turnip: any variety

One of the best things about growing vegetables in containers is the lowered need to weed, but you will need to do plenty of watering.

DECIDING WHAT TO GROW

There are many factors to consider when deciding what and how much to grow in your vegetable garden. Usually the main limiting factor is the size of your garden, but you must also limit yourself to things that will do well in your climate. For this you need to know the length of your growing season, which is the average number of days from the last spring frost to the first frost in autumn. (For more information on this, see chapter 1.) Seed packets will list the typical number of growing days required for a variety, either from seeding or from the transplanting date.

In addition to the more practical matters, you should also consider your family's likes and dislikes. No sense wasting time and space on cabbage and Swiss chard if no one's going to eat them. Also consider what is worth growing yourself and what may be just as easily bought at your local farmers' market and for a better price. Some crops, such as sweet corn and potatoes, taste great fresh from the garden but require a lot of space to get enough to make a meal. On the other hand, one zucchini plant is usually all you need for an entire family—and many neighbors!

The number of vegetable varieties available for your garden is almost endless, and it can be quite overwhelming to try to decide what to grow. It is a good idea to start with varieties that have shown to do well in your geographic area. The plant list at the end of this chapter lists recommended varieties. State and county extension websites often have lists of recommended varieties. Also, talk to your neighbors and ask them what they are growing.

What you decide to grow will depend on the size of your garden, what your family likes to eat, and how much time you want to spend tending your garden.

DECIDING WHICH TOMATOES TO GROW

There are many choices to make when selecting tomatoes. Here are some things to consider.

FRUIT COLOR
- Red
- Orange
- Pink
- Yellow
- Green
- Bicolor
- Streaked

FRUIT SHAPE
- Large
- Small
- Round
- Flattened
- Elongated

USE
- All-purpose
- Salad
- Slicing
- Canning
- Paste or sauce
- Juice
- Stuffing

SIZE OR CLASS
- **Beefsteak** or very large types
- **Medium** or standard types
- **Paste**, **plum**, or **pear** types
- **Cherry** types

BREEDING
- **Hybrid** types are usually more productive and many have enhanced disease resistance.
- **Open-pollinated** types come true from seed and many are locally adapted to a certain region.
- **Heirloom** types are open-pollinated varieties that have been around for many years.

GROWTH HABIT
- **Indeterminate** types continue to grow in length and produce fruits until the vines die. They should be staked or trained to some type of support.
- **Determinate** types stop growing at a certain point and tend to produce their fruits in a more concentrated time. Most types do not require support.
- **Dwarf** types have short stems and smaller fruits and are good for container use or small spaces.

DAYS TO MATURITY
- **Early** types mature in 65 days or less from the time they are transplanted.
- **Midseason** types require 66 to 79 days.
- **Late** season types require 80 days or more.

DISEASE RESISTANCE
Tomatoes are susceptible to many diseases. Cultivars that have resistance to certain diseases will have the following letters in their name or in their descriptions.

- **V** Verticillium wilt
- **F** Fusarium wilt
- **N** Nematodes
- **A** Alternaria
- **As** Alternaria stem canker
- **L** Gray Leaf Spot
- **T** Tobacco mosaic virus

There are thousands of tomato varieties to choose from and they come in many colors, shapes, and sizes. Start by choosing one suitable for your climate and the length of your growing season.

Another consideration when deciding what varieties to grow is resistance to disease and insects. Breeders have developed cultivars that are resistant to most major diseases, such as leaf spots, wilts, and mildews, as well as many insect pests. If you are plagued with a certain problem, or if you just want to avoid potential problems, look for selections that are "resistant" or at least "tolerant" of problems.

A PLANTING PLAN

Once you've figured out what you want to grow, it's time to figure out where to plant it. It's a good idea to develop a blank master plan of your vegetable garden that you can easily carry out to the garden with you. Outline your garden to scale, draw in the beds, and note any perennial vegetables or permanent structures. Make a new photocopy each year and pencil in what you planted, where you planted it, and the dates you planted it. This will make it easy for you to practice crop rotation from year to year, which is very important in reducing pest problems in vegetable gardens. You can transfer your information to a computer database so that you can sort and organize your data, making it even more useful.

GROWING HEIRLOOMS

Heirloom varieties are open-pollinated varieties that have been around for many years, at least 50 but often 100 or more. Many have been handed down from one family member to another for many generations. They often have distinct characteristics not found in today's modern cultivars, such as intense flavor or interesting colors. They are becoming more and more readily available in traditional seed catalogs and are widely available from specialty growers. The major downside of heirlooms is their lack of resistance to diseases and insect pests.

Here are a few heirlooms to try:

- Bean 'Kentucky Wonder'
- Cabbage 'Early Jersey Wakefield'
- Corn 'Golden Bantam'
- Cucumber 'Improved Long Green'
- Lettuce 'Paris White Cos'
- Lettuce 'Tennis Ball'
- Muskmelon 'Jenny Lind'
- Radish 'French Breakfast'
- Squash 'Blue Hubbard'
- Tomato 'Brandywine'

'Blue Hubbard' heirloom winter squash was introduced in 1909 and is still a good choice for many gardens.

PLANTING YOUR GARDEN

Prepare the garden bed as described in chapter 1, removing all existing vegetation and amending soil as needed based on a soil test. Most vegetables do best in a well-drained soil rich in organic matter. Take the time to get the soil right before planting. Since vegetables are heavy feeders, plan to amend the soil with compost or fertilizer every year.

TIMING

Vegetable gardens require close attention to planting dates. You can't just plant your entire garden in one day each spring. And many crops require successive sowings throughout the growing season to ensure a continual harvest.

Cool-season vegetables, such as cabbage, broccoli, and lettuce, require cool temperatures to do well and many actually have better quality when grown in cool weather; it's said that the frost "sweetens" their fruit. They will languish in the heat of summer. They should be planted in early to midspring and again in mid- to late summer for a fall or winter crop. Warm-season vegetables, such as tomatoes,

PERENNIAL VEGETABLES

Most vegetables are annuals that you plant in spring and pull out in fall. There are a few vegetables, however, that are hardy perennials. If you want to include them in your garden, you must find a permanent spot for them where they can grow undisturbed for many years. They are all ornamental enough to be included in other areas of your landscape if you don't have room in your vegetable garden.

Asparagus is a tough, hardy plant that will grow well in USDA Zones 3 to 8. It does require a lot space, however, since you need a large planting to get a good harvest. Plan on 25 plants for enough fresh table use for a family of four.

Rhubarb grows best in USDA Zone 7 or colder. One or two plants is usually all you need. Plants can live 20 years or longer, so choose a site carefully.

Artichokes do best in mild climates in USDA Zones 8 or 9, but they can be grown as annuals in colder climates as far north as Zone 4 if they are started early enough indoors. Most cultivars take 125 days or more to produce chokes.

Horseradish is a tough and hardy plant that can be grown in areas as cold as USDA Zone 3. The roots spread vigorously and plants can overtake nearby plants, so you should plan to grow it in a secluded area or provide some type of root barrier around it to keep it from spreading.

Asparagus is a perennial vegetable that requires a lot of space. Once established, it is long-lived and can be very productive. The wispy foliage provides decorative color and texture long after the familiar stalks have gone to seed and are no longer edible.

squashes and peppers, should not be planted outside until all danger of frost has passed and the soil has warmed up to at least 50°F.

After harvesting early-maturing vegetables such as salad greens, radishes, peas and spinach, you can plant other crops in the same space for fall harvest. Unfortunately, nurseries don't usually carry vegetables after spring, so you will have to direct seed or start your own transplants. It's important to know the average first frost date in your area (see chapter 1) in order to calculate when to plant these late vegetables so they'll mature before being killed by cold weather.

Leafy vegetables, such as Swiss chard, kale, and beet greens can be harvested before the leaves reach full size. Often these small leaves are more tender and tasty than mature ones. These crops can be planted in succession every few weeks over the course of the spring and summer to provide a steady supply of young leaves. Lettuce tends to bolt and taste bitter when grown in the heat of summer, so just enjoy it in spring or wait until temperatures cool to plant a late crop. Shade from taller plants may help improve the quality of summer-grown lettuce, as will selecting varieties suited for warm weather.

Before sowing these second crops, turn over the soil and mix in some balanced fertilizer to replace what earlier plants have used up. Left-over debris like stems or roots from the first planting can cause problems in seed germination if they aren't removed or allowed to break down, so wait a week or two before seeding the second crop, or be sure to remove this material as completely as possible.

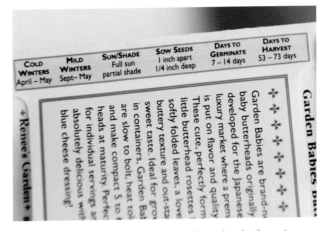

The number of days to harvest are given on the seed packet for each vegetable. This number can refer to days from transplanting or days from seeding, depending on the crop. To make sure your plants are garden-ready at transplanting time, read each seed packet carefully and make a list of start dates. Your goal is to have strong, stocky vegetable plants when you put them in the ground.

HARDENING OFF

Hardening off is the process of acclimating your tender, indoor-grown seedlings or store-bought transplants to the harsher conditions and brighter light awaiting them in the garden. A week or so before planting outdoors, start exposing your plants to outside conditions. Set them outside in a shady, sheltered spot for a couple of hours. Gradually increase the time they spend outdoors and the amount of sunlight they receive over the course of the week. If you are away from home during the week, you will need to start this process on a weekend. Keep a careful eye on the young plants. It doesn't take much for them to wilt or even die if they get too much wind or sunlight too quickly.

SOWING SEEDS

Many vegetables and herbs grow best when direct-seeded into the garden. Prepare your seed bed or rows by loosening the soil to a depth of 6 to 12 inches, depending on your crop. For tiny seeds, moisten but don't soak the soil before planting. Watering after planting can wash the seeds away. Do your best to evenly space the seeds in the row or bed. The seed packet will tell you how far apart to plant them. Don't sweat it if you plant them too closely, however. You will need to do some thinning after they come up.

As a rule of thumb, bury seeds only about as deep as their diameter. Sprinkle soil on top of the seeds, pressing gently to ensure they have contact with the soil. A few seeds, such as lettuce and dill, need light to sprout, so cover them sparingly. Consult the seed packet to see if they need light to germinate. Sprinkle water on the seedbed whenever the surface is dry until all the seeds have sprouted.

BASICS OF TRANSPLANTING

When your seedlings are hardening off and the garden is ready, it's time to plant. Keep in mind that this is a traumatic experience for even the toughest of plants. Try to plant on an overcast day; misty rain is perfect. If cloudy weather isn't in the forecast, transplant later in the day.

1 WATER THE PLANT well while it is still in its pot. Prepare a planting hole as deep as the plant's container and about double the diameter.

2 REMOVE THE PLANT from the pot by placing your hand on top of the pot, with your fingers around the plant's stem. Turn the pot upside down and gently squeeze it or push the plant out from the bottom with your other hand. If you must tug it out, pull it by its leaves rather than the stem (if a leaf comes off, no harm done; damage the stem, and the plant will not survive).

3 **IF THE ROOTS HAVE WRAPPED AROUND** and around the plant, gently pull a few loose with your fingers. Set the plant in the hole at the same depth it was in its pot, generally where the stem meets the roots. Tomatoes are an exception—plant them a bit deeper.

4 **BACKFILL THE HOLE** with the soil you removed and press gently to ensure that the roots have solid contact with the soil. Water well. Do not compact the soil too aggressively or the surface will shed water.

CUTWORM COLLARS

Cutworms are the caterpillars of several types of moths. They feed at night and hide in the soil during the daytime. They can be devastating to young seedlings, severing the stems at the soil level. Protect your young tender plants with cutworm collars made from sections of cardboard toilet-paper or paper-towel tubes. Push collars over transplants and about 2 inches into the soil. Allow the tubes to disintegrate naturally.

An easy and chemical-free way to protect plants against cutworm damage is to place cardboard collars around plants when transplanting them to the garden.

PLANTING PATTERNS

Vegetable gardens are typically laid out in rows, but this isn't always the best way to maximize space. While it's important that plants have adequate spacing between them, this may not need to come in the form of rows. Many heat-loving plants such as cucumbers and melons do best in warm soil that drains well, so they are often planted in hills.

Large seeds such as beans and peas are easy to space out in rows.

Plants with tiny seeds, like carrots and lettuces, are often easier to sow scattered in wide rows. You can get a lot more food per square foot in wide rows.

Warm-season crops such as melons and squashes are often sown three to five seeds at a time in hills. The hill has better air exposure so the soil warms sooner.

INTERCROPPING

Intercropping is growing two or more crops together that mature at different times. This technique not only increases yields, but can also help reduce pest problems if the crops are from different families. To be successful, you must pick vegetables and herbs that mature at different speeds. They should also have similar cultural needs and you must be able to harvest the early crop without damaging the later crop. Some root crops can be quite disruptive when they are being pulled out of the soil.

Here are some ideas:

- Leaf lettuce with tomatoes, peppers, bulbing onions, pole beans, or late-season cabbage
- Green onions with tomatoes, peppers, or basil
- Spinach with Brussels sprouts or garlic
- Radishes with peppers or tomatoes

Make maximum use of your space by seeding a crop of quick-growing lettuce in between rows of later-maturing crops, such as peppers.

HOW TO PLANT POTATOES

There are many ways to plant potatoes, but hilling is usually the best for beginners. The important thing is to make sure the seed potatoes or pieces are buried deep enough so the newly forming tubers are always protected from sunlight.

1 **DIG A TRENCH** about 10 inches deep, reserving the removed soil nearby.

2 Space the seed potatoes or cut pieces 12 to 15 inches apart and plant them 3 inches deep. As the new shoots poke through the soil, gently cover them with loose soil until the trench is filled.

3 After 2 to 3 weeks, when shoots are 6 to 8 inches tall, place soil around the stems within ½ inch of the lower leaves. Continue to mound the soil up around plants as they grow.

CARE OF YOUR VEGETABLE GARDEN

THINNING

Seeds, especially tiny ones, are usually sown thicker than is needed with the assumption that not all will germinate. The result is that most crops will need to be thinned out after the seeds have germinated. Removing some plants in a row to make room for others to grow is not always an easy task for gardeners, since you're getting rid of growing plants, but it is important. Plants grown too closely together will not mature properly and your harvest will be greatly reduced.

Thinning can be done with your fingers or you can use tweezers or small scissors. These tiny seedlings can often be replanted into another area of the garden, if you have the room. If you are going to do this, you will need to gently pull the seedlings to retain the roots. If you are not going to replant the seedlings, it is better to just cut them off at ground level so the roots of the remaining plants are not disturbed. You can toss the rootless thinnings from lettuces, onions, radishes, and carrots into a salad or soup and make use of them.

Thinning is easier and the root disturbance is less if the soil is moist. Water several hours before thinning if the soil is dry.

Leaf mulch not only suppresses weeds, it also conserves water and keeps vegetables clean by limiting mud splashing. To keep your garden healthy, avoid wood mulches that won't decompose in one season.

MULCHING

Mulching goes a long way toward controlling weeds in the vegetable garden and it improves the soil as it breaks down. It also helps keep plant foliage clean. Good material for mulch includes partially decomposed compost or leaves, weed-free straw or hay, or dried grass clippings. Be sure to put it on thick enough to smother weeds, at least 3 or 4 inches but preferably 5 or 6. Keep it a few inches away from the stems of the crops.

Timing is important with mulching. You can mulch cool-season crops soon after planting, but warm-season crops should not be mulched until the soil has thoroughly warmed. If you lay the mulch down on a weed-free soil, you should not have to weed your vegetable garden again all summer. Plants that you want to overwinter should have a winter mulch applied to them after the ground freezes.

SIDE-DRESSING

Most vegetables will benefit from an extra boost of fertilizer about midway through their growing season, a technique known as side-dressing. The best time is usually when they begin to put on a lot of growth or when they are forming blossoms and fruit. To side-dress individual plants, dig a shallow circular trench about 3 inches deep around the plant and about 5 inches away from the stem. Place an inch or so of aged manure or compost in the trench, replace the soil, and water the plant thoroughly. For row crops, dig trenches along both sides of the rows. You can also use a granular fertilizer based on the package directions.

WATERING

It is very important to maintain a consistent and even supply of water to your vegetables. Most vegetables require 1 inch of water a week. Many crops will suffer greatly if the soil is allowed to dry out. Tomatoes often develop blossom-end rot when they are exposed to a very dry period after a wet period. And peppers will drop their blossoms if the soil is too dry.

If your garden is small and reachable with a garden hose, you can use a sprinkler or watering wand. Just be sure to water deeply so the plants will develop deep root systems. Frequent shallow watering encourages shallow root systems that are unable to survive even the smallest dry period. Larger gardens will benefit from soaker hoses or a drip irrigation system. But make sure your system allows you to cultivate around the plants as needed and then remove the equipment in fall so you can turn the garden. These systems have the advantage of wetting the soil rather than the foliage.

Water in the morning so plants have a chance to dry off before the cooler evening temperatures set in. Moist foliage and cool temperatures set the stage for disease development.

Apply a side-dressing of compost, manure, or granular fertilizer to give vegetables a midseason boost.

SUPPORTING YOUR PLANTS

Some vegetables will require some type of support to grow and produce at their best. Tomatoes are usually staked or caged, while pole beans and pea vines require some type of trellis or support system. Supports can also be used to grow vines and save space in smaller gardens. Stakes should always be put into the ground before seeding or transplanting to avoid root damage to half-grown plants. Heavy fruits such as melons require support for each individual fruit. You can use mesh bags or cloth slings that you tie to the trellis.

USING FLOATING ROW COVERS

Floating row covers are made of spun plastic and are permeable to light, air, and water. These covers have a variety of uses in the vegetable garden. They can be used to shield young plants from strong drying winds. They warm the air around plants in spring and fall, offering between 2 and 10 degrees of added warmth. They can also be used to provide shade for plants that need a break from full sun conditions in midsummer.

Snap peas require gentle training to get them started growing up a support.

Determinate types of tomatoes are easily supported by traditional tomato cages, but indeterminate types keep growing all season so they will need something more substantial.

Floating row covers can be laid directly on plants or suspended on hoops above plants, which allows for better air circulation.

Floating row covers provide a barrier against insect pests such as flea beetles, radish maggots, cucumber beetles, and more. But they must be removed as flowers start to set on insect-pollinated crops such as cucumbers, squashes, and melons, or the bees won't be able to get to the flowers. They are light enough that you can place them directly on the plants without damaging them. They should be spread with plenty of slack so they don't hinder plant growth. And the edges need to be secured so they don't blow away.

CLEAN UP

Always remove all dead plants and anything you won't be overwintering. Insects and diseases often overwinter in garden debris, so get it off your garden and into the compost bin. Turn the soil so that weed seeds are exposed to the elements. In spring, turn the soil again as soon as it is dry enough to be worked.

REAPING THE REWARDS

HARVEST

Harvest time is the reward for your efforts. You and your family get to enjoy the juicy tomatoes and freshly dug potatoes. And any extra produce you can't eat can be shared with friends or donated to a local food bank.

It can be tricky knowing when is the best time to harvest some crops to get the greatest payoff for your hard work. As a general rule, crops grown for their leaves, stems, stalks, and roots should be harvested when they are still young and tender, but most are still quite edible after they reach larger sizes. Fruit crops, including beans, cucumbers, eggplants, and summer squashes, taste better when picked slightly immature. Tomatoes should be left on the fine until they are fully ripe for maximum flavor but they will continue to ripen if picked before they have full color.

You should pick ripe fruits even if you aren't able to eat them or give them away. Overripe fruits attract insect and disease problems and overripening reduces the plant's ability to produce more fruits. Regular cutting of leafy crops such as lettuces and spinach helps delay flowering and keeps them producing new leaves.

Try to harvest all vegetables when the plants are dry to reduces chances of spreading diseases. Use a sharp shears or knife to cut broccoli and cabbage heads and fruiting crops, including a small portion of the stem to extend storage life. Avoid bruising or puncturing tender skins. Harvest in the morning when the sugar content of most vegetables is higher.

Leafy crops like lettuces and spinach should be cut rather than pulled to avoid uprooting plants, which will continue to produce fresh leaves for future use.

STORAGE

Your homegrown produce will taste best right out of the garden, but we can't always eat everything we pick right away. Most produce will keep for several days or more in the refrigerator, and some vegetables can be stored for months.

Directions for storage vary with each crop, but there are a few general rules to follow. Most crops should be cooled as soon as possible after harvest to prolong storage life. However, if your produce isn't quite ripe, leave it at room temperature. Wash only the produce you plan to use immediately. Remove the tops from root crops to prevent them from drying out.

Some crops need to be cured before they can be stored for more than a few weeks. These include garlic, onions, potatoes, pumpkins, sweet potatoes, and winter squashes. Cure these crops by subjecting them to warm temperatures and dry conditions for 10 days to 2 weeks after harvest. If the weather cooperates, this can be done right in the garden. After curing, they can be stored in a cool dry place (40 to 50 degrees Fahrenheit) for several months.

If you want red, yellow, orange, or brown peppers, you need to allow your green peppers to fully ripen on the plant. Green peppers are actually picked before they are fully ripe.

Onions for storage should be "cured." Do this by removing their stalks and air-drying them at warm temperatures for several days.

GROWING CULINARY HERBS

Herbs are the perfect complement to all the great vegetables you will be growing. There are many culinary herbs, but the best-known and easiest to grow are basil, dill, chives, parsley, thyme, oregano, rosemary, cilantro, and sage. Some are annual, some biennial, and some perennial. They can be incorporated into the vegetable garden or grown in their own space, where they provide an interesting variety of shapes, textures, leaf colors, and in some cases, flowers.

Growing herbs is similar to growing leafy vegetables, but there are some differences. They all like lots of sun and well-drained soil. They do very well in raised beds, where they benefit from the improved drainage. Most grow best in a leaner soil than most vegetables. Rich soil produces lots of foliage but leaves have reduced oil content and less flavor and fragrance. Most do very well in containers, which you can place right outside your kitchen door or use to decorate your patio or deck.

Herbs benefit from regular harvesting, which encourages more leafy growth and delays flowering. Even if you don't have a use for your herbs in the kitchen, you should give them a good trimming about once a month during the growing season to encourage new leaf growth. Herbs can be harvested throughout the growing season but have their best flavor when picked just before they bloom. If you plan to dry herbs for winter use, this is the time to pick the stems.

Herbs don't have to be relegated to their own garden. Many, such as sage, oregano, and thyme, are ornamental enough to be incorporated into flower gardens.

OUT TO DRY

Herbs for drying should be picked when their leaves are dry. You can dry picked herbs by hanging them in bunches or by spreading them on drying screens. Place them in a dry, well-ventilated place out of the sun. Herbs will take a few days to a couple weeks to dry. You can tell when they are dry by rubbing a leaf between your fingers. A completely dry herb will crack and crumble.

If you are drying herbs for their seeds (dill, coriander), be sure that the seeds are ripe when you pick the plants. On most herbs the seeds turn from green to tan or light brown when ripe. Place a paper bag over the hanging bunches to catch the seeds as the ripen and fall.

When the herbs are completely dried, strip the leaves from the stems and pack them in clean jars with tight-fitting lids. Store the jars away from heat and light. They should last about a year—until next year's harvest!

Regularly prune the flowers off basil and other leafy herbs to encourage more foliage growth.

MICROWAVE DRYING

Microwave drying is a quick and easy way to dry small amounts of herbs. Lay a single layer of clean, dry leaves between paper towels and place in the microwave for 1 to 2 the minutes on high power. Allow the leaves to cool. If they are not completely dry, reheat for 30 seconds and retest. Repeat as needed until herbs are completely dry.

BASIL

Basil is a tender perennial grown as an annual. The standard type, sometimes called sweet basil, grows about a foot tall. It has tasty leaves and attractive foliage from early summer to first frost and is pretty enough to be used in containers and in flower beds. Small-leaved types make good edging plants. In addition to the standard cooking basil, there are varieties that have the taste of cinnamon, lemon, and lime.

Planting: Basil is very frost-sensitive. Sow seeds indoors 4 to 6 weeks before last frost date. Do not plant outside until a week after all danger of frost has passed. Space garden plants a foot apart or slightly less.

Care: Plants should not be allowed to dry out. Fertilize every 2 weeks with a water-soluble fertilizer. Pinch seedlings to encourage branching and bushy growth. Always cut stems back to right above another set of leaves. Remove flower stalks. Rejuvenate plants by cutting back by about half in midsummer. Basil is generally problem-free, but plants are susceptible to damping off, cold temperature damage, and fungal diseases.

Harvest: Pick leaves whenever you need them. For long-term storage, harvest leaves just before flowers appear and dry or freeze.

Cultivars: 'Large Leaf', 'Genovese', and 'Lettuce Leaf' are good standard types. 'Dark Opal' has purple leaves and 'Purple Ruffles' has ruffled purple leaves. They both make beautiful vinegars and are ornamental enough to use in flower gardens. 'Siam Queen' is also ornamental and a good choice for Thai and Vietnamese cooking. 'Spicy Globe' is an ornamental type that forms a neat, 8-inch globe of small leaves.

SNAP BEANS

Also called string and green beans, snap beans are available as both bush and pole types. Bush beans grow 1 to 2 feet tall and are usually grown in rows. Pole beans can grow up to 15 feet tall, require some type of support, and produce more beans than bush types. Snap beans can be yellow (also called wax beans) or purple. Romano beans have broader, flat pods.

Planting: Sow seeds a week or two after all danger of frost has passed and the soil has warmed to at least 55°F. Seeds will rot in cold, wet soil. Sow seeds 1 inch deep, 2 to 3 inches apart. Bush beans bear heavily but briefly. To extend the harvest, sow successive crops every 2 weeks up to 12 weeks before the first expected frost. Plant pole beans along the north side of the garden where they won't shade other vegetables.

Care: Thin bush beans to 5 to 6 inches in rows spaced 3 feet apart. Beans have the ability to fix nitrogen from the air, as long as the right bacteria are present in the soil. You can treat seeds with an inoculant to make sure the bacteria are present. Beans rarely require additional nitrogen fertilizer but usually benefit from additional phosphorus and potassium. Have the support system in place before planting pole beans. Possible problems include damping off, bean rust, leaf spots, bacterial blights, aphids, beetles, leafhoppers, leafminers, and whiteflies.

Harvest: Pick beans when they are thin and tender, before the seeds swell. Pinch or cut the pods off carefully to avoid uprooting the plant. Pick every few days to encourage plants to produce more.

Cultivars: 'Bush Lake 274', 'Provider', 'Derby', 'Tendercrop' (bush). 'Blue Lake', 'Romano' (pole). 'Gold Crop', 'Gold Rush' (yellow)

BROCCOLI

With this cool-season crop, the part of the plant that is eaten is the flower head, before the buds open. Modern hybrids produce large center heads and abundant side shoots after the center head is harvested.

Planting: Start seeds indoors 6 to 8 weeks before the last expected spring frost or purchase plants in spring. Plants can go into the garden about 2 weeks before the frost-free date. Place a cutworm collar around young plants. Spacing can range from 8 to 18 inches, depending on the variety and how big you want your central heads to be. A second fall crop can be direct seeded in early summer; make sure seedlings have plenty of moisture as they go through the summer heat.

Care: Plants decline in summer heat, so pull up spring plantings and replace with heat-loving vegetables. Fall crops will endure a few light frosts. Leaves may develop a bronze or purplish cast if potassium is lacking. Possible problems are club root, cabbage worms, aphids, and flea beetles. Cabbage worms usually stick to the leaves. If you find them in your heads, simply pick them off or soak the head in strong salt water. The insects will float to the top.

Harvest: Harvest broccoli while the buds are still tight and before there is any yellow color. Use a sharp knife to cut about 2 inches of the stem with the head. Continue harvesting the side shoots after the central head is cut to encourage more shoots.

Cultivars: 'Green Comet', 'Packman', 'Premium Crop', 'Waltham'

CABBAGE

Cabbage is a cool-season crop found in many shapes and sizes and colors, with green, blue-green, and red cultivars available. Leaves can be smooth or wrinkled (savoy). Heads develop in cool weather, so it should be planted for a spring or fall crop. Cultivars are available that mature early (50 to 60 days from transplanting), midseason (70 to 85 days), or late season (85 days or more). Late-season varieties are best suited to storage and should be timed for fall harvest. Cabbage is one of the few vegetables that can tolerate light shade. It can also withstand light frost.

Planting: Best grown from transplants purchased or started 4 to 6 weeks before the average frost-free date. Hardened-off seedlings can go into the garden 3 to 4 weeks before the last expected frost date, providing the garden is dry enough to work in. Space plants 10 to 20 inches apart depending on the head size. Place a cutworm collar around seedlings.

Care: Side dress with a heavy nitrogen fertilizer 3 weeks after transplanting. Plants like ample potassium; a bronze tinge to the leaves signals a deficiency. Practice crop rotation to reduce your chances of club root, a fungal disease. Other possible problems are black rot, fusarium wilt or yellows, aphids, cabbage loopers, cutworms, cabbage root maggots, flea beetles, and slugs.

Harvest: Heads can be harvested as soon as they are firm, even if they are small. Use a sharp knife to cut off the heads, leaving as much stem on the plant as possible to encourage the production of a second crop of smaller heads.

Cultivars: 'Golden Acre', 'Market Prize', 'Stonehead' (green). 'Ruby Ball', 'Red Dynasty' (red). 'Alcosa', 'Savoy King' (savoy)

CARROTS

This root crop comes in the traditional size and shape as well as smaller types call fingerlings. There are also round varieties. Smaller types can be ready to eat in 50 days or so. The frilly foliage of carrots makes them pretty enough to use in flower gardens. Small cultivars can be grown in containers at least 12 inches deep.

Planting: Direct seed in spring 2 to 3 weeks before the last expected frost and then again 10 to 12 weeks before the first fall frost date for a fall storage crop. Sow seeds about ¼ inch deep in wide bands to maximize space, then thin to 3 to 4 inches. You can make succession plantings every week until midsummer. Seeds can be presoaked in water for 6 hours before sowing to hasten germination, which can take up to 10 days.

Care: Carrots require a deeply dug soil (at least 12 inches) free of rocks and other debris. Even the tiniest impediment can cause the root to become stunted or forked. Pulling weeds around carrots or while thinning can disturb the plants. It may be better to cut weeds off instead. Avoid high nitrogen, which can cause roots to branch and become "hairy." Hill soil around any carrots that are exposed to prevent the shoulders from becoming green and bitter tasting. Possible problems include blight, aster yellows, damping off, wireworms, carrot rust fly, and leafhoppers. Use row covers to protect against insects. Rotate crops to protect against wireworms in the soil.

Harvest: Begin harvesting as soon as carrots are large enough to use or when they are a good orange color. You may need to use a trowel to gently pry up larger roots.

Cultivars: 'Chantenay', 'Orbit', 'Royal Chantenay', 'Scarlet Nantes'

CHIVES

Chives is a hardy (USDA Zone 3) perennial that is very easy to grow. Plants grow into thick, grasslike clumps 8- to 10-inches tall and will live for many years. All plant parts are edible, but it is usually grown for the green leaves, which have a mild onion flavor. Leaves can be cut throughout the growing season as needed and will grow back quickly. Plants are quite ornamental, especially when the showy purple flowers appear in late spring, and are nice additions to flower gardens.

Planting: The easiest way to start plants is to get a clump from a friend or neighbor; plants are easily divided at just about any time during the growing season. You can also grow chives from seeds, but germination is slow, so be patient.

Care: Choose a permanent site in full sun to light shade with well-drained soil. Chive is a vigorous self-seeder. Pick off flowers when they start to turn brown to prevent having hundreds of seedlings next year. This also prevents plants from going dormant. Divide clumps every 3 to 4 years to keep plants vigorous. To extend the season, pot up a small clump in fall about a month before the first frost and bring it inside once winter hits. Chive has no serious pest problems and rarely needs additional fertilizer.

Harvest: Use a sharp knife to cut leaves above 2 inches above the ground once plants have reached a height of 6 inches. If you cut back an entire clump, allow it several weeks to regenerate before harvesting again.

Cultivars: The species (*Allium schoenoprasum*) is usually grown for cooking use. There are some cultivars selected for their showier flowers. 'Forescate' has bright rose-red flowers.

CILANTRO, CORIANDER

When grown for its leaves, this annual plant is called cilantro. When grown for its dried brown seeds, it goes by coriander. Cilantro has very fragrant leaves and stems. The young leaves resemble parsley. Plants grow quickly, eventually reaching about 18 inches in height, and go to seed in about 2 months. It is ornamental enough for the flower garden while green, but not so much once it turns brown. It can take partial shade and it does well in containers.

Planting: Sow seeds in spring after frost danger, 1/2 inch deep where you want the plants; seedlings do not transplant well. Sow seeds every 3 weeks until late summer to have a regular supply of leaves. Plants dry out easily, so plan to water as needed.

Care: Seeds need adequate water to germinate, so keep soil moist. Plants will bolt (go to seed) quickly in hot weather, after which the foliage is not as tasty. If you want coriander seeds, allow plants to go to seed. Let a few plants self-sow so you will have plants again next year. No pest problems.

Harvest: Pinch off leaves as needed for cilantro. Seeds ripen in late summer or fall; collect them before they fall to the ground for coriander.

Cultivars: 'Caribe', 'Slo Bolt', 'Santo', and 'Leisure' all tend to go to seed slower than the species.

CUCUMBERS

This warm-season crop is available as traditional vining plants or as compact bush types. Vines require 6 to 8 feet to sprawl while bush types only require 2 to 3 feet. Vining cultivars produce more fruits per plant, but the bush types bear slightly earlier and are easier to care for and harvest. "Picklers" bear earlier, but only for 2 weeks or less. "Slicers" bear later but produce longer, up to 6 weeks. Both types can be used for eating or pickling when small.

Planting: Can be direct seeded, but starting seeds indoors about 3 weeks before the last frost date gets an earlier harvest. Do not seed or set out plants until at least 2 weeks after the last frost or the soil temperature has reached 65°F. Extend the harvest by sowing seeds at the same time you set out plants. Plant in rows, beds, or in hills, spaced according to the package. Vining types can be trellised and bush cultivars can be grown in large containers.

Care: Plants need warmth and ample water to produce. Use black plastic to warm the soil to get a jump start on planting. Pale foliage indicates a lack of nitrogen and bronzing indicates potassium deficiency. Misshapen fruit is a sign of water stress. Possible problems include anthracnose, mosaic virus, cucumber beetles, aphids, and squash vine borer.

Harvest: Fruits grow quickly and bearing plants should be checked daily. Pick fruits while they are still small; picklers 3 to 4 inches and slicers 6 to 8 inches. Large fruits are seedy and bitter.

Cultivars: 'Alibi', 'Calypso', 'Wisconsin SMR #55' (pickling). 'Bush Champion', 'Burpless Hybrid', 'Marketmore 76' (slicing). 'Salad Bush', 'Spacemaster' (containers)

DILL

Dill is an annual with tasty leaves from early summer to first frost and seed heads that mature in late summer. It can grow 3 feet or taller when it is happy. The feathery leaves and lacy yellow flowers are attractive midsummer. Dill's delicate foliage and tall flowers make it attractive enough for mixed plantings and containers, but it does reseed prolifically. Black swallowtail butterflies use dill as a larval food.

Planting: Start sowing seeds outdoors in a sunny spot as soon as the ground can be worked in spring and sow successive crops every 3 to 4 weeks to ensure a continuous supply. If you want fresh dill for pickling, sow seeds in late spring. Seeds germinate better with some light, so only cover lightly, if at all.

Care: Dill will tolerate afternoon shade. When seedlings are 2 inches tall, thin to 6 to 8 inches apart. Dill does not transplant well. It will self-seed if you allow some seed heads to remain. No pest problems.

Harvest: Pick dill weed as you need it, but do not remove more than one-fifth of the plant's foliage or you will weaken the plant. Harvest flower heads when they are half open and seeds when they are brown. To store, hang bunches upside down in paper bags to catch seeds and dried leaves. Whole leaves can be frozen.

Cultivars: 'Dukat', 'Tetra', and 'Superdukat' are slow to bolt. 'Fernleaf' is bushier and has more ornamental foliage.

GARLIC

This onion relative grows from a bulb that is divided into cloves. It is very hardy, surviving winters in USDA Zone 2. It is best planted in fall and will take about 8 months from planting to harvest. The two main types are softneck and hardneck. **Softnecks**, most often found at supermarkets, have pliable stems and store well. **Hardnecks** have stiff central stems that curl at the top. They are more cold-hardy but do not store as well. You can save some of your largest cloves for replanting the next fall. Do not plant supermarket garlic.

Planting: Plant individual cloves outdoors about 6 weeks before the soil freezes, around early October. Plant cloves, pointed end up, 2 inches deep, spaced 5 inches apart.

Care: Mulch after planting to retain moisture. Apply a second layer of winter mulch after the ground freezes. Plants need well-drained soil. Stop watering once the foliage begins to turn yellow or fall over. Cut off flower stalks to encourage bulb development. No pest problems.

Harvest: Leaves can be harvested and used as you would chives, but don't remove more than a quarter of the foliage at one time. Bulbs can be harvested when about three-quarters of the tops have yellowed. Carefully dig up a couple plants and see if bulbs have well-segmented cloves that are beginning to separate. Spread plants, including roots, in a single layer on a screen in a warm, dry, airy location to dry. After 2 to 3 weeks, when bulbs are dry, remove excess dirt, roots, and tops, leaving 1 inch of stem.

Cultivars: 'Rocambole', 'Purple Stripe', 'Porcelain' (hardneck). 'Artichoke', 'Silverskin'(softneck)

LETTUCES

The most popular types of lettuce for the home garden are leaf, butterhead, and romaine. Romaine lettuces need a longer growing season but are heat-resistant and can tolerate summer temperatures. Leaf and butterhead lettuces like the cool conditions of late spring and early fall, but modern breeding has produced cultivars that are "bolt-resistant," meaning they are slow to go to seed, and have extended the season for these lettuces.

Planting: The small seeds should be scattered on the surface of a smooth seed bed and pressed lightly into the soil. They need light to germinate. Sow seeds as soon as the soil can be worked, as early as a month before the last frost date, and again in mid- to late summer for a fall crop. Make successive sowing every 10 days to extend your harvest.

Care: Lettuces require an even supply of water. Cultivate carefully around plants to avoid damaging the shallow roots. Plants will benefit from regular applications of nitrogen. Once hot weather arrives, most lettuces will bolt and need to be ripped out. Lettuces are essentially safe from most insects and diseases, but over-moist soil can lead to rot. Rabbits are attracted to lettuces. Scatter blood meal around plants after every rain to repel rabbits and deer. Other possible problems include damping off, downy mildew, mosaic virus, fusarium wilt, aphids, leaf miners, leaf hoppers, slugs, and wireworms.

Harvest: Begin harvesting leaves as soon as they are large enough, cutting from the outside of the plant first. Pick head lettuces when firm and fully formed.

Cultivars: 'Black-Seeded Simpson', 'Red Sails', 'Ruby', 'Salad Bowl', 'Grand Rapids' (leaf lettuce). 'Buttercrunch', 'Dark Green Boston', 'Summer Bibb' (butterhead). 'Little Gem', 'Paris Island Cos' (romaine)

MELONS

Melons are vining plants native to tropical areas. They will do well in this region as long as you select short-season varieties and give plants a head start with indoor seeding. Warming the soil with black plastic will also help. Muskmelons have netted skins and salmon, white, or green flesh. They are the easiest and most popular type for home gardens. Full-size watermelons require a very long growing season and lots of space. If you want to grow watermelons, select a smaller "icebox" type that has compact vines.

Planting: Don't plant too early. Start seeds indoors 1 to 2 weeks before the last expected frost date. Plant hardened-off plants in the garden 2 to 3 weeks after the frost-free date. Plants produce anywhere from two to five melons that usually ripen about the same time. Since plants don't store well, don't plant more than you can enjoy or give away. Plant in raised hills to increase soil warmth, placing three plants in a hill. Plants can be trellised, but you'll need to provide support for each melon.

Care: Melons do well planted in black plastic ground cover. It warms the soil, retains moisture, keeps the weeds down, and protects fruits. Make sure there are ample holes in the plastic for water to get to the roots. Possible problems include mildews, leaf spots, fusarium wilt, cucumber beetle, aphids, squash bugs, and flea beetles. Floating row covers and proper growing conditions deter diseases and insects.

Harvest: Muskmelons will "slip," or separate, from the vine when they are fully ripe. To avoid over-ripening the fruits, harvest when just a little pressure on the stem separates it from the fruit.

Cultivars: 'Ambrosia', 'Burpee Hybrid', 'Harper Hybrid', 'Saticoy Hybrid' (muskmelon). 'Sugar Baby', 'Yellow Baby', 'Blue Belle', 'Crimson Sweet', (watermelon).

ONIONS

Onions are day-length sensitive, with different types requiring different amounts of light and dark to form bulbs. Choose long-day onions to ensure success. They like cool temperatures in the beginning, but require warmer temperatures for the bulbs to mature. Onion colors can be white, yellow, or red and are also classified by their use: storage, slicing, pearl, and scallions or green onions.

Planting: Onions are usually planted as sets, which are smallish dormant bulbs, but they can also be started from transplants. Seeds usually take too long to mature when planted outdoors and seeds are challenging to start indoors. Sets can be planted about 4 weeks before the frost-free date. Gently push them into the softened ground, pointed end up, so that you can just see the top of the set. Space sets 2 to 6 inches apart depending on the mature bulb size. Scallions can be planted an inch apart.

Care: Weeding onions is challenging. Remove weeds while they are still small to avoid pulling up the onion bulbs with the weeds. Onions are shallow rooted and require an even supply of moisture. Possible problems include damping off, downy mildew, pink root, smut, onion maggots, thrips, and wireworms.

Harvest: Harvest scallions as soon as the tops are about 6 inches tall. Bulbs can be pulled as soon as they're big enough to use. Storage onions must stay in the ground until their tops die back and fall over. After harvesting, spread onions in a single layer for 2 to 10 days to cure.

Cultivars: 'Early Yellow Glob', 'Stuttgarter', 'Sweet Sandwich', 'Sweet Spanish' (bulbing). 'Tokyo Long White', 'White Lisbon' (scallion)

OREGANO

This attractive, shrubby perennial is reliably hardy in USDA Zone 5 but often survives winters in Zone 4. It can be grown as an annual in colder climates. Plants have gray-green leaves and loose clusters of purplish-pink flowers in summer. Not all plants have aromatic, tasty leaves, however. The best type for culinary use has white flowers and will have the botanical name *Origanum vulgare* spp. *hirtum* or *O. heraceloticum* and is usually sold as Greek or Italian oregano. Taste a leaf or two before you buy a plant to make sure it has good flavor. It is quite ornamental and can be used in flower gardens. Marjoram is related to oregano but is more frost-tender and must be grown as an annual.

Planting: Start with nursery-grown plants and plant after all danger of frost has passed.

Care: Place this perennial herb in a spot where it can be left alone. Its only requirements are full sun and a well-drained soil. Once established, oregano is easy to grow, drought-tolerant, and trouble-free. Plants will self-sow, but the offspring are often flavorless. Watch for spider mites.

Harvest: Leaves are most flavorful before plants flower. Pick leaves as soon as the plant is large enough to be harvested. You can also cut back entire plants when they are about 6 inches tall, again just before they begin to flower, and a third time in late summer.

Cultivars: 'Compactum' stays 2 to 3 inches tall and has good flavor. It is a good container variety. There are many ornamental types that are good for flower gardens but rarely have tasty leaves.

PARSLEY

Parsley is a biennial grown as an annual. It has tasty leaves early summer to early winter and attractive bright green foliage all season. It is a larval food source for swallowtail butterflies. Flat-leaved parsley is also called Italian parsley. Curly parsley is often used for garnish.

Planting: Parsley grows best in cool weather. Sow seeds outdoors several weeks before last frost date. Rake the seed bed smooth and sow seeds ¼ inch deep. Use care if transplanting, as these taprooted plants resent being disturbed. Mark the site by planting quick-germinating radish seeds, since parsley germination is slow. Seeds can be started indoors in individual pots 8 to 10 weeks before last frost date. Sow seeds overnight in warm water to speed up germination, which can take 3 weeks. Cover seeds, since darkness aids germination.

Care: Parsley grows best in full sun in rich, evenly moist, well-drained soil, but it tolerates partial shade. Thin seedlings to 8 inches. Parsley is tolerant of spring and fall frosts. Usually problem-free, but watch for crown rot. Try to plant enough to share with the large parsley worms, which turn into swallowtail butterflies.

Harvest: Plants mature 2 to 3 months from sowing. Harvest leaves by cutting rather than pulling as soon as they are large enough to use. Plants will survive winter in most areas, but the flavor is not as good the second year.

Cultivars: The species (*Petroselinum crispum* Neapolitanum group) is fine for garden use. 'Pagoda', 'Dark Green Italian', and 'Plain Italian' are good flat-leaved cultivars. 'Sherwood' is a curly-leaved type (*P. crispum* Crispum group) with good heat resistance.

PEAS

Garden peas are grown for their seeds and must be shelled. **Snow peas** are harvested before the seeds mature and both pods and seeds are eaten. **Snap peas** have plump sweet seeds and tender pods, both of which are eaten. Vines range from 1 to 8 feet in length; smaller types can be grown without support. Pea flowers are quite ornamental and plants can be used in flower gardens.

Planting: Peas tolerate cold temperatures but seeds rot in wet, cold soil. Direct-seed up to 5 weeks before the last expected frost, in single or double rows. Put supports in place before planting. Plant every 10 days to spread out the harvest. Plant again in late summer for fall.

Care: Plants benefit from supports. It makes harvest easier and improves air circulation. Use wires or strings, or simply stick a row of branches in the ground for the peas to grow up into. Generally free of insect pests, but watch for blights, wilts, powdery mildew, and root rot. Birds will pull up seedlings to get the seeds.

Harvest: Pods are usually ready to harvest about 3 weeks after plants flower. Use a small pair of scissors to cut off the pods. Garden peas should have filled pods and still be bright green, not dull. Snow peas can be picked as soon as the pod is full-sized but before the seeds begin to swell. Snap peas should be picked after the seeds have filled out but before the pods are large and hard. Harvest daily.

Cultivars: 'Frosty', 'Green Arrow', 'Little Marvel', 'Progress No. 9', 'Wando' (garden). 'Mammoth Melting Sugar', 'Oregon Sugar Pod' (snow). 'Sugarbon', 'Sugar Snap', 'Sugar Ann', (snap)

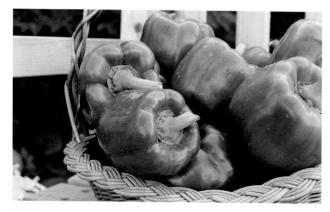

BELL PEPPERS

Most bell peppers start out green and turn red or orange when mature, but there are also yellow, purple, and even brown cultivars. In addition to bell peppers, you can grow jalapeno, Serrano, and poblano types for use in Mexican cooking. All peppers like warm weather, so choose short-season cultivars for best results. Most do well in containers and are quite ornamental.

Planting: Sow seeds indoors 8 to 10 weeks before the last frost or purchase plants. Plants cannot be direct seeded. Place hardened-off plants 12 to 18 inches apart in the garden 2 to 3 weeks after the frost-free date.

Care: Plants need a constant supply of moisture. Tall types may need support, but be sure to get stakes in place before planting to avoid damaging the shallow roots. Plants usually don't need additional nitrogen. Narrow leaves with a grayish cast are a sign of phosphorus deficiency. Plants also require adequate magnesium. Problems include tobacco mosaic virus, bacterial leaf spot, blossom end rot, sunscald, aphids, flea beetles, cutworms, and tomato hornworms.

Harvest: Keep plants picked to extend the harvest. They can be picked at the immature green stage or allowed to ripen to their next color. Hot peppers can be picked green, but they will continue to increase in flavor and heat as they mature. Use a pair of scissors to cut fruits from plants. If frost is forecast, pick all remaining fruits.

Cultivars: 'New Ace', 'Gypsy', 'King of the North', 'Lady Bell' (ripening to red). 'Sweet Chocolate' (ripening to brown). 'Golden Bell', 'Orobelle' (ripening to yellow)

POTATOES

Potatoes require quite a bit of space, but it is usually worth it to get to enjoy the taste of homegrown potatoes. Choose a variety based on the season of maturity and how you want to use them. Early types are ready to dig about 65 days after planting; midseason about 80 days; and late 90 days or more. Early potatoes are best eaten soon after harvest, while mid- and late potatoes are better for storage. Fingerlings are smaller in size and are usually mid- to late season cultivars.

Planting: Potatoes are not grown from seeds or plants, but rather small whole potatoes or pieces, called seed potatoes. Purchase disease-free certified seed potatoes from a grower. Potatoes form underground.

Care: Potatoes do best in cooler temperatures. Plant in spring 2 to 4 weeks before the last frost date or when soil has warmed to 40°F. The main pest problem is the Colorado potato beetle. Other problems include blights, mosaic virus, wilts, flea beetles, aphids, cucumber beetles, cutworms, Japanese beetles, leafhoppers, and wireworms. Floating row covers will greatly reduce pest problems.

Harvest: Harvest early types when still small, 7 to 9 weeks after planting, and main crops after the tops have died back but before a hard frost. Use a garden fork or your hands, working carefully to avoid damaging the tender skins. It is usually better to harvest a entire plant, but you can pluck a few potatoes from several plants. Potatoes to be stored should be cured by spreading them in a single layer in a dark, cool place for 2 weeks.

Cultivars: 'Norland', 'Red Pontiac', 'Early Cobbler', 'Superior', 'Chippewa', 'Katahdin', 'Kennebec', 'Yukon Gold', 'Green Mountain'

RADISHES

This cool-season root crop is very easy to grow. There are several colors and types. The most familiar is the red globe, or spring radish. These grow quickly and are often ready for the table in a month or less. Long-season, or winter radishes, include the Asian radishes (daikon, Oriental, Japanese, Chinese, and lo bok). These are larger and take 2 months or more to reach full size.

Planting: Sow seeds outdoors 4 to 6 weeks before the last expected frost. Make successive sowings every week to 10 days until weather is consistently above 65°F. Because spring radishes mature so quickly, they are perfect for intercropping with slower-maturing vegetables. Seeds can be sown again in late summer for a fall crop. Long-season radishes should be planted in spring or summer depending on the cultivar. Winter-storage types should mature around first frost.

Care: Thin seedlings to 2 to 4 inches or you won't get nice round globes. Maintain even moisture. Water-stressed plants can get bitter and tough. You shouldn't need additional fertilizer with this quick crop. Few problems, but watch for club rot, cabbage root maggots, and flea beetles.

Harvest: Begin pulling spring radishes as soon as they are large enough to use. Their quality quickly goes downhill as they get large. Winter types can be harvested as soon as they are large enough use, but a mild frost or two will improve their flavor.

Cultivars: 'Champion', 'Cherriette','Icicle', 'Summer Cross', 'Red Meat' (spring types). 'April Cross', 'Misato Rose' (long season)

SAGE

Sage is a hardy (USDA Zone 4) perennial with tasty leaves early summer to early winter. The textured, gray-green foliage is attractive all season. Culinary sage is *Salvia officinalis*. There are many other plants that have "sage" as part of their common name but are not suitable for culinary use. Pineapple sage (*S. elegans*) is a tender perennial with pineapple-scented leaves that can be used in the kitchen.

Planting: Plant outside after all danger of frost has passed.

Care: Choose a site in full sun with average to rich, well-drained soil. Poorly drained or wet soil can lead to root rot. Sage is tolerant of partial shade and drought once established. In colder areas where sage doesn't overwinter, grow plants against a south-facing wall for protection or take cuttings in late summer to be overwintered indoors. Space sage 12 to 24 inches apart. Water as needed to keep soil moist, but not wet. Cut plants back by one-third each spring to promote new growth. Even though garden sage is a perennial, plan to replace the woody plants every 3 to 4 years to keep them healthy and vigorous. No serious pest problems but root rot can be a problem.

Harvest: Pinch leaves off as needed, but stop in early fall to harden plants for winter. For storage, dry leaves in a single layer in a dry location out of sunlight.

Cultivars: There are several cultivars that have showier leaves, including 'Aurea', 'Kew Gold', 'Tricolor', and 'Purpurea', but they are not as hardy.

SPINACH

This cool-season leafy green comes in two general types: smooth-leaved or savoyed. Smooth types have thin, tender leaves that are good for salad use. Savoyed types have broader, thicker crinkled leaves and hold up better in cooking.

Planting: Sow seeds directly in the garden 4 to 6 weeks before the last expected frost. Seeds can be started indoors a few weeks earlier if you want an even earlier crop, but it is usually not worth the effort. Sow seeds every 2 weeks in spring to get a continuous harvest and then start again in late summer for a fall crop.

Care: Thin seedlings to 6 inches, using the thinnings for salads. Spacing that is too tight can lead to bolting, so give plants ample room. These plants usually don't require supplemental fertilizer. This quick-maturing crop is good for succession planting.

Plants will bolt when day length gets over 12 hours or they are exposed to extremely high or low temperatures. No serious pest problems. Blight, downy mildew, and fusarium wilt may show up and plants may be bothered by aphids, flea beetles, leafhoppers, and leaf miners. Row covers go a long way in reducing insect damage.

Harvest: Spring spinach is usually harvested by picking the entire plant before it bolts, but you can cut individual leaves at any time, starting with the outside leaves and moving inward. Fall crops can be harvested either way.

Cultivars: 'Bloomsdale Long Standing', 'Melody', 'Tyee'

SQUASHES & PUMPKINS

Summer squash is picked while immature and the skins are still tender. They generally grow on bushy plants that produce many fruits. **Winter squashes** and **pumpkins** are left on the vine until they are mature and have tough, firm skins. They usually grow on long vines with only a few fruits per plant.

Planting: Squashes like warm soil and warm temperatures. Plant three to five seeds in hills spaced 3 to 4 feet apart, 2 to 3 weeks after the last frost date. Seeds can be started indoors a few weeks before outdoor planting, but it's not always worth the effort, especially with winter squashes.

Care: Plants need plenty of room. Adequate spacing reduces disease problems. Small-fruited plants can be trained on a trellis, but this isn't a good idea for heavy-fruited plants. Squashes are heavy feeders so plan to top dress with a low-nitrogen fertilizer. They also need a regular, plentiful water supply. Potential problems include aphids, cucumber beetle, leaf hopper, squash vine borers, anthracnose, bacterial wilt, mildews, mosaic, and scab.

Harvest: Begin picking summer squashes as soon as they are large enough to use. Winter squashes should be full-colored with skins tough to pierce with a thumbnail; pick all before a hard frost.

Cultivars: 'Gold Rush', 'Seneca Prolific', 'Seneca Zucchini' 'Zucchini Elite', 'Early Prolific Straightneck' (summer). 'Butternut', 'Blue Hubbard', 'Sweet Mama', 'Table Queen' 'Blue Ballet', 'Cream of the Crop' (winter). 'Big Autumn', 'Small Sugar', 'Howden', 'Atlantic Giant', 'Connecticut Field', 'Big Max', 'Ghost Rider', 'Triple Treat' (pumpkins)

THYME

There are many types of thyme available for garden use. Most cooks prefer common thyme (*Thymus vulgaris*), which is a shrubby plant growing 12 to 18 inches tall. This hardy (USDA Zone 4) perennial has tasty leaves early summer to fall and attractive foliage all season. Tiny pink flowers appear late spring into summer. These attractive plants can be incorporated into the perennial border or rock garden or used in containers. The low-growing types make attractive ground covers and can take light foot traffic, which releases their heady fragrance.

Planting: Thyme plants can be set outside late spring to early summer. They can tolerate light spring frosts. Thyme is difficult to start from seeds. Plant in full sun in well-drained soil. They are tolerant of dry soils once established. In colder areas, where garden thyme doesn't always overwinter, grow plants against a south-facing wall for extra protection or take cuttings in late summer to be overwintered indoors. Space plant 6 to 12 inches apart.

Care: Cut plants back after they flower to encourage bushiness. After 3 or 4 years, thyme becomes woody and less productive and should be renewed if you are using it for culinary purposes. Either replace plants or divide plants in spring or fall. No pest problems.

Harvest: Cut leaves as needed. Plants benefit from regular shearing. For long-term storage, hang upside down in a dry location out of sunlight. Strip off leaves and flowers and store in a cool, dark place.

Cultivars: 'Argenteus' has white-edged leaves. 'Orange Balsam' has orange-scented leaves. 'German Winter' is more compact.

TOMATOES

For help deciding which tomatoes to grow, see page 70. Choose a variety based on your tastes, your intended use, your available garden space, the length of your growing season, and resistance to diseases. Most gardeners grow several types.

Planting: Plant hardened-off plants outside after all danger of frost has passed. Sow seeds indoors 6 to 8 weeks before last frost date. Space plants 3 feet apart if staked; 6 feet apart if allowed to sprawl.

Care: Plants need even water throughout the growing season; cracked and deformed fruits and blossom end rot are the result of an uneven water supply. They are heavy feeders. Don't overdue the nitrogen, however, or you will have all vines and no fruits. All types will grow best if they are staked or caged to get their fruits off the ground. Tomatoes are susceptible to a variety of disease problems, including several wilts, leaf spots, blights, and tobacco mosaic virus. Grow resistant cultivars when available, and provide optimum cultural conditions, including rotating your tomatoes every 2 to 3 years. Insect pests include tomato hornworms, aphids, Colorado potato beetles, cutworms, flea beetles, mites, slugs, and whiteflies.

Harvest: Harvest fruits when they are evenly colored and slightly firm or soft. Green fruits will continue to ripen but aren't usually as tasty.

Cultivars: 'Early Girl', 'Better Boy', 'Big Beef', 'Jet Star', 'Quick Pick', 'Celebrity', 'Lemon Boy', 'Brandywine', 'Ultra Boy'. 'Sweet 100', 'Sweet Million' (cherry)

JUST FOR FUN

GROWING FLOWERS, GRASSES, AND GROUNDCOVERS

Growing ornamental plants—annual and perennial flowers, bulbs, ornamental grasses, and groundcovers—is where you can really let your creativity shine. In most cases these plants will be chosen for their beauty, but they can also serve important roles in gardens. Groundcovers, grasses, and even some tough perennials can be used to cover problem sites, and tall grasses can be used for screening and windbreaks. Annuals are good for providing quick color or filling in bare spots.

In this chapter you will learn how best to use these ornamental plants in your garden. You'll learn what to plant to get season-long color as well as what tasks you'll need to do to keep your plants healthy. The chapter ends with a list of recommended annuals, perennials, bulbs, grasses, and groundcovers best suited to your region.

Showy ornamental plants include flowers, ornamental grasses, and groundcovers. They can be used in a variety of ways in the landscape, but are often combined in mixed borders.

ANNUALS

As you learned in chapter 1, an annual is any plant that completes its life cycle in one growing season. The term "annual" is usually used to refer to long-blooming flowering plants that often hail from tropical areas. These flowers have the ability to bring instant gratification anywhere they are placed—from your doorstep to the mailbox at the end of the driveway. They are often used as exclamation points in a landscape.

Annuals, like the zinnias, marigolds, and wax begonias here, often conjure up an air of nostalgia. Many people's first flower memories are of pots of smiling-faced pansies or brick-red geraniums at grandma's house. These annuals are all still around and ready for modern garden use, but many of them have been updated to make them even easier to cultivate and maintain..

Annuals come in almost any color imaginable, and most of their impact comes from their showy flowers. But this group of plants also offers a wide range of leaf colors, growth habits, and textures. You can use them in mixed plantings for a bouquet effect or in mass groupings where you want a large area of a single color. They make great container plants and are good anywhere you want an instant show. You will often see annuals named as part of a "series." Annuals that are part of a series all have similar growth characteristics but tend to have different flower colors.

Like vegetables, annuals can be classified as cool-season or warm-season plants based on their tolerance of cool air and soil temperatures. Cool-season annuals, which include pansies, snapdragons, and calendulas, do better in mild temperatures and can quickly deteriorate in hot weather. Warm-season annuals such as marigolds, zinnias, and impatiens grow and flower best in warm weather and do not tolerate any frost.

GROWING ANNUALS

Most annuals prefer well-drained soil that is rich in organic matter. Add a 2- to 4-inch layer of compost and mix it into the top 8 to 12 inches of soil the first year, adding a 1- to 2-inch layer of compost before planting in subsequent years. You can cover the bed with organic mulch, such as shredded bark, pine straw, or cocoa bean

When purchasing annuals at a garden center, look for healthy seedlings that haven't overgrown their container. Don't buy them too early. These young plants require daily watering and regular fertilizing, and the garden center or nursery is much better able to give this regular care than you are at home.

hulls, to reduce moisture evaporation and suppress weed growth. Just make sure the mulch doesn't overwhelm the small plants and adds to their beauty rather than detracting from it.

Some larger-seeded annuals are easy to start from direct-seeding. These include cosmos, marigold, morning glory, nasturtium, sunflower, and zinnia. Smaller-seeded annuals such as petunia, impatiens, and lobelia are more difficult to sow and require longer growing times before they flower. They need to be started indoors or purchased as plants in spring in order to get flowers by midsummer.

Most warm-season annuals should be seeded indoors 6 to 8 weeks before the last spring frost, but some require 10 to 12 weeks or more. Tender annuals should not be planted outdoors until all danger of spring frost has passed. Even if they are not injured by low temperatures, they will not grow well until the soil warms. Cool-season annuals will tolerate lower temperatures, but even they don't like a hard frost. They can usually be planted outdoors about a week or two before the last expected spring frost date.

Plants started inside or purchased from a garden center need to be hardened off before planting them outdoors. Move the plants outside to a sheltered spot for a few hours, taking them back inside at night. Increase the outside time a little each day. After about a week, the plants should be tough enough to plant outdoors.

ANNUALS THAT AREN'T ANNUAL

There are some plants that are called "annuals" even though they technically live more than one year. Biennials, those plants that complete their life cycle in two years, are usually grouped with annuals. Hollyhocks and Canterbury bells, both technically biennials, will bloom their first year if set out early enough. Tender perennials such as geraniums and verbenas are also usually treated as annuals, even though they will survive from year to year in mild-winter climates. Because they are quick to bloom like true annuals, they are usually grown for one season and thrown out at the end. Lantana is an example of a woody shrub that is often grown as an annual in cold climates.

Foxglove (*Digitalis purpurea*) is a biennial, meaning it doesn't flower until its second summer after seeding. But it is often grouped with annuals in references and at nurseries.

CARE OF ANNUALS

WEEDING

Weeding is probably the biggest maintenance chore with annuals; these plants do not compete well with weeds. Keep garden beds weed free by pulling regularly or covering the soil with organic mulch. Remember to keep the mulch away from the plants' stems.

WATERING

Most annuals need at least 1 to 1½ inches of water per week from rain or irrigation. More may be needed during very hot weather and as the plants get larger. Water thoroughly and deeply to promote strong root growth. Allow the soil surface to dry before watering again. Soaker hoses and drip irrigation that apply water directly to the soil are best. Overhead irrigation destroys delicate blooms and can contribute to many fungi and molds. Watering is best when completed in the morning hours, so foliage has a chance to dry before cooler evening temperatures set in.

FEEDING

Annuals put a lot of energy into blooming and require regular applications of nutrients. An easy way to provide annuals with the nutrients they need is to use a slow-release, or time-released, fertilizer at planting time. One application will slowly release nutrients with every watering. Although these fertilizers cost more than other types, they are usually worth the investment to save yourself from having to apply biweekly liquid fertilizer applications.

The newer annuals require high soil fertility to do their best. Apply a slow-release fertilizer at planting time, mixing it in with the soil, and plan to follow up with biweekly applications of a water-soluble fertilizer.

GROOMING

Because they are only around for a few months, most annuals don't require a lot of grooming. Some of the taller types may need staking or support systems of some type. Staking is best done at planting time to avoid damaging roots. Some annuals benefit from pinching to promote bushiness. This list includes petunias and chrysanthemums. In general, pinching any plant that has become too leggy or too tall will make it bushier and more compact. One grooming task almost all annuals will benefit from is deadheading.

NEW KIDS ON THE BLOCK

A recent boost to annuals' popularity can be attributed to Proven Winners™, a cooperative effort between several annual producers. The introduction of their "new" annuals has made names like bacopa, calibrachoa, and scaveola commonplace among gardeners. Another boost to annual popularity has come from the Simply Beautiful™ introductions from Ball Horticultural Company. You'll find the Proven Winners and Simply Beautiful logos on many of the annuals you see at garden centers.

Not all of the new annuals are about flowering. Recent years have seen an increase in annuals with interesting leaf colors, shapes, and textures introduced primarily as fillers in containers, but also well-suited to garden beds.

OFF WITH THEIR HEADS!

Deadheading is the process of removing spent flowers from annual plants to help stimulate prolonged and repeated blooming. Although tedious and completely optional, it is a good idea for a number of reasons. Removing spent flowers encourages rebloom, eliminates seed production and self-seeding, and makes your garden and landscape look a lot nicer. Cut back to the next set of leaves to encourage new buds to open.

Pruning can invigorate some species. Petunias can be cut back in midsummer to within a few inches of the ground, fertilized and heavily watered, and they will be full and attractive again in just a few weeks.

1 **TO REMOVE ANNUAL SEEDLINGS**, gently pop the young plants from their cell-packs by squeezing the bottoms and pushing up. Do not grab plants by their tender stems or leaves.

2 **WHEN PLANTING ANNUALS**, plant at the same depth they were growing in the containers. If your growing medium is properly prepared, it will be loose enough that you can easily dig shallow planting holes with your fingers. For gallon pots, use a trowel, spade, or cultivator.

 **PLANTS GROWING IN PEAT POTS** can be planted pot and all, but remove the upper edges of peat pots so that the pot will not act as a wick, pulling water away from the roots.

4 **PINCH OFF** any flowers or buds so the plant can focus its energy on getting its roots established rather than flowering, then water well.

PERENNIALS

A plant that is perennial will survive more than one year, and technically can include trees, shrubs, grasses, bulbs, and even some vegetables. In gardening, the term "perennial" is usually used to describe herbaceous flowering plants that are grown specifically for their ornamental beauty. Typical perennials include daylilies, hostas, delphiniums, and yarrow.

Unlike annuals, perennials do not bloom throughout the growing season. Their bloom period can range anywhere from a week to a month or more. Many people shy away from perennials because of their higher initial cost. The extensive choices can also be overwhelming. But the fact that perennials live on from year to year provides several advantages. You will save the labor, time, and expense involved in replanting every year. Your garden will have continuity and a framework to work within. But the most appealing thing about using perennials is the astonishing array of colors, shapes, sizes, and textures available.

The tops of herbaceous perennials often die in the fall, but the roots survive the winter and send up new growth during the spring. Some herbaceous perennials grow a rosette of foliage (small leaves that grow along the base of the plant, similar to what biennials grow) after the stems die off.

Perennials can be divided into evergreen and deciduous.

Perennials are a very diverse and versatile group of plants. There are perennials that will thrive in every soil type, from full sun to full shade. This sunny border includes daylilies, chrysanthemums, and coneflowers.

With a little planning, your perennial border can have something going on from early spring through fall, as in this garden, which includes coneflower, Joe-pye weed, and ornamental grasses.

Perennials that keep their foliage all year-round are evergreen perennials. Deciduous perennials lose their foliage during the fall or winter and produce new top growth in spring.

It is essential to know your hardiness zone when selecting perennials for your garden. (See page 19.) You also need to choose plants based on your soil conditions and available sunlight. After that, it's all about what you like. Choose plants with an eye for color, plant height, bloom time, and even fragrance.

CREATING A PERENNIAL BORDER

As versatile as perennials are, the spot where they really shine is in a perennial border. A perennial border is a wonderful way to bring beauty to your landscape and enjoy these fascinating plants throughout the year. The goal with a perennial border is to create a garden with interest from early spring through fall, and even into the winter. A border is usually more interesting if it contains a wide variety of heights, colors, and textures, but some beautiful borders can be created with all one-color plants or with a target peak bloom time, such as spring.

The trick to designing a beautiful perennial border is to select plants that bloom at different times so you have something blooming throughout the growing season. This may take you a few seasons to master, but it is quite gratifying when it all comes together. Start by reviewing the recommended plants at the end of this chapter and select a mix of early, mid-, and late bloomers that match your soil and sunlight conditions.

A perennial border doesn't have to be all about flowers. Be sure to include showy foliage plants so you have something interesting happening all the time. This border includes Japanese forest grass, ferns, and pulmonaria.

You may want to start with a plan on paper, or you may just want to start planting a few things you like and see how it looks. The nice thing about perennials is that most of them are easily moved. Try to get a good combination of various heights, forms, and textures (spiky, feathery, clumpy, etc). Also consider foliage color because that is important when flowers are not in bloom.

Perennials range in height from well under a foot to 10 feet or more. The standard rule is to stair-step the plantings, placing the tallest in the back to shortest in front. But don't follow this rule too closely. For a more natural look, mix it up a little. Tall, spiky plants can be brought forward for accent and taller see-through plants will add interest in the middle section.

Resist the temptation to plant one of everything. Instead, plant in groups of three or more and, if your border is large, repeat the groupings. Fill areas with textural plants and plants with calming foliage such as chartreuse-leaved sedges, hostas, or ferns. Use flat, ground-hugging plants to fill in gaps in the front of the garden. Billowing plants can be used to link more dramatic plants together. They create a path for the eye to follow. Tall, spiky plants break up the horizontal flow of the garden, adding energy and lift to the overall design.

THE MIXED BORDER

A garden border made up of perennials, shrubs, grasses, roses, and even trees is often more interesting and usually easier to maintain than a border of all perennials. Shrubs, grasses and trees extend the seasons of interest, often into winter, and require less maintenance than perennials. Stick with nonsuckering shrubs and clumping grasses to make sure these plants don't overtake nearby perennials. Trees should be small and upright so they don't create too much shade.

Since it usually takes a few years for perennials to establish and really put on a show, consider planting some annuals among your perennials to fill in the gaps. This border includes wax begonias and dusty miller among the yarrow and black-eyed Susans. Add spring bulbs to bring color to the border before the perennials are up and blooming.

THE SHADY PERENNIAL BORDER

Shade gardens depend more on good foliage, especially in summer after the flush of spring-blooming plants is over. Incorporate plants with interesting texture, form, and foliage colors to keep the border interesting throughout the summer. Variegated plants also make nice additions to shade borders.

Dry shade is found in areas where rainfall is reduced due to some type of obstruction. Examples include under the canopies of large trees or right along the north side of a house. This is an especially challenging place to garden, but it's even more difficult to grow lawn grasses. Mulching is key in these areas to help conserve what water there is in the soil. And careful plant selection is also vital.

Top: A mixed border is dominated by perennials but includes ornamental grasses and shrubs, as well as annuals, ferns, bulbs, and even trees.

Middle: Native woodland plants, such as wild ginger and ferns, are good choices for shady spots.

Bottom: Ferns are usually grouped with perennials, even though they don't have showy flowers. There are many beautiful ferns in a range of greens and yellows that work well in shady perennial borders.

A cottage garden is a charming way to incorporate perennials into a landscape. It typically has a looser, more relaxed style and usually includes a lot of old-fashioned and fragrant flowers. It is a good style for people who like to have a lot of different plants. Included in this garden are coreopsis, monarda, and blazing star.

Most perennials are best planted in spring so they have an entire growing season to develop roots and become established before they have to face winter. Rainfall is also usually more abundant in spring. But container-grown plants can be planted almost any time during the growing season, as long as you can provide them with adequate moisture. If you plant in the heat of summer, you may need to provide some type of shading until the plants become established. Fall planting should be finished at least 6 weeks before hard-freezing weather occurs. Early spring is a good time to plant perennials in colder climates.

Plant spacing depends on each individual species and how long you want to wait for your garden to fill in, but generally about 12 inches is good for most herbaceous perennial plants. Obviously the more plants you can afford the sooner your garden will be more attractive and the fewer weed problems you will have. However, planting too densely can be a waste of money and effort.

Good soil preparation is extremely important for perennials, since they may be in place for many years. Dig the bed to a depth of 8 to 10 inches and work in at least 2 inches of organic matter before planting.

SELECT A VARIETY OF PERENNIALS with varying bloom times, flower colors, and plant heights, as well as a few plants with interesting foliage to fill in.

BEFORE REMOVING PLANTS from their containers, place them in the prepared garden to see how they will look together. Experiment with different groupings until you find an arrangement that pleases you.

DIG A HOLE about twice as wide as each container and deep enough so the plant is just a little higher than it was in the container, to allow for soil settling. Dig holes one at a time to make it easier to maintain the arrangement.

GENTLY REMOVE THE PLANT from its container and pull apart any circling roots. Fill in with soil and tamp it around the plant.

WATER THE ENTIRE GARDEN thoroughly to settle the soil around the roots. Make sure the plants get plenty of water until they are established.

TIP: Create a shallow well ringing around the base of the stem to trap water so it doesn't run off as quickly.

Mulch in perennial gardens will reduce the amount of time you need to spend weeding and watering.

CARE OF PERENNIALS

Pay especially close attention to watering the first few weeks while perennials develop their root systems. Most perennials require at least 1 to 1½ inches of water per week from rain or irrigation. To promote deep root growth, water thoroughly and deeply. Allow the soil surface to dry before watering again. Soaker hoses and drip irrigation are ideal watering methods since they save water and avoid wetting leaves and flowers.

Mulch with a 1- to 2-inch layer of compost, shredded leaves, pine bark, or pine straw to help keep down weeds and conserve moisture. Pull weeds as you see them.

An annual spring application of compost is often all many perennials need. Additional fertilization should be done as needed, based on the results of a soil test. An application of a fertilizer such as 8-8-8 or 10-10-10 at the rate of 1 to 2 pounds per 100 square feet of bed area just before new shoots emerge in the early spring is a common recommendation. Avoid touching any emerging leaves with fertilizer to limit leaf damage.

GROOMING PERENNIALS

Most perennials require grooming to make them produce their best flower show. Grooming activities include controlling tall plants, deadheading flowers, and thinning of plants.

Some taller plants may need staking, especially if your garden is located in an open, windy area. Plants that produce flowers on a single stalk (delphinium, hollyhock) are best supported with individual stakes. Place the stake about an inch from the stem when you plant or very early in spring when the plant is just coming up. Tie the stem to the stake as it grows using a loose figure-eight pattern that won't damage the stem. Use inconspicuous green or brown twine. It may look unsightly for a few days, but in a week or so plant foliage will cover the string and stakes.

Plants with many floppy stems (asters, phlox, shasta daisies, carnations) or heavy blossoms (peonies, phlox, dahlias) should have the entire plant supported by a hoop or series of stakes connected with twine. Many support systems using hoops and sticks of wood or metal are available from nurseries and home-improvement stores. Small tomato cages work well for bushy plants. Get the support system in place early in the growing season to prevent root damage and make it easier on yourself. Once plants get tall and floppy, it is very difficult to make them behave. If you want a more relaxed look or just don't like the idea of stakes all over your garden, try to plant your tall, skinny plants next to sturdier ones that they can lean on for support.

Cutting back taller summer- and fall-flowering species in spring reduces plant height and encourages more compact growth, making these plants more suitable for landscape use. It will also reduce or eliminate the need for staking. Cutting back can also be used to stagger bloom times, extending the period of bloom for certain species. Cutting back of plants by one-half to two-thirds must be done early enough in the growing season so as not to delay flowering too long. This timing will vary in different areas of the country; in the Midwest, for example, it is best not to do any cutting or pinching back after early June. Where the growing season is longer, you could cut back plants up to about mid-June.

Deadheading some perennials will encourage more flowers. It will also reduce unwanted seed production on plants that tend to set a lot of seed and can become weedy. Cutting off spent flower heads eliminates seeds that provide food for wildlife. However, if you allowed every flower to set seed you would be overwhelmed with seedlings in just one growing season

All perennials will need to be cut back at some point. This can be done in spring or fall. Spring is usually a better time. A lot of plants offer winter interest as well as important food sources and shelter for birds and other wildlife. With some plants, fall cutting back is recommended to reduce diseases and keep problem insects from overwintering. Some gardeners like to cut back some of the rougher-looking plants in fall and allow the showier plants to remain until spring to help spread out the maintenance.

If you don't want the maintenance of staking, look for dwarf or compact cultivars of taller-growing species. 'Purple Dome' is a compact cultivar of New England aster that only grows 18 to 24 inches tall and does not require staking.

Peony hoops can be used on any of the bushy perennials that tend to get floppy if they are not supported.

Most perennial plants will benefit from being divided every three or four years. Dividing prevents overcrowding and keeps the plants healthy, vigorous, and more prone to flower production. Some plants with deep tap roots do not respond well to attempts to divide or replant them. Be sure to give careful thought to using these plants before planting, especially in a small garden.

The best time to divide most plants is spring so they have a full growing season to recover. But some plants are better divided in fall.

Water the soil around the plant a few hours before dividing. Prepare the new planting site before digging so you can plant the new divisions right away. Transplant on a cloudy or even rainy day.

1 **CUT BACK THE FOLIAGE** on an overgrown perennial by about one-half to reduce water loss in the transplanting process.

2 **USE A SHARP SPADE** to cut around the plant and gently lift as much of the root ball out of the ground as possible.

3 **SMALLER ROOT BALLS** can usually be cut into pieces using a sharp knife. Larger clumps can be sliced with a sharp spade or pried apart using two back-to-back garden forks.

4 **REMOVE EXCESS SOIL** from the root ball so you can see what you are working with and remove any rotted or damaged roots.

5 **REPLANT THE NEW PLANTS** as soon as possible at the same depth the plant was growing at or slightly higher to allow for settling, and water the soil thoroughly. If you can't replant the same day, pot up the divisions and keep well-watered until they are established.

BULBS

Bulbs are perennial plants with specialized storage roots. In addition to "true bulbs," such as lilies, daffodils, and tulips, other plants that develop thick underground storage parts and are often called bulbs include corms (crocus, gladiolus, autumn crocus, and crocosmia), tubers (tuberous begonia, elephant's ear, and caladium), rhizomes (windflower, canna, iris, tuberose, and lily of the Nile), and tuberous roots (foxtail lily, Persian buttercup, and dahlia).

Bulbs usually bloom for about three weeks and at predictable times each year. They are often classified by the time of year they flower: spring flowering, summer flowering, or autumn flowering.

Spring bulbs are a welcome sight after a long, boring winter. They make dramatic displays wherever they are planted, but are especially nice to see at the bases of large shrubs and trees and in the fronts of flower borders. Although they are full-sun plants, many can be grown in the shade of deciduous trees, where they bloom early enough that the trees have not fully leafed out. They are planted in fall and most are long-lived perennials.

Summer bulbs are often treated like herbaceous perennials and incorporated into borders. Many of them are quite shade tolerant. Their planting times vary; some require spring planting and some do best when planted in fall. Some are hardy, but many need to be dug out and stored over winter or treated as annuals and replaced each year.

Hardy bulbs such as daffodils are a smart investment, especially if you purchase them by the dozens or even hundreds. In the right location, they will multiply and bloom for years.

THE COMPLETE GUIDE TO MID-ATLANTIC GARDENING

There aren't as many fall-blooming bulbs, but they are a welcome sight, bringing color to fall gardens. Most are hardy perennials that should be planted in mid- to late summer. They have rather unattractive foliage that emerges in spring, so it is best to plant them among shrubs or perennials that will mask the leaves until the plants bloom.

PLANTING BULBS

Purchase spring bulbs while supplies are good during September or October. They can also be ordered by mail at any time for fall planting. When buying bulbs, always go for the largest ones you can afford; large bulbs produce bigger and more bountiful flowers. The bulb, corm, rhizome, or tuber should be firm and blemish-free; avoid any that are shriveled, bruised, soft, or moldy. Store bulbs in a cool area below 60°F until planting. Summer-flowering bulbs should be planted in the spring after danger of frost is past. The soil temperature should be at least 55°F. Fall bulbs are usually planted in mid- to late spring.

Roots will grow out of the basal plate at the bottom of bulbs. Make sure this basal plate is down when you plant the bulb or corm.

Prepare the bed well before planting these long-lived plants. Bulbs will rot if they stand in water, so make sure there is good soil drainage. In heavy soil, incorporate 2 to 3 inches of organic matter to a depth of 10 to 12 inches. Remove all weeds and debris before planting. The soil pH for most bulbs should be between 6 and 7. Permanent bulb plantings should be fertilized by mixing a slow-release complete fertilizer or bone meal with an application of quick-release fertilizer at the rate of 1 to 2 pounds per 100 square feet in the rooting area at planting time. It is not necessary to fertilize bulbs that are planted for only one season's flowering.

In general, bulbs are planted three to four times as deep as the width of the bulb. Set the bulbs in place with their pointed ends up and gently press them into the soil. Large bulbs should be 3 to 6 inches apart, small bulbs 1 to 2 inches. For best appearance, plant in masses, especially spring-flowering bulbs. Cover the bed with 2 to 3 inches of organic mulch after planting.

DESIGN TIPS FOR PLANTING BULBS

Spring bulbs should be planted in groups of at least twelve; more if you can afford it. The smaller the bulb, the more you should plant.

Do not plant bulbs in a straight line or a single-width circle around a tree or shrub.

Large drifts of one or two colors look better than a hodgepodge mix of many different colors.

Summer-blooming bulbs look best when interplanted with perennials, annuals, or shrubs instead of in their own exclusive beds.

GARDEN BULBS

Tulips and hyacinths are popular hardy spring bulbs. Both are "true bulbs."

Lilies are hardy summer-flowering bulbs that are best planted in perennial borders.

Autumn crocus, a corm, is hardy in USDA Zones 4 to 11.

SPRING BULBS

Allium species, ornamental onions
Anemone blanda, windflower
Camassia species, wild hyacinth
Chionodoxa forbesii, glory-of-the-snow
Crocus species, crocus
Eranthis hyemalis, winter aconite
Eremurus hybrids, foxtail lily
Fritillaria species, fritillarias
Galanthus nivalis, snowdrop
Hyacinthus orientalis, hyacinth
Iris species, dwarf iris
Leucojum species, snowflakes
Muscari species, grape hyacinth
Narcissus species, daffodils
Ornithogalum umbellatum, star of
   Bethlehem
Puschkinia scilloides, striped squill
Scilla siberica, Siberian squill
Tulipa species, tulips

SUMMER BULBS

Agapanthus africanus, lily of the Nile
Alocasia macrorrhiza, elephant ear
Belamcanda chinensis, blackberry lily
Begonia tuberhybrida, tuberous begonia
Caladium bicolor, caladium
Canna x *generalis*, canna lily
Colocasia esculenta, elephant ear
Crinum species, crinum lily
Crocosmia x *crocosmiiflora*, crocosmia
Cyclamen species/*C. purpurascens*,
   cylcamen
Gladiolus cultivars & hybrids, gladiolus
Hymenocallis latifolia, spider lily
Iris cultivars & hybrids, bearded iris
Lilium species, lily
Ornithogalum thrysoides, chincherinchee
Oxalis species, oxalis
Polianthes tuberosa, tuberose
Ranunculus asiaticus, Persian buttercup
Tigridia pavonia, tiger flower
Triteleia laxa, triplet lily
Zantedeschia species, calla lily

LATE SUMMER & FALL BULBS

Colchicum autumnale, autumn crocus
Dahlia cultivars & hybrids, dahlias
Lycoris species, spider lily
Schizostylis coccinea, crimson flag
Sternbergia lutea, winter daffodil
Zephyranthes candida, zephyr lily

1 REMOVE THE SOIL to the proper depth so that the bottom of the bulbs will be three to four times as deep as the width of the bulbs. Incorporate any needed soil amendments, including organic matter, fertilizer, and bone meal.

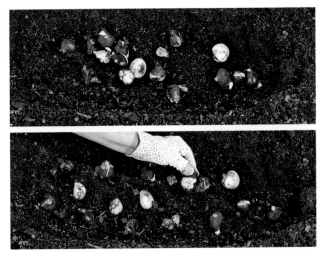

2 TOSS THE BULBS into the garden (top photo). Even out spacing as needed but avoid straight planting lines. Make sure the bulbs have their basal plate facing down, pointed side up (bottom photo).

3 COVER THE BULBS with soil and water well.

Many spring bulbs naturalize lawns well, including snowdrops, Siberian squill, crocus, grape hyacinth, daffodils, most species of tulips, and ornamental onions. Scatter several dozen bulbs, planting them wherever they fall; some bulbs will be far apart, others close together, giving an uncontrolled look. You can naturalize more than one type of bulb but make sure they complement each other. Don't cut the grass until the leaves of the bulbs have begun to yellow, about 4 to 6 weeks after the flowers fade.

CARE OF BULBS

Normal rainfall usually provides enough moisture for spring-flowering bulbs, but in a hot or dry spring, additional water will help prolong blooming. Summer- and fall-flowering bulbs need plenty of water while growing. Bulbs can be mulched to keep down weeds and conserve soil moisture.

Most bulbs will continue flowering for years. These perennial plants should be top-dressed with compost each spring. Some tulips may only bloom well for a year or two and should be replaced as needed.

Do not remove bulb foliage after bulbs finish flowering. Allow the leaves to die down on their own. The leaves manufacture the food the bulbs store to produce flowers next year.

Many bulbs eventually become overcrowded and must be divided and replanted for best effect. Wait to dig bulbs until the foliage has turned yellow and withered. Divided bulbs can be replanted immediately or stored in a dry, cool area for a short while. Discard any bulbs that appear diseased.

Remove the flowers of large-flowered bulbs after they fade to prevent seed formation, but keep the leaves on the plant for at least 6 weeks after bloom is finished or until they turn brown. This allows the energy from the leaves to build up the bulb for next year's bloom. You can plant leafy perennials or showy annuals around bulbs to hide the browning bulb foliage.

DIGGING & STORING TENDER BULBS

Summer-flowering bulbs that are not winter-hardy need to be dug and stored before the first fall frost.

1 **AFTER THE LEAVES HAVE BEEN KILLED BY FROST,** loosen soil with a garden fork and gently lift bulbs out of the soil, being very careful not to damage the bulbs.

2 **SHAKE OFF MOST OF THE SOIL** and trim off all but an inch or two of the stem.

3 **LET THE PLANTS DRY** for a few days until the stems shrivel, then trim the stems off completely.

4 **PUT THE BULBS IN A PLASTIC BAG** with dry wood shavings, peat moss, or shredded leaves. Label the bag and store the bulbs in a cool area away from frost.

GROUNDCOVERS

Groundcovers are low-growing, spreading plants that require little maintenance once established. They quickly cover the ground and hold the soil in place and are often used where other plants—especially traditional lawn grasses—don't do well, such as in heavy shade or on steep slopes. They can be herbaceous or woody and grow in full sun to full shade. Some can take light foot traffic. Groundcovers are also good for camouflaging the dying foliage of spring bulbs. In addition to their practical uses, groundcovers can also become design elements, unifying areas of your garden.

Many groundcovers are just a few inches tall, forming a tight mat over the soil's surface. Some are taller and form spreading clumps that have a more delicate appearance. They are usually green, but can also have purple, maroon, or chartreuse foliage, and many types have variegated leaves. Some even have showy flowers. You can combine several different groundcovers with similar cultural requirements to create a tapestry effect.

Groundcovers are not completely maintenance-free. However, if you take a little time to remove all existing vegetation and prepare the ground before planting, you'll be rewarded with a cool carpet that mostly takes care of itself. Once plants are established, you shouldn't have to do much more than pull an occasional weed and water during very dry periods. Top-dressing with compost every other year or so in spring will eliminate the need for additional fertilizer.

By their nature, groundcovers are

Rather than fighting the conditions and having to regularly reseed and fertilize turfgrasses, consider installing a groundcover, such as hostas, in shady areas that don't get much foot traffic.

aggressive plants. Several popular groundcover plants such as gout weed, English ivy, and vinca have become problems in natural areas, choking out native plants. If your garden is near a natural area, be very careful about plants you use as groundcovers.

ORNAMENTAL GRASSES

Ornamental grasses bring both practical and aesthetic benefits to the landscape. On the practical side, they come as close as possible to being no-maintenance. They are very adaptable, growing in poorer soils than most garden plants, and once established they require very little care beyond the annual cutting back. They rarely need watering or fertilizing and are seldom bothered by insects, diseases, or deer. On the aesthetic side, grasses come in a wide range of heights, colors, and textures and offer more than one season of interest. They also bring movement and sound to the landscape, two elements lacking in most plants.

Ornamental grasses can be annual or perennial, and are often classified according to their main growth periods: warm season or cool season. Cool-season grasses grow best in spring. They like ample water, and may turn brown during times of drought. Warm-season grasses don't really come into their own until midsummer, but once they do, they take center stage right through winter. They tend to be drought-tolerant.

Grasses are also classified according to their growth habits: clump forming or rhizome forming. Clump-forming grasses grow in nice, neat mounds, increasing in width slowly over time. They tend to mix better with other perennials and rarely become invasive. Rhizome-forming grasses are spread by underground stems and can become invasive. These grasses have their place (many make excellent groundcovers on tough sites), but it usually isn't in a formal landscape situation. Obviously, it's important to know the characteristics of each grass before you choose which ones to use in your landscape.

Ornamental grasses can be used as accent or specimen plants, groundcovers, and screens. Many mix well in perennials borders. Some are suitable in

Continued on p. 126

'Dragon's Blood' sedum is a good groundcover for hot, sunny sites.

Ornamental grasses are among the easiest of plants to grow and they often have a multi-season impact in the garden.

1 PREPARE YOUR PLANTING AREA using one of the methods described on page 26. Rake the soil smooth and cover with 3 to 4 inches of organic mulch such as shredded leaves or bark.

2 LAY OUT PLANTS WITH THE PROPER SPACING for their species. This will differ greatly from plant to plant, so carefully read the instructions that came with the plant to avoid overcrowding or isolation. Though not a common groundcover, these pachysandra plants demand a wide berth.

PLANTING UNDER A LARGE TREE

If you are going to install a groundcover under a large shade tree, you don't want to dig up the entire area. This can be too stressful for an established tree, which doesn't like to have its roots disturbed in any way. Instead, plant individual plants among the roots. To find pockets of soil among roots, pound a 2-foot-long steel stake into the ground. In spots where the stake will easily go down at least 6 inches, use a narrow spade or trowel to dig out a small hole for planting.

3 SPREAD APART THE MULCH AND DIG HOLES for the plants to the same depth the plants were at in their containers. Space the plants according to the instructions, set them into their holes, and place soil around the bases of the stems.

4 GIVE THE ENTIRE BED A GOOD SOAKING. Water as needed the first year to make sure plants receive at least an inch of water each week.

The term "ornamental grass" is used to include not only true grasses but also close relatives such as sedges (shown here) and rushes.

water, Japanese gardens, and rock gardens. Native grasses are essential in prairie gardens and natural landscapes. Crafters like to grow grasses for use in dried and fresh arrangements, and some work well in containers. Most grasses, especially those with delicate, airy seed heads, look best against a dark background and placed where they can catch morning or evening light.

PLANTING AND CARE OF ORNAMENTAL GRASSES

The best time to plant ornamental grasses is spring, but container-grown plants can be planted any time during the growing season, providing you can give them adequate water.

When it comes to the care of ornamental grasses, less is often better. A big problem gardeners have is that they want to give them too much water or too much fertilizer. These can lead to lodging (falling over) or root rot in poorly drained soils.

To keep ornamental grasses looking their best, they should be thinned out by dividing every 3 to 4 years. Divide in the spring by digging a whole clump, cutting it up like a pie, removing any dead parts in the center of the clump, and then replanting what is needed. Dividing mature clumps can be difficult and may require the use of an ax or saw to separate the large clumps into useable transplants.

Ornamental grasses grow well on a wide variety of soils with a pH range of 5.0 to 8.0. Established grasses rarely need fertilization; too much nitrogen can result in lodging or flopping over. Leaf color and vigor are good guides to nitrogen requirements. An application of a slow-release fertilizer in spring is usually adequate.

Established plants rarely need watering or weeding, but young plants need a little of each. Water newly planted specimens during dry periods. Covering the soil with mulch in midspring will help reduce weed problems.

1 THE MAIN MAINTENANCE TASK with ornamental grasses is cutting back the browned foliage each spring.

2 YOU CAN USE AN ELECTRIC HEDGE TRIMMER, hand pruners, or even a mower, depending on how big your plants are and how many. Cut back to about 2 inches from the ground.

3 BE SURE TO CUT THE CLUMPS BACK early enough so that you don't cut off any new green growth. Avoid cutting back grasses in the fall as winter injury may result and the winter beauty of the plants and their value to wildlife is lost.

ANNUALS, PERENNIALS, BULBS, GROUNDCOVERS, AND GRASSES FOR THE MID-ATLANTIC

PLANTS FOR PARTIAL TO FULL SHADE

Maidenhair fern, *Adiantum pedatum*

Lady's mantle, *Alchemilla mollis*

Dwarf lady's mantle, *Alchemilla glaucescens*

Japanese anemone, *Anemone* xhybrida

Grape-leaf anemone, *Anemone tomentosa*

Columbine, *Aquilegia* xhybrida

Wild columbine, *Aquilegia canadensis*

Fan columbine, *Aquilegia flabellata*

Wild ginger, *Asarum canadense*

European wild ginger, *Asarum caudatum*

Astilbe, *Astilbe xarendsii*

Chinese astilbe, *Astilbe chinensis* var. *pumila*

Sprite astilbe, *Astilbe simplicifolia* 'Sprite'

Japanese painted fern, *Athyrium nipponica* var. *pictum*

Lady fern, *Athyrium felix femina*

Wax Begonia, *Begonia semperflorens*

Tuberous begonia, *Begonia tuberhybrida*

Bleeding Heart, *Dicentra spectabilis*

Fringed bleeding heart, *Dicentra eximia*

Cranesbill, Geranium, *Geranium sanguineum*

Bigroot cranesbill, *Geranium macrorrhizum*

Wild geranium, *Geranium maculatum*

Hellebore, *Hellebores orientalis*

Christmas rose, *Hellebores niger*

Heuchera, Coralbells, *Heuchera* cultivars

Foamy bells, x*Heucherella*

Hosta, *Hosta* cultivars

Fragrant plantain lily, *Hosta plantaginea*

Impatiens, *Impatiens walleriana*

Martagon lily, *Lilium martagon*

Woodland phlox, *Phlox divaricata*

Pulmonaria, lungwort, *Pulmonaria saccharata*

Long-leaved lungwort, *Pulmonaria longifolia*

Coleus, *Solenostemon* cultivars

Foamflower, *Tiarella cordifolia*

PLANTS FOR GROUNDCOVER USE

Maidenhair fern, *Adiantum pedatum*

Lady's mantle, *Alchemilla mollis*

Wild gingers, *Asarum* species

Chinese astilbe, *Astilbe chinensis* var. *pumila*

Japanese painted fern, *Athyrium nipponica* var. *pictum*

Lady fern, *Athyrium felix femina*

Blue Fescue, *Festuca glauca*

Cranesbill, Geranium, *Geranium sanguineum*

Bigroot cranesbill, *Geranium macrorrhizum*

Wild geranium, *Geranium maculatum*

Hellebore, *Hellebores orientalis*

Christmas rose, *Hellebores niger*

Daylily, *Hemerocallis* cultivars

Hostas, *Hosta* cultivars

Sedum, *Hylotelephium spectabile* [*Sedum spectabile*]

Creeping phlox, *Phlox subulata*

Little bluestem, *Schizachyrium scoparium*

Two-row stonecrop, *Sedum spurium*

Foamflower, *Tiarella cordifolia*

NORTH AMERICAN NATIVE PLANTS

Maidenhair fern, *Adiantum pedatum*

Nodding wild onion, *Allium cernuum*

Blue star, *Amsonia tabernaemontana*

Wild columbine, *Aquilegia canadensis*

Wild ginger, *Asarum canadense*

Butterfly milkweed, *Asclepias tuberosa*

Swamp milkweed, *Asclepias incarnata*

Lady fern, *Athyrium felix femina*

Baptisia, *Baptisia australis*

White false indigo, *Baptisia alba*

Harebell, *Campanula rotundifolia*

Coreopsis, *Coreopsis verticillata*

Large-flowered tickseed, *Coreopsis grandiflora*

Fringed bleeding heart, *Dicentra eximia*

Purple coneflower, *Echinacea purpurea*

Narrow-leaved coneflower, *Echinacea angustifolia*

Wild geranium, *Geranium maculatum*

Blazing star, *Liatris spicata*

Rocky Mountain blazing star, *Liatris ligulistylis*

Eastern blazing star, *Liatris scariosa*

Bee balm, Monarda, *Monarda didyma*

Switchgrass, *Panicum virgatum*

Phlox, *Phlox paniculata*

Wild sweet William, *Phlox maculata*

Woodland phlox, *Phlox divaricata*

Creeping phlox, *Phlox subulata*

Black-eyed Susan, *Rudbeckia hirta*

Cutleaf coneflower, *Rudbeckia laciniata*

Blue Salvia, *Salvia farinacea*

Little bluestem, *Schizachyrium scoparium*

New England Aster, *Symphyotrichum novae-angliae*

Smooth aster, *Symphyotrichum laeve*

Aromatic aster, *Symphyotrichum oblongifolius*

Foamflower, *Tiarella cordifolia*

'Prelude White' wax begonia and
'Non-stop Yellow' tuberous begonia

Swan River daisy

Begonia semperflorens

WAX BEGONIA

Plant Type: Annual
Height: 6–12 inches
Bloom Time: Late spring through first fall frost.
Site: Does best in well-drained soil in partial to full shade but can be grown in full sun if given ample moisture.

This very popular bedding plant has single or double flowers in shades of red, pink, or white that cover plants all summer. The succulent stems support rounded green or bronze leaves, which can be just as ornamental as the flowers. Bronze-leaved types are better adapted to more sun. This prolific bloomer can be massed as a flowering groundcover or used in containers.

Care: The tiny, dustlike seeds take 3 to 4 months to reach flowering size, so indoor seeding is not recommended. Plant hardened-off transplants after all danger of frost. Plants don't usually require deadheading to flower more, but it does help keep the plants looking neater. If you didn't use a slow-release fertilizer at planting time, fertilize every few weeks with a balanced fertilizer. Possible problems include mealybugs, spider mites, thrips, powdery mildew, and stem rot.

Cultivars: There are many selections available. The Pizzazz Series is early blooming with good foliage. The Cocktail Series features dwarf plants with bronze foliage and a wide range of colors.

Related Species: Tuberous begonias (*B. tuberhybrida*) have lush leaves and much larger, very showy flowers in many colors. They require partial to full shade. Tubers can be lifted in fall and overwintered indoors. The 'Non-Stop' Series has very large flowers on plants 8 to 10 inches tall.

Brachyscome hybrids

SWAN RIVER DAISY

Plant Type: Annual
Height: 12–18 inches
Bloom Time: Late spring through first fall frost.
Site: Prefers moist, organically rich, well-drained soil in full sun. Tolerates some drought.

This compact, bushy, mounded, warm-season annual is covered with fragrant daisy-like flowers with lavender, blue, violet, yellow, or white petals and yellow to almost black center disks. Some have double flowers. The gray-green leaves are divided into narrow linear segments. Use this Proven Winners plant as a bedding plant in borders or in containers.

Care: Plant hardened-off transplants outside after all danger of frost has passed. Shear back when bloom begins to decline to encourage an additional flush of bloom and to shape the plant. If you didn't use a slow-release fertilizer at planting time, fertilize every few weeks with a balanced fertilizer. No pest problems.

Cultivars: Blue Zephyr™ has double purple flowers. 'City Lights' has dark pink flowers. Surdaisy White™ has white flowers and greenish centers. 'Toucan Tango' has lavender flowers with green centers.

Calibrachoa

MILLION BELLS®

Plant Type: Annual
Height: 4–10 inches
Bloom Time: Late spring through first fall frost.
Site: Well-drained soil in full sun.

These petunia relatives are prolific bloomers and come in a wide range of colors, from white to yellow to pink to blue. The plants are more compact and smaller than petunias, with flowers about an inch across and daintier leaves. There are trailing types, which are best used in containers, and mounding types, which can be used in containers or as bedding plants. The flowers are attractive to hummingbirds.

Care: Plants are only propagated vegetatively; seed is not available. Put hardened-off plants outside after the last spring frost. If you didn't use a slow-release fertilizer at planting time, fertilize every few weeks with a balanced fertilizer, especially container plants. Plants are self-cleaning and do not require deadheading. No pest problems.

Cultivars: Terra Cotta is a more upright form with flowers in shades of bronze, apricot, and brick-red. Other selections, named for their flower colors, are called 'Cherry Pink', 'Crackling Fire', 'Red Tangerine', 'Trailing Blue', 'Trailing Magenta', 'Trailing Pink', 'Trailing Sky Blue', 'Trailing Yellow', and 'Yellow'. The Callie® Series has an attractive mounding growth habit that is nice in containers.

Impatiens walleriana

IMPATIENS

Plant Type: Annual
Height: 6–18 inches
Bloom Time: Late spring through first fall frost.
Site: Well-drained soil in partial to full shade.

These showy plants are the best annuals for brightening shady spots. They come in a wide range of flower colors from white to pink to orange to purple and some have double flowers. They can be used in containers, in foundation plantings, and underneath large shade trees as long as they get adequate moisture.

Care: Plants take a long time to grow from seed, so it is best to start with plants. Plants are very frost sensitive. Plant hardened-off transplants after all danger of frost has passed. Pinch back stems of young plants to encourage bushier plants. Plants wilt quickly if they do not receive adequate rainfall, so be prepared to water. If you didn't use a slow-release fertilizer at planting time, fertilize every few weeks with a balanced fertilizer. No serious pest problems. Slugs may feed on plants.

Cultivars: Impatiens are usually available as strains of mixed colors. The Super Elfin Series has abundant blooms and a compact growth habit. The Blitz Series has large flowers and is good for containers. The Mini Series only grows 6 to 8 inches tall. 'Victoria Rose' has frilly, rose-pink, double flowers. The Little Lizzy Series features 6-inch, well-branched plants with small flowers in a variety of colors.

Related Species: 'New Guinea Impatiens' have larger, showier leaves, many variegated, and larger, but fewer, flowers. Plants are also a little larger and they can take a little more sun. 'Tango' has orange flowers and bronzy green leaves on 2-foot plants.

Sweet potato vine

Nicotiana

Ipomoea batatas

SWEET POTATO VINE

Plant Type: Annual
Height: 10 inches
Bloom Time: Late spring through first fall frost (showy foliage)
Site: Well-drained soil in full sun.

This tender perennial is grown as an annual for its showy dark purple, chartreuse, bright green, or variegated (green with pink or white) leaves. The leaves are heart-shaped to palmately-lobed and can get up to 6 inches long. Plants usually do not flower. Use it as a groundcover or in containers or window boxes. Groundcover plants typically mound to 10 inches tall and spread by trailing stems to 8 to 10 feet wide, rooting in the ground as they go. It can also be grown up a support as a vine but will require training.

Care: This tuberous plant is not grown from seed. Purchase container plants in spring and set out hardened-off plants after the last frost date. Plants can be trimmed back at any time if they get too vigorous. If you didn't use a slow-release fertilizer at planting time, fertilize every few weeks with a balanced fertilizer. No serious problems, but watch for thrips and flea beetles. Fungal leaf diseases can occur if plants are grown in the same garden area year after year.

Cultivars: 'Blackie' has lobed purplish-black leaves. 'Black Heart' has very dark purple, heart-shaped leaves. 'Margarite' has chartreuse leaves and a nice cascading habit. 'Tricolor' has green-and-white leaves tinged in pink. The Sweet Caroline Series stays more compact and does not produce large tuberous roots, so it better for container use.

Nicotiana alata

NICOTIANA, FLOWERING TOBACCO

Plant Type: Annual
Height: 1–2 feet
Bloom Time: Late spring through first fall frost.
Site: Well-drained soil in full sun to partial shade.

This tender perennial is grown as an annual. The somewhat spindly plants are covered with long-tubed flowers in shades of white to pink to red. Some types have a sweet fragrance at night. Mass it in beds and borders and use it in containers and window boxes. Plant fragrant types near patios and decks. The flowers are attractive to hummingbirds and butterflies.

Care: Start seeds indoors 6 to 8 weeks before the last frost date or purchase container plants and set out hardened-off transplants a week or so before the last expected frost. Plants are more tolerant of cold temperatures than most annuals. Plants often reseed. No serious insect or disease problems, but plants are susceptible to tobacco mosaic virus.

Cultivars: Domino, Havana, Merlin, Metro, Nicki, and Starship are all popular series with more compact growth habits, mixed flower colors, and long blooming periods. 'Perfume Deep Purple' has very fragrant, dark purple flowers.

Related Species: White Shooting Stars (*N. sylvestris*) is a vigorous plant that typically grows 3 to 5 feet tall and has pendant clusters of trumpet-shaped, white flowers that are strongly fragrant. It blends nicely into perennial borders.

African Daisy

Geranium

Osteospermum hybrids

AFRICAN DAISY

Plant Type: Annual
Height: 1–3 feet
Bloom Time: Late spring through first fall frost.
Site: Well-drained soil in full sun.

This tender perennial is grown as an annual. Plants are covered with daisylike flowers all summer long. The central disc can be blue, yellow, or purple. The petals range from white, cream, pink, purple, mauve, and yellow. They sometimes have a different shade at the tips or towards the end of the petal. Some varieties have spoon-shaped petals. Use it in beds and borders. It is a great container plant and does well in window boxes.

Care: Plant hardened-off transplants outside after all danger of frost has passed. Deadhead spent flowers to prolong bloom. Plants can be cut back in midsummer to approve appearance. If you didn't use a slow-release fertilizer at planting time, fertilize every few weeks with a balanced fertilizer. No serious insect or disease problems.

Cultivars: The Asti Series has abundant blooms and good drought tolerance. Plants come in white, purple, and lavender and a mix. The Margarita Series has well-branched plants with flower colors that include purple, pink, and a bronze bicolor. The Sundora® Series has a wide range of colors, including oranges and yellows. The Symphony Series has sapphire blue centers with petals in shades of yellow, orange, and white.

Pelargonium cultivars

GERANIUM

Plant Type: Annual
Height: 1–3 feet
Bloom Time: Late spring through first fall frost.
Site: Well-drained soil in full sun.

This perennial is grown as an annual for use as bedding or container plants. Geraniums are also great in window boxes. The cheery red, purple, pink, orange, or white flowers appear in clusters atop long flowering stalks throughout the growing season. The rounded to kidney-shaped leaves often have dark circular zonal bands.

Care: Deadhead spent flowering stems to promote additional flowering and to maintain appearance. Pinch stems to promote bushiness. If you didn't use a slow-release fertilizer at planting time, fertilize every few weeks with a balanced fertilizer. Poorly drained soils lead to stem and root rots. Plants are susceptible to leaf spots and gray mold. Caterpillars may chew holes in the leaves.

Cultivars: The Allure Series has strong plants that support large, semi-double flowers. The Designer Series has extra large flowers in a wide range of colors. 'Sincerely Yours' is one of the best red selections. 'Melody Blue' is lavender-blue. 'Sassy Dark Red' has dark crimson flowers. 'Regal White' has large lacy white flowers with orchid-colored eyes. 'Maiden Burgundy' has deep burgundy blooms.

Related Species: Ivy geraniums (*P. peltatum*) have trailing stems that spread to as much as 3-feet-wide and lobed, ivy-like leaves and clusters of single or double flowers in shades of red, pink, lilac, or white. They are great in hanging baskets. They need consistent soil moisture, not too wet, not too dry. The Colorcade Series has well-branched plants with long bloom.

'Tidal Wave Silver' and 'Lavendar Wave' petunias

Blue Salvia

Petunia hybrids
PETUNIA
Plant Type:
Height: 10–14 inches
Bloom Time: Late spring through first fall frost.
Site: Well-drained soils in full sun to light shade.

This tender perennial, grown as an annual, has been popular for many years due to its ease of culture and prolific flowering. Plants are bushy to spreading, some as much as 2 to 3 feet wide. The funnel-shaped, single to double flowers come in virtually all colors except brown and black with some picotees and bicolors. Common hybrid groupings include Grandiflora hybrids with large flowers to 4 inches; Multiflora hybrids with smaller but more abundant flowers to 2 inches; and Cascading hybrids, pendulous-stemmed varieties. Most flowers have some fragrance. Use them in beds and borders and for edging and groundcover. They are great in containers, especially window boxes and hanging baskets.

Care: Plants may be grown from seed sown indoors 10 to 12 weeks before last frost date, but are usually bought as bedding plants and planted outside after all danger of frost. Purchased plants often benefit from pinching at the time of planting. Deadhead spent flowers. Cut back leggy plants. If you didn't use a slow-release fertilizer at planting time, fertilize every few weeks with a balanced fertilizer. No serious insect or disease problems. Susceptible to root rot, gray mold, late blight, and tobacco mosaic virus. Watch for aphids, flea beetles, slugs, and snails.

Cultivars: Wave petunias can grow up to 4 feet wide in just a few weeks and are prolific bloomers. The Supertunia® Series are fast growers and expand the color range of petunias; there are double and mini forms available. Surfinia® petunias are similar to Supertunias.

Salvia farinacea
BLUE SALVIA
Plant Type: Annual
Height: 1–3 feet
Bloom Time: Late spring through first fall frost.
Site: Well-drained soil in full sun to partial shade. Tolerates poor soils and drought.

This tender perennial is grown as an annual. It is an erect, branching plant with violet-blue flowers growing in spikes at the tops of the branches. It blends well into perennial borders and natural plantings, but can also be used as a bedding plant and in containers. It is a nice cut flower and it dries well. Butterflies like the flowers.

Care: Plants need to be purchased or seeds started indoors 10 to 12 weeks before the last frost date. Set out hardened-off transplants after all danger of frost. No serious insect or disease problems, but powdery and downy mildew may show up during wet periods.

Cultivars: Selections are available in shades of blue, purple, white, and bicolor. 'Victoria Blue' is a compact cultivar that typically stays under 2 feet tall and has large, deep blue flowers. 'Rhea' is even shorter, 12 to 14 inches, with violet-blue flowers. 'Strata' has blue flowers on silver spikes.

Related Species: Red salvia (*S. coccinea*) has looser spikes of red, blue, orange, pink, or white flowers that are attractive to hummingbirds. Plants grow 1 to 2 feet tall. 'Lady in Red' and 'Forest Fire' are nice red selections.

Coleus

Marigolds

Solenostemon cultivars
COLEUS

Plant Type: Annual
Height: 1–3 feet
Bloom Time: Late spring through first fall frost.
Site: Well-drained soil in partial to full shade.

This tropical perennial is grown as an annual for its very showy multi-colored foliage. Leaf colors include every shade of green, red, yellow, white, purple, and pink. Plants grow in neat mounds. It is one of the best annuals for shady spots. It looks great massed, but individual plants can also be used as specimens. It does very well in containers. Newer types do better with some sun, and some prefer full sun.

Care: Sensitive to frost, so wait until all danger has passed to set out hardened-off plants. Do not allow soil to dry out. Pinch stem tips to keep plants compact and to promote bushiness. Remove flower heads as they appear to highlight the showy foliage. Plants grown in too much sun may wilt. Plants grown in too much shade may become leggy. If you didn't use a slow-release fertilizer at planting time, fertilize every few weeks with a balanced fertilizer. Generally free of pest problems.

Cultivars: The ColorBlaze Series has good branching and is more heat-tolerant. The Wizard Series is self-branching and does not require pinching. The Saber Series has long, saber-like leaves. The Fiji Series has fringed leaves. 'Fishnet Stockings' has wide, bright green leaves with sharply contrasting deep purple veining. 'Flame Thrower' has fiery orange and magenta leaves with a border of purple and a fine edge of green. It is a compact grower good for hanging baskets or urns. 'Kingswood Torch' has magenta foliage that is overlaid with orange and burgundy. 'India Frills' has small, colorful, irregular leaves on a full, compact plant. The Kong™ Series is very shade-tolerant and has very large showy leaves. Plants grow about 18 inches tall, forming a neat mound without constant pinching.

Tagetes erecta cultivars
MARIGOLD

Plant Type: Annual
Height: 1–4 feet
Bloom Time: Late spring through first fall frost.
Site: Well-drained soil in full sun; even partial shade will reduce flowering.

These nearly carefree annuals have cheery flowers in shades of yellow, orange, and mahogany. Use marigolds as bedding plants, in herb and vegetable gardens, and in beds of mixed annuals. They can also be used in containers. French marigolds blend well into perennial borders. Butterflies like the flowers, especially single forms. Marigold flowers are edible and can be tossed in salads or used as a garnish.

Care: Marigolds can be started from seed sown directly in the garden after all danger of frost has passed and soil has warmed to at least 50°F. Plants will bloom in about 6 weeks. Seeds can also be started indoors 4 to 6 weeks before the last frost date and planted outside after all danger of frost. Deadhead spent flowers to encourage more blooms and improve appearance. Plants can also be pinched when young to promote branching. The heavy flower heads on some types may snap when exposed to strong winds and/or heavy rains. Taller types may need staking. If you didn't use a slow-release fertilizer at planting time, fertilize every few weeks with a balanced fertilizer. Aster yellows can be a problem. Susceptible to powdery mildew, botrytis, leaf spot, and stem and root rots. Watch for spider mites and thrips.

Cultivars: The Safari Series produces 8- to 10-inch mounds of delicate leaves covered by broad-petaled flowers. The Inca II Series has very large, fluffy, double flowers.

Related Species: French marigolds (*T. patula*) are more compact, typically growing 6 to 12 inches tall. They have attractive fernlike foliage. They are not quite as heat-tolerant and may stop flowering in very hot weather. The Disco Series has loads of tiny flowers.

Pansy

Zinnias

Viola wittrockiana

PANSY

Plant Type: Annual
Height: 6–12 inches
Bloom Time: Midspring to midfall with deadheading.
Site: Well-drained soil in full sun to partial shade.

Pansies are short-lived perennials grown as annuals. They are a welcome sight to northern gardeners after a long winter. They come in a variety of single colors and combinations, from white to almost black, including purples, reds, yellows, oranges, blues, and pinks; many are bicolored or blotched. The edible flowers make tasty additions to salads. Plant a second crop in mid-August for a few more weeks of color after other annuals have been killed by frost.

Care: Pansies can be planted outside about a month before the last expected spring frost date. They tolerate cool temperatures, but if temperatures threaten to dip below freezing, they'll need some protection. Summer plants will need shelter from afternoon sun. Water as needed to keep soil evenly moist but not wet. If you didn't use a slow-release fertilizer at planting time, fertilize every few weeks with a balanced fertilizer. Give summer plants an organic mulch to help keep the soil cool. Deadhead regularly to prolong flowering, and cut back plants in late June to promote late-summer and autumn bloom. Pest free.

Cultivars: Crystal Bowl, Universal, and Maxim Series are among the most cold-tolerant types. 'Delft' has 2-inch blooms of porcelain blue and white.

Related Species: Violas (*V. cornuta*) are similar but the plants are smaller with smaller flowers. The Jewel Series is especially hardy.

Zinnia elegans cultivars

ZINNIA

Plant Type: Annual
Height: 8–36 inches
Bloom Time: Late spring through first fall frost.
Site: Well-drained soil in full sun; even light shade will reduce flowering and weaken stems.

This old-fashioned favorite is a bushy, leafy plant with strong, upright flower stems. Flowers can be single, semi-double, and double and come in shades of red, yellow, orange, pink, rose, lavender, green, or white. They are great as bedding plants and in containers, especially lower-growing narrow-leaf zinnia. Include taller varieties in your cut-flower garden.

Care: One of the few annuals that can be directly sown in the garden after the last frost and still produce a good show of flowers; most types bloom in 6 to 8 weeks from seed. You can also start seeds indoors 4 to 6 weeks before last frost, but transplant carefully as the young plants resent being moved. Deadhead faded flowers. If you didn't use a slow-release fertilizer at planting time, fertilize every few weeks with a balanced fertilizer. Tall varieties may need staking. Powdery mildew can be a problem. Reduce the risk by providing ample spacing to increase air circulation and avoid overhead watering.

Cultivars: The Button Box Series has double flowers on plants 12 inches tall. The Lilliput Series has small double flowers on plants up to 18 inches tall.

Related Species: Narrow-leaf zinnia (*Z. angustifolia*) has profuse single, daisy-like flowers and small, narrow leaves on bushy plants 8 to 16 inches tall. The flowers do not fade in summer as is sometimes the case with common zinnia, and deadheading is not required. 'Classic' is a nice white-flowered selection. The Crystal Series has a very compact growth habit. The Star Series has star-shaped flowers on plants to 14 inches tall.

Moonshine Yarrow Maidenhair fern

Achillea x 'Moonshine'

MOONSHINE YARROW

Plant Type: Perennial
Hardiness Zones: 3–8
Height: 1–2 feet
Bloom Time: Early to late summer
Site: Well-drained soil in full sun. Tolerates alkaline and dry soils.

This plant has dense, terminal clusters of lemon yellow flowers and beautiful gray-green, fernlike foliage. It is a great plant for the perennial or mixed border. The flowers attract butterflies and are not usually bothered by deer.

Care: Many yarrows are rapid spreaders that become floppy and weedy, but 'Moonshine' is a well-behaved compact selection that does not need staking. Yarrows do not require high soil fertility. Deadhead to promote extended bloom. Divide in spring every 3 years or so, discarding any woody stems. Yarrows make good cut and dried flowers. These plants have very few insect problems. They can suffer from root rot if the soil is poorly drained. Foliage may turn brown at the end of wet summers. You can cut plants back to the ground after blooming to improve the appearance. A nice mound of new foliage will quickly grow back.

Cultivars: 'Anthea' is a more upright version (36 inches tall) with lighter yellow blooms and better disease resistance. 'Coronation Gold' grows to 3 feet tall with sturdy stems and large golden yellow flowers. 'Schwellenburg' has gold flowers and silver-gray foliage on 2-foot plants.

Related Species: Common yarrow (*A. millefolium*) is a rapid spreader. The cultivars are better behaved, but should still be used with caution. 'Fanal' has red flowers. 'Heidi' has pink flowers. 'Summer Pastels' is a mix of flower colors, including white, purple, apricot, and yellow. They all grow about 2 feet tall. Zones 3–8.

Adiantum pedatum

MAIDENHAIR FERN

Plant Type: Fern
Hardiness Zones: 2–8
Height: 1–2 feet
Site: Prefers moist, slightly acidic soil in partial to full shade but tolerates alkaline soil and dry shade.

Maidenhair fern has horizontal, lacy, fan-shaped, arching branches and wiry, black stems. This delicate fern is attractive from spring through fall and its fine texture brings softness to a shade garden. With time, 2-foot-wide clumps will cover the ground. Use it in shade gardens and under large shrubs and small trees. It also makes a nice edging plant. It is a nice complement to bolder shade plants such as hostas.

Care: Transplant it carefully to avoid damaging the thin stems. It requires adequate water during establishment, but is quite drought tolerant once established; fronds may turn brown in late summer during dry years. It does not require high soil fertility but will do best in a rich, organic soil.

Lady's mantle

'Blue Ice' blue star

Alchemilla mollis

LADY'S MANTLE

Plant Type: Perennial
Hardiness Zones: 3–8
Height: 1–2 feet
Bloom Time: Late spring to early summer
Site: Prefers a rich, well-drained soil in light shade but will tolerate sun if there is ample soil moisture.

This low-growing, clumping plant has interesting scalloped leaves all summer long. The chartreuse flowers appear in delicate sprays in late spring and are especially pretty with purple-flowered plants. The leaves are stunning when drops of dew or rain collect on them. Great in the front of a border or as a slow-spreading groundcover. It grows well under shallow-rooted trees and shrubs. It is a good cut flower.

Care: Divide every 6 years or so, in spring. Plants may reseed. The flowers look quite tired by midsummer and may be cut off to better show off the attractive foliage and reduce unwanted seedlings. No insect or disease problems.

Cultivars: 'Auslese' has pale yellow, upright flowers and stays about 18 inches tall. 'Thriller' is a slightly larger selection, to 24 inches, with more prolific bloom.

Related Species: Dwarf lady's mantle (*A. glaucescens*) has smaller leaves and less-showy flowers and stays about 10 inches tall. Zones 3–8.

Amsonia tabernaemontana

BLUE STAR

Plant Type: Perennial
Hardiness Zones: 3–9
Height: 2–3 feet
Bloom Time: Late spring to early summer
Site: Prefers evenly moist soil in full sun or partial shade. Tolerates some drought.

This North-American native is an erect, clumping plant with clusters of light blue, starlike flowers in late spring. The narrow, willow-shaped foliage turns an attractive golden yellow in fall. The dense clumps add structure and long-season interest to a perennial border. A massed planting is stunning in fall.

Care: Plants may require staking, especially if they are in shade. Plants can be cut back by one-half to one-third after flowering for a neater appearance. Divide in fall as needed. No serious pest problems.

Cultivars: 'Blue Ice' and 'Montana' are more compact growing than the species and have deeper blue flowers.

Anemone xhybrida

JAPANESE ANEMONE

Plant Type: Perennial
Hardiness Zones: 4–8
Height: 2–5 feet
Bloom Time: Late summer into fall
Site: Rich, moist soil in sun or light shade. Avoid hot, dry sites. Too much shade will cause the flower stalks to lean.

This late-blooming perennial has beautiful flowers in shades of pink, rose, or white with gold centers. They arise well above the large mounds of foliage on wiry stalks. The dark green, divided leaves are handsome and offer bold texture. The silvery flower buds add interest before flowers open. The flowers last until frost. This is an excellent border plant, especially when the flowers are set off by a dark background. Try it in the woodland garden.

Care: Japanese anemones will spread to form large clumps that can be divided in spring as needed. An early fall frost may damage the flowers. No need to deadhead this late bloomer. No serious pest problems.

Cultivars: 'Honorine Jobert' grows 3 to 4 feet tall and has abundant single white flowers. 'Whirlwind' has semidouble white flowers on 3-foot plants. 'Queen Charlotte' has silvery pink, semidouble flowers on 3-foot plants. 'Alice' stays about 2 feet tall with semidouble light pink blossoms. 'September Charm' has silvery pink flowers with darker rose areas on the petals.

Related Species: Grape-leaf anemone (*A. tomentosa*) has white flowers and dark green leaves. 'Robustissima' is a popular cultivar with mauve-pink flowers. It is hardier, into Zone 3.

Aquilegia xhybrida

COLUMBINE

Plant Type: Perennial
Hardiness Zones: 3–9
Height: 2 to 3 feet
Bloom Time: Spring to early summer
Site: Prefers well-drained soil in partial shade but will tolerate full sun. They do not do well in heavy, compacted soils.

These open, airy plants have unique flowers that dance above lush mounds of foliage. The nodding, upside-down flowers have upward-spurred petals and dangle from the tips of branching stems. They bloom for a month or more and attract hummingbirds. Some are fragrant. Use them freely in borders. They make nice cut flowers.

Care: Plants are rather short-lived, usually about 3 years, but they do reseed. Deadhead if you don't want plants to self-sow. Plants do not usually need staking unless planted on very windy sites. Leaf miners may attack the foliage, causing tan tunnels or blotches. Remove and destroy affected leaves as soon as you see them. Plants can be cut back after flowering if they are heavily infested.

Cultivars: 'Biedermeier' hybrids are compact, 1-foot plants with a variety of bicolor flowers. The Clementine Series grow 18 inches tall with a mix of colors. The Songbird Series grow to 3 feet with a mix of flower colors. 'Nora Barlow' has double flowers, each a mix of red, pink, and green. 'Leprechaun Gold' has violet flowers atop variegated foliage.

Related Species: Wild columbine (*A. canadensis*) is a native plant that grows 1 to 3 feet tall with nodding red and yellow flowers that are very attractive to hummingbirds. It takes quite a bit of shade. It reseeds readily and will naturalize. 'Corbett' is a nice pale yellow selection. Zones 3–8. Fan columbine (*A. flabellata*) stays under 18 inches in height and has blue or white flowers and attractive blue-green foliage. 'Alba' is a white-flowered form that grows 10 inches tall. Zones 3–9.

Wild ginger

Asarum canadense
WILD GINGER

Plant Type: Groundcover
Hardiness Zones: 2–8
Height: 6 to 8 inches
Bloom Time: Early spring
Site: Prefers consistently moist, humus-rich soil in partial to full shade but tolerates drier, less-acidic soils.

Wild ginger is a rhizomatous creeping native plant with large, textured, heart-shaped leaves up to 8 inches wide. The leaves are up early in spring, and they cover the interesting nodding, maroon flowers that also appear in spring. It is an excellent groundcover for the edges of gardens in shady areas and is good for hiding empty spots left by spring ephemerals.

Care: Plants may wilt during dry spells but they quickly recover with watering. Wild ginger spreads quickly but is easy to pull and rarely becomes invasive. No serious pest problems. Snails and slugs may feed on leaves. Deer usually avoid it.

Related Species: *A. caudatum* (western wild ginger) is slightly smaller and has shinier, evergreen leaves. Zones 5–8. European wild ginger (*A. europeum*) grows 6 to 8 inches tall and has semi-evergreen heart-shaped leaves that are shinier. Zones 4–7.

Butterfly milkweed

Asclepias tuberosa
BUTTERFLY MILKWEED

Plant Type: Perennial
Hardiness Zones: 3–9
Height: 1–3 feet
Bloom Time: Mid- to late summer
Site: Well-drained soils in full sun or light shade. Mature plants can withstand drought. Good drainage is essential; plants may rot in overly rich or damp soil.

This native prairie plant has dense clumps of leafy stems topped with broad, flat clusters of fiery orange, red, or sometimes yellow flowers. Older plants will have larger and more numerous flowers. Plants may send up additional stems from the crown as they get older, giving mature plants an almost shrublike appearance. Plant it in perennial gardens, mixed borders, or prairie gardens. It is particularly striking when planted with complementary-colored blue and purple flowers. It attracts butterflies and their larvae, as well as hummingbirds, bees, and other insects. It makes a nice cut flower and the seed pods look nice in dried arrangements.

Care: Set out young container-grown plants in their permanent locations, as the deep taproot makes plants difficult to move. Plants are slow to emerge in spring, so cultivate carefully until new growth appears; you may want to mark the site each fall. Plants can get a little top-heavy and may require gentle staking. Plants rarely need dividing. No major insect or disease problems.

Cultivars: 'Gay Butterflies' is a seed-grown strain of mixed yellow, red, pink, and orange flowers and 'Hello Yellow' is golden yellow.

Related Species: Swamp milkweed (*A. incarnata*) has flat, terminal clusters of pale rose to rose-purple flowers on 2- to 4-foot, sturdy plants. It grows best in constantly wet soil in full sun. 'Ice Ballet' has white flowers and 'Cinderella' and 'Soulmate' have rose-pink flowers. These cultivars do not produce as many seedlings as the species and tolerate drier soils. Zones 3–9.

Astilbe

'Burgundy lace' Japanese painted fern

Astilbe xarendsii

ASTILBE

Plant Type: Perennial
Hardiness Zones: 3–9
Height: 2–4 feet
Bloom Time: Summer
Site: Prefers fertile, moist soil in partial shade, but can take heavy shade (reduced flowering) and full sun, with ample soil moisture.

This large group of showy shade plants has a place in any garden. The smaller types make nice edging plants or groundcovers under shrubs and trees. Astilbes look nice next to water features, but they should not be grown in wet soil. Flowers come in shades of violet, pink, red, and white. They are good cut flowers and they dry well.

   Care: This long-lived, easy-care perennial does well as long as it has ample soil moisture; leaves will turn brown in dry conditions. It may need dividing every 3 years or so. Crowns may lift out of the soil as plants grow older. Cover the crown with topsoil or lift and replant. Plants may reseed but they usually do not resemble the parent plant. Deadheading does not extend the bloom and the dried flower heads add winter interest. No serious pest problems.

   Cultivars: Many cultivars are available. 'Bridal Veil' has pure white flowers. 'Bressingham Beauty' has bright pink flowers. 'Cattleya' has rose pink flowers. 'Country and Western' has soft pink flowers. 'Fanal' has red flowers and deep bronze leaves. 'Rheinland' has pink flowers. 'Sister Theresa' has salmon-pink flowers. 'White Gloria' has creamy white flowers.

   Related Species: Chinese astilbe (*A. chinensis*) is a vigorous plant that tolerates dry soil better. Var. *pumila* is a low groundcover staying about 10 inches tall and bearing dark pink flowers. 'Purple Candles' has reddish-purple flowers on 3-foot plants. 'Visions' grows 16 inches tall with red flowers. Zones 4–8. Sprite astilbe (*A. simplicifolia* 'Sprite') has arching, airy plumes of pink flowers above bronze, finely textured foliage. Zones 4–9.

Athyrium nipponicum var. pictum

JAPANESE PAINTED FERN

Plant Type: Fern
Hardiness Zones: 4–8
Height: 10–12 inches
Site: Prefers a slightly acidic, moisture-retentive soil in partial shade away from afternoon sun.

This showy, well-behaved fern has silver-gray and green fronds with reddish midveins. It spreads slowly from rhizomes. Use it in any shady garden as an edging plant or along pathways. It can also be used in containers.

   Care: Divide as needed, about every 3 years. Fronds will turn brown if there is too little or too much soil moisture or too much sunlight. Snails and slugs may be minor problems.

   Cultivars: 'Burgundy Lace' has silvery purple-bronze fronds. 'Pewter Lace' has pewter-colored fronds and showy pink midribs.

   Related Species: Native lady fern (*A. felix femina*) grows 2 to 3 feet tall and forms a cool green carpet of lacy, deeply cut fronds that arch from the crown, spreading slowly from rhizomes. 'Lady in Red' has attractive deep red stems. Zones 3–9. 'Ghost' is a hybrid between the two species that has soft grayish-green fronds with an overlay of silvery hues accented by contrasting dark maroon midribs. It typically grows to 30 inches in height. 'Branford Beauty' is another hybrid with upright silvery gray fronds and reddish stems. It typically grows to about 2 feet. Cultivars hardy in Zones 4–8.

Baptisia

'Blue Clips' and 'White Clips' bellflowers

Baptisia australis
BAPTISIA
Plant Type: Perennial
Hardiness Zones: 3–9
Height: 3–4 feet
Bloom Time: Spring to early summer
Site: Prefers slightly acidic, well-drained soil in full sun or very light shade.

This North American native has attractive bluish-green, compound leaves on nicely shaped, almost shrublike, plants. The deep blue, pealike flowers occur on spikes up to 1 foot long in late spring and are very showy. They turn into ornamental charcoal gray seedpods that persist into winter.

Care: This long-lived perennial starts out slowly but eventually forms huge clumps that are difficult to transplant, so choose a site carefully. Plants rarely need dividing and resent disturbance. Trimming or shearing foliage to shape after bloom helps maintain the rounded appearance but eliminates the attractive seedpods. Peony hoops placed over plants in early spring will support larger plants or those grown in shadier spots. No serious pest problems.

Cultivars: var. *minor* is a smaller version, staying about 2 feet in height. 'Purple Smoke' grows a little over 4 feet tall and has violet blooms with dark purple centers. 'Solar Flare' Prairieblues™ is a hybrid with interesting flowers, lemon yellow upon opening and aging to orange to violet. 'Twilite' Prairieblues™ is another hybrid with deep violet-purple flowers highlighted with lemon-yellow on 4- to 5-foot plants. Zones 4–8.

Related Species: White false indigo (*B. alba*) grows 2 to 3 feet tall and has white flowers. Zones 4–8.

Campanula carpatica
BELLFLOWER
Plant Type: Perennial
Hardiness Zones: 3–8
Height: 4–12 inches
Bloom Time: Early to midsummer
Site: Well-drained soil in sun to partial shade.

This charming plant has cup-shaped, blue-lilac flowers on tall stems that arise from a neat mound of foliage. Use it at the front of the perennial border or in rock gardens. It is a nice edging plant.

Care: Plants do not require deadheading, but it may extend bloom time. Divide every 3 years or so for best growth. Slugs and snails may damage foliage, especially during moist weather. No disease problems.

Cultivars: 'Blue Clips' has violet-blue flowers. 'Pearl Deep Blue' has darker blue flowers. 'Pearl White' and 'White Clips' have white flowers. 'Birch Hybrid' reaches only about 6 inches and has numerous upward-facing, purple-blue flowers from spring into summer. 'Sarastro' has purple-blue nodding flowers on 18-inch plants.

Related Species: Clustered bellflower (*C. glomerata*) is an upright plant growing 1 to 3 feet tall with clusters of flowers at the tops of stems in summer. It has a coarser appearance and it will spread. 'Joan Elliott' has intense violet-blue flowers on 15- to 18-inch stems. 'Crown of Snow' has white flowers. Zones 3–8. Peach-leaved bellflower (*C. persicifolia*) has nice foliage topped by large, outward facing flowers. It grows 18 to 36 inches tall and may require staking. 'Chettle Charm' has white flowers with a blue edge. Zones 3–7. Harebell (*C. rotundifolia*) is a very hardy native species with wiry flowering stems arising from rosettes of small, roundish leaves. The charming, blue-violet flowers begin blooming in late spring and continue sporadically into fall. Zones 2–8.

Coreopsis verticillata

COREOPSIS

Plant Type: Perennial
Hardiness Zones: 3–9
Height: 1–3 feet
Bloom Time: Late spring to late summer
Site: Well-drained soil in full sun. Very drought-tolerant but does not like poorly drained soils.

Threadleaf coreopsis is a North American native with bright yellow flowers in summer and attractive fine-textured leaves throughout the growing season. It is low maintenance and attracts a wide range of insects, including bees and butterflies. It is a nice cut flower.

Care: Divide plants when the centers begin to die out and blooms are fewer. It will spread by rhizomes and older dense clumps are difficult to weed out. No serious pest problems, but aphids may be a problem. Plants may develop root or crown rots if drainage is poor.

Cultivars: 'Zagreb' has golden yellow flowers on 18-inch plants. 'Crème Brulee' is a hybrid with clear yellow, single flowers on 20-inch plants. It has a long bloom time. 'Moonbeam', another hybrid, has soft yellow single flowers and also blooms for a long time but is not as hardy. It does not require division as frequently as other types.

Related Species: Large-flowered tickseed (*C. grandiflora*) is a short-lived perennial that reseeds. It blooms for a very long time if deadheaded. 'Early Sunrise' has double gold-yellow flowers on 18-inch plants. 'Sunfire' has dark yellow single flowers with a burgundy ring. Zones 4–9.

Dicentra spectabilis

BLEEDING HEART

Plant Type: Perennial
Hardiness Zones: 3–8
Height: 2–3 feet
Bloom Time: Spring to summer
Site: Well-drained soil in full to partial shade.

This garden favorite has soft green, divided foliage and rose pink, nodding, heart-shaped flowers with protruding white inner petals. The flowers hang in a row along on long, arching stems above the foliage. Plants become almost shrublike. It is good for the shaded border or woodland garden. Because foliage yellows and goes dormant midsummer, it is best to plant this it with later developing perennials such as hostas, ferns, and bluestars, which will fill in as the bleeding heart foliage begins to die back. It is a good cut flower.

Care: Cut foliage to the ground when it starts to deteriorate. Divide only if you want more plants. Plants do reseed. No serious insect or disease problems, but is susceptible to aphid infestations.

Cultivars: 'Alba' is a white-flowered form. 'Gold Heart' has beautiful gold foliage and rose-pink flowers. The Hearts Series are hybrids with a compact growth habit, long flowering times, and showy ferny foliage.

Related Species: Fringed bleeding heart (*D. eximia*) is a North American native with beautiful fernlike, grayish-green foliage that persists throughout the growing season. Pink to purplish red, nodding, heart-shaped flowers are carried above the foliage on long, leafless, leaning stems. Plants grow 12 to 18 inches tall. It requires a consistently moist, rich soil to do well. 'Alba' and 'Snowdrift' have white flowers.

Purple Coneflower

'New Hampshire Purple' cranesbill

Echinacea purpurea
PURPLE CONEFLOWER
Plant Type: Perennial
Hardiness Zones: 3–8
Height: 3–4 feet
Bloom Time: Summer
Site: Growth is best in fertile loam, but the soil can contain some gravel or clay, in full or partial sun.

This North American native plant has showy, 3- to 4-inch flowers with purple-pink petals and bristly orange center cones. It begins blooming early- to mid-summer and often continues into fall. Plants are shrubby and branching with dark green leaves and fibrous root systems. The plant itself isn't that attractive, so use lower-growing plants in front as a distraction. The seed heads are attractive well into winter. Butterflies visit the flowers for nectar.

Care: Deadheading doesn't really give more flowers and takes food from goldfinches. Divide only when you have to, since divisions usually don't produce as many flowers. A better way to get more plants is to dig up seedlings in spring, which can be prolific when plants are happy. Very drought-tolerant. Aster yellows can be a serious problem.

Cultivars: The species is beautiful in its own right, but there are many cultivars available. 'Elton Knight', 'Fatal Attraction', 'Pica Bella', Pixie Meadowbrite™, Summer Sky™, and 'Vintage Wine' are good choices for the Mid-Atlantic. If you are interested in a white-flowered coneflower, 'Alba', 'White Lustre', and 'White Swan' have white ray petals and coppery centers. Most cultivars are only reliably hardy in Zones 4–8.

Related Species: Narrow-leaved coneflower (*E. angustifolia*)) is a native prairie species 1½ to 2 feet tall and has stout, hairy, nearly leafless stems topped with paler rose-pink petals that are droopier and appear earlier (late spring). Zones 3–8.

Geranium sanguineum
CRANESBILL, GERANIUM
Plant Type: Perennial
Hardiness Zones: 3–8
Height: 6–18 inches
Bloom Time: Late spring into summer
Site: Needs well-drained soil. Does well in full sun to partial shade.

Cranesbills are free-flowering plants that are covered with showy purple to pink flowers for a long time. Plants are bushy or mounding with deeply lobed leaves that turn deep red in autumn, quite showy in their own right.

Care: Plants often rebloom if they are deadheaded. Foliage can be cut back in late summer to keep plants neater. Plants can remain undivided for 6 to 10 years. Japanese beetles can be a problem.

Cultivars: 'Album' has white flowers. 'John Elsley' has carmine flowers on 10-inch plants. 'New Hampshire Purple' has deep reddish-purple flowers on 18-inch plants and has intermittent flowers throughout the summer.

Related Species: Bigroot cranesbill (*G. macrorrhizum*) has spreading underground stems and is good for groundcover use. 'Ingwersen's Variety' has soft pink flowers. Zones 3–8. Wild geranium (*G. maculatum*) is a hardy native species that grows 1 to 2 feet tall and has loose clusters of purple flowers rising above grayish-green leaves in late spring. Zones 3–8.

Hybrid hellebore

Daylilies

Hellebores orientalis

HELLEBORE

Plant Type: Perennial
Hardiness Zones: 5–9
Height: 12–18 inches
Bloom Time: Late winter to early spring
Site: Does best in rich, humusy, well-drained soil in part shade, but tolerates full shade. Keep them away from cold winter winds.

This clump-forming plant has large, cup-shaped, rose-like, usually nodding flowers with center of conspicuously contrasting yellow stamens. Flowers usually appear in clusters of one to four on thick stems rising above the foliage. They sometimes appear while there is still snow on the ground and bloom for a 2 months or more. Flower color ranges from white to pink to rose-purple, often with interior spotting. Leathery, glossy, dark green leaves are evergreen in warm climates but deciduous in extremely cold winters. Leaves, stems, and roots are poisonous. Clumps will slowly spread through self-seeding and will eventually become an attractive groundcover.

Care: Cut back flower stems after blooming to help plants look neater. The evergreen foliage looks scorched and tattered in extremely harsh winters, particularly if not protected from cold winter winds and/or insulated by snow cover. Plants never really require division and grow best when left undisturbed. No serious insect or disease problems. Crown rot and leaf spot are occasional problems

Cultivars: There are many garden hybrids described as *H.* x *hybridus*. 'Ivory Prince' has ivory flowers tinged with pink that sit well above the foliage. 'Red Lady Strain' has large red flowers. 'Onyx Odyssey' has double flowers in shades of dark purple.

Related Species: Christmas rose (*H. niger*) is small, staying under a foot in height. Plants are slower to establish and only self-seed sparingly in optimum growing conditions. It blooms later than *Helleborus orientalis* but has a similar flower. Zones 5–8.

Hemerocallis cultivars

DAYLILY

Plant Type: Perennial
Hardiness Zones: 3–9
Height: 1–4 feet
Bloom Time: Late spring through summer
Site: Prefers well-drained soil in full sun to light shade, but tolerates a wide range of conditions, including dry soil.

These plants are not true lilies and do not grow from bulbs. They grow from thick tuberous roots, with mounds of long, straplike leaves. The individual flowers only last a day or two, but plants produce flowers for a long time. Peak bloom on most cultivars is midsummer. They are great plants for borders or for massing and some types can be used as groundcovers.

Care: Daylilies are very easy to grow. They do not need staking. Division every 3 to 6 years in early spring will promote better bloom. Snipping off the spent flower blossoms makes plants look neater and encourages more bloom on some types. Few insects bother daylilies, but plants grown in poorly drained soil may get crown or root rot.

Cultivars: There are over 50,000 daylily cultivars available, with flowers in almost every color and a variety of forms, including doubles and bicolors, and a range of heights. Here are some good choices for the Mid-Atlantic: 'All American Chief' (red and yellow). 'Barbara Mitchell' (lavender-pink and yellow-green). 'Bitsy' (lemon yellow). 'Dream Soufflé' (pink and creamy yellow). 'Going Bananas' (yellow). 'Joan Senior' (near white). 'Judith' (lavender pink and green). 'Lady Lucille' (deep orange). 'Moonlit Masquerade' (creamy white, purple, and green). 'Parade Queen' (creamy yellow). 'Siloam Double Classic' (peachy pink). 'Strawberry Candy' (coral pink, red, and yellow). 'Strutter's Ball' (dark purple and green).

Related Species: Tawny daylily (*H. fulva*) is the common orange daylily often seen in ditches. Do not plant this species; it is invading natural areas.

'Green Spice' heuchera

Hostas

Heuchera cultivars

HEUCHERA, CORALBELLS

Plant Type: Perennial
Hardiness Zones: 3–8
Height: 1–2 feet
Bloom Time: Summer
Site: Prefer moist, well-drained soil in partial shade, but tolerates full sun and dry soil.

These versatile plants are mainly grown for their showy maple- to heart-shaped leaves, which comes in shades of green, purple, and orange, with many having overlaying silver and gray tones. Plants send up delicate sprays of tiny flowers in shades of white, pink, or red that attract hummingbirds. Plants grow from neat mounds that slowly increase in size.

Care: Easy to grow. Many people remove the spent flower stalks to better show off the foliage. Plants benefit from dividing every 3 to 5 years; discard the central woody part. Plants can heave out of the soil in winter and may need to be replanted in spring. No serious pest problems.

Cultivars: 'Palace Purple' a very popular selection with dark purple leaves. 'Green Spice' has green-purple leaves with silver accents. 'Caramel' has unique apricot foliage and light pink flowers. 'Plum Pudding' has plum-colored, ruffled foliage with darker purple veins. 'Chocolate Ruffles' has deeply cut, ruffled leaves that emerge coppery pink and mature to a deep purple. 'Electra' has gold foliage with red veins.

Related Species: Foamy bells (xHeucherella) is a hybrid cross between *Heuchera* and *Tiarella* with showier blooms and interesting foliage. It does best in shade. 'Bridget Bloom' has pink flowers. Zones 4–8.

Hosta cultivars

HOSTA

Plant Type: Perennial
Hardiness Zones: 3–8
Height: 6–48 inches
Bloom Time: Summer to fall
Site: Most types do best in well-drained soil in full to partial shade, but some like a little more sun.

Hostas are the standbys of the shade garden. They are mainly grown for their showy leaves, which can be various shades of green, blue, yellow, and white, but many hostas also have showy, fragrant blooms. The more unique types are used as specimens, but other types also make good groundcovers.

Care: Easy to grow if given proper conditions. Leaves will sunburn if plants get too much light. Most do not need division on a regular basis, but it can be done every 3 to 5 years to increase your numbers or reduce plant size. Most plantings are not bothered by diseases, but viruses can appear. Deer, slugs, and snails can be devastating to foliage.

Cultivars: There are hundreds to choose from. 'Elegans' has blue-gray foliage. 'Gold Standard' has gold leaves edged in green. 'Krossa Regal' is a large plant with blue leaves. 'Royal Standard' is a large plant with green leaves and nice white flowers. 'Sum and Substance' is a large plant with shiny gold foliage. 'Golden Tiara' has gold margins and purple flowers. 'Ginko Craig' is a small plant with narrow green leaves edged in pure white .

Related Species: Fragrant plantain lily (*H. plantaginea*) has shiny green leaves and large, fragrant white flowers. Zones 3–9.

'Caesar's Brother' Siberian iris

'Alaska' shasta daisy

Iris siberica

SIBERIAN IRIS

Plant Type: Perennial
Hardiness Zones: 3–8
Height: 3–4 feet
Bloom Time: Late spring into summer
Site: Well-drained, slightly acidic soil in full sun.

Siberian iris are easy to grow, long-lived, have nice green foliage, and—compared to their more challenging relatives the bearded iris—are pest-free. They have the same showy flowers, but in a more limited color range and for a shorter bloom period. The flowers are held well above the upright, grasslike plants and they come in shades of white, blue, red, and violet. Unlike bearded iris, which grow from rhizomes, Siberian iris grow from fibrous roots. Use this plant in perennial gardens; it looks nice next to water features. It is a nice cut flower, but short-lived. Cut just as buds start to open.

Care: The only real maintenance the Siberian iris requires is division every 3 to 5 years in spring to keep the plants from dying out in the centers. Cut back foliage in late fall to eliminate hiding places for rodents, which will feed on the roots. No pest problems.

Cultivars: 'Caesar's Brother' is a popular selection with deep purple flowers. 'Ego' is medium blue. 'Gull's Wing' has white flowers.

Related Species: Dwarf crested iris (*I. cristata*) is a low-growing, spreading plant that typically grows 3 to 6 inches tall. It has pale blue, lilac, or lavender flowers with gold crests on the falls and blooms early to midspring. It will form dense colonies in optimum growing conditions. 'Alba' has white flowers. 'Powder Blue Giant' has pale blue flowers. 'Summer Storm' has deep blue flowers. Zones 3–9.

Leucanthemum Superbum Group

SHASTA DAISY

Plant Type: Perennial
Hardiness Zones: 4–8
Height: 16–36 inches
Bloom Time: Summer
Site: Well-drained soil in full sun to light shade. Too much shade results in floppy plants.

This cottage-garden favorite has large flowers with the classic daisy look. The outside white ray flowers surround yellow center disks. Plants have lance-shaped, dark green leaves and spread slowly to form large clumps. Plants bloom for a long time. Use it in borders and rain gardens. It is a good cut flower.

Care: Remove spent flower heads to promote additional bloom and keep plants looking neat. Divide clumps every 3 years or so to maintain vigor. Taller types may need staking. Plants can be pinched back in early spring to produce more compact growth. No serious insect or disease problems. Leaf spots, aster yellows, stem rots, aphids, and leaf miners may occur.

Cultivars: 'Alaska' has large flowers. 'Becky' grows to 4 feet tall on rigid stems that do not require staking and is a prolific bloomer. 'Sunshine' ('Sonnenschein') has large, pale lemon yellow blooms with golden yellow centers. 'White Knight' is a compact, semi-dwarf selection that stays under 2 feet tall.

Related Species: The weedy, invasive oxeye daisy (*L. vulgare*) should not be planted.

'Kobold' blazing star

'Gardenview Scarlet' bee balm

Liatris spicata

BLAZING STAR

Plant Type: Perennial
Hardiness Zones: 3–8
Height: 2–4 feet
Bloom Time: Midsummer to early fall
Site: Well-drained soil in full sun.

This native perennial has very showy red-violet to mauve terminal flower spikes. The alternate, grasslike leaves increase in size from top to bottom. The root system consists of corms, which occasionally form offsets near the mother plant. The flowers of all *Liatris* species open from the top down and can be one of two general forms: spike or button. All species have strong stems with thin, closely set leaves whorled on the stem. It is a great for perennial borders, cutting gardens, rain gardens, and cottage gardens. Flowers are very attractive to butterflies.

Care: Plants reseed but never become weedy and seldom need dividing. Cut back plants in spring rather than fall so birds can feast on the seed heads. Lower leaves may turn yellow and wither away if conditions become too dry. *Liatris* species may need a little pampering when young, but once established they are easy to maintain. Taller types may need staking. Rabbit and deer like tender young plants and mice and voles eat the roots.

Cultivars: 'Kobold' is a popular compact cultivar that is less likely to need staking than the species, usually staying under 2 feet. 'Floristan Violet' grows 2 feet tall with violet flowers. 'Floristan White' has creamy white flowers.

Related Species: Rocky Mountain blazing star (*L. ligulistylis*) is a button type with dark violet flowers. It grows 3 to 5 feet tall. Zones 3–8. Eastern blazing star (*L. scariosa*) is a button type growing 1 to 4 feet tall. 'White Spire', 'Alba', and 'Gracious' have white flowers. Zones 4–8.

Monarda didyma

BEE BALM, MONARDA

Plant Type: Perennial
Hardiness Zones: 4–9
Height: 2–4 feet
Bloom Time: Summer
Site: Well-drained but evenly moist soil in full sun to very light shade.

This tough, North American native grows from a spreading root system to form clumps. The interesting flowers come in shades of purple, red, pink, and white. It is a great plant for the perennial border, prairie garden, or rain garden. Flowers are favorites of bees, butterflies, and hummingbirds and are good for cutting.

Care: Deadheading prolongs bloom time and improves the plant's appearance. Some types spread rapidly and require frequent division in spring. Cut back some plants in late spring to extend bloom time and encourage compact growth. No insect problems, but some types are very susceptible to powdery mildew. Newer cultivars are quite disease resistant, however. Give plants good air circulation and avoid overhead watering to reduce your chances of disease.

Cultivars: 'Coral Reef' has coral-pink flowers on 3-foot plants. 'Gardenview Scarlet' has bright red flowers on 4-foot plants. 'Grand Parade' has lavender-purple flowers on 18-inch plants. 'Jacob Cline' has deep red flowers on 4-foot plants. 'Marshall's Delight' has bright pink flowers on 4-foot plants. 'Raspberry Wine' has bright purplish-red flowers on 4-foot plants. 'Violet Queen' has deep purple flowers on 3- to 4-foot plants.

Peony

'David' phlox

Paeonia cultivars
PEONY

Plant Type: Perennial
Hardiness Zones: 3–8
Height: 2–3 feet
Bloom Time: Late spring to early summer.
Site: Well-drained soil in full sun.

Peonies are long-lived plants that bring an old-fashioned charm to any border. The sweet-scented flowers are available in shades of pink, red, white, and pale yellow. The mounded plants have nice foliage and the plants are attractive even after flowers fade. They are great cut flowers.

Care: Easy to grow if planted correctly. Peony roots should be planted in late summer. Each division should have three to five "eyes" or buds. Dig holes 18 inches deep and fill all but 8 inches with a good organic soil mix with some superphosphate mixed in. Fill the hole with loose, unfertilized soil. Plant the roots so the eyes are 2 inches below the soil surface. Plants too deep or too shallow will not flower. If you are planting potted plants in spring, make sure the eyes are no more than 2 inches deep when you are finished planting. Staking is necessary, at least for the double-flowered types. Place peony hoops over plants in early spring to avoid damaging plants. Remove spent flowers but do not cut plants back until after a fall freeze. Ants are often seen on flowers but they do not harm plants. Japanese beetles are the main insect pest. Peonies are susceptible to blights and wilts. Fall cleanup and good air circulation help reduce problems.

Cultivars: 'Angel Cheeks' has white double blooms blushed with pink. 'Charm' has red petals flecked with gold. 'Do Tell' has large flowers with light pink outer petals and darker rose pink to red centers. 'Many Happy Returns' has red flowers. 'Miss America' has semi-double flowers with creamy white outer petals surrounding a center of golden yellow. 'Red Charm' has dark red flowers.

Phlox paniculata
PHLOX

Plant Type: Perennial
Hardiness Zones: 3–8
Height: 2–4 feet
Bloom Time: Mid- to late summer.
Site: Well-drained soil in full sun to light shade. Needs good air circulation.

This staple of the perennial border has fragrant, five-petaled tubular flowers densely arranged in large clusters atop stiff, upright stems with narrow leaves. Flowers are attractive to hummingbirds and butterflies and they make good cut flowers.

Care: Intolerant of drought, so water during dry spells but avoid overhead watering. Remove faded flowers to prolong bloom and to prevent unwanted self-seeding. Taller types may need staking. Powdery mildew and root rot can be serious problems. Spider mites and plant bugs can also be a problem, particularly in hot, dry conditions.

Cultivars: 'Bright Eyes' has soft pink flowers with red centers. 'David' has white flowers and good resistance to mildew. 'Franz Shubert' has lilac flowers with white centers. 'Katherine' has lavender flowers with white centers. 'Red Riding Hood' has cherry red flowers.

Related Species: Wild sweet William (*P. maculata*) is a native species growing 2 to 3 feet tall with large, conical clusters of fragrant, pink, lavender, or white flowers in summer. It is a good alternative in areas where powdery mildew thrives. 'Alpha' has rose-pink flowers with darker eyes. 'Rosalinde' has deep pink flowers. Zones 3–8. Woodland phlox (*P. divaricata*) is a shade-tolerant native that has showy blue-purple flowers in spring. Zones 3–8. Creeping phlox (*P. subulata*) makes an attractive groundcover. It grows about 6 inches tall and is covered with pink, lavender, or white blooms in spring. Zones 3–9.

'Janet Fish' pulmonaria

'Goldsturm' black-eyed Susan

Pulmonaria saccharata

PULMONARIA, LUNGWORT

Plant Type: Perennial
Hardiness Zones: 3–8
Height: 12–18 inches
Bloom Time: Spring
Site: Rich, well-drained soil in partial shade. Leaves will turn brown in too much sun.

This nice, neat, mounded perennial has charming flowers in shades of blue, pink, white, or red and plants can have more than one color of flowers. Buds usually start out pink and then mature into the given colors. Plants spread nicely but are not invasive. They are beautiful in small groupings in shade and woodland gardens. Some types are striking enough to be specimen plants. They can also be used as groundcovers in shady areas. The flowers attract hummingbirds.

Care: Remove flower stalks when plants are finished blooming to make plants look neater and highlight the showy foliage. Usually pest free, but powdery mildew and slugs may be problems.

Cultivars: There are many beautiful selections, some with more silvery-gray markings than others. 'Mrs. Moon' has pink flowers that turn blue as they mature and silvery spotted leaves. 'Blue Ensign' has rich blue flowers. 'Majeste' has silvery-gray leaves with narrow green edging. 'Janet Fisk' has blue flowers. 'Benediction' has silver-speckled leaves and abundant cobalt blue flowers.

Related Species: Long-leaved lungwort (*P. longifolia*) has long, narrow leaves marked with silver. 'Bertram Anderson' has violet-blue flowers. Zones 3–8.

Rudbeckia cultivars

BLACK-EYED SUSAN

Plant Type: Perennial
Hardiness Zones: 4–9
Height: 1–3 feet
Bloom Time: Late summer to early fall.
Site: Well-drained soil in full sun.

Black-eyed Susan is well-known by all for its cheery golden yellow petals surrounding a conical cluster of rich brown disc florets. It blooms for a long time, starting midsummer and continuing well into fall.

Care: This species is rhizomatous and will form colonies. It also self-sows and produces abundant offsets. The foliage of *Rudbeckia* species is susceptible to several diseases, including botrytis and powdery mildew.

Cultivars: 'Goldsturm' is a popular compact form. Var. *speciosa* spreads more slowly.

Related Species: *R. hirta* (black-eyed Susan) grows 1 to 3 feet and is a short-lived perennial. Once a planting is established plants will self-seed to keep the color coming year after year. Deadhead spent flowers to encourage additional bloom and/or to prevent any unwanted seedlings. Plants never become aggressive. Showy tetraploid hybrids called gloriosa daisies are derived from *R. hirta*. They have large yellow, orange, red, or multicolored flowers on 2- to 3-foot plants. They bloom all summer and are good for cutting and containers. 'Becky' stays about 8 inches in height. 'Indian Summer' has larger flowers on compact plants. 'Prairie Sun' has 5-inch flowers with golden petals tipped in primrose yellow surrounding a light green cone. 'Cherokee Sunset' is a mix of fully double flowers in shades of yellow, orange, bronze, and russet. Zones 3–7. Cutleaf coneflower (*R. laciniata*) has droopy petals and a green cone. 'Autumn Sun' ('Herbstonne') grows 4 to 7 feet tall with large flowers with drooping yellow rays and bright green center cones. 'Gold Drop' has bright yellow double flowers. Zones 4–9.

Perennial salvia

Sedum

Salvia nemorosa

PERENNIAL SALVIA

Plant Type: Perennial
Hardiness Zones: 3–8
Height: 1–3 feet
Bloom Time: Early to late summer.
Site: Well-drained soil in full sun.

This long-flowering perennial matures into nice clumps. The very showy flowers come in shades of violet-blue, reddish purple, pink, or white. The plants are in the mint family and have fragrant leaves and stems. Use them in perennial borders. They are good cut flowers and they are attractive to bees and butterflies. Plants may be short-lived if not given proper growing conditions.

Care: Pinch back growing tips of taller varieties when they are about 6 inches tall if you want shorter plants. Cut off spent blooms to keep plants neater and encourage more bloom. Plants can be cut back after blooming to get a second bloom. Divide in spring when mature plants start to die out in the middle. No insect problems; powdery mildew can be a problem.

Cultivars: 'May Night' is a popular selection with indigo-blue flowers on 18-inch plants. 'Rose Queen' has rose pink flowers on 30-inch plants. 'Viola Klose' has violet-blue flowers on 18-inch plants. 'Pink Friesland' has rose pink flowers on 18-inch plants.

Related Species: Lilac sage (*S. verticillata*) is a more erect plant growing about 2 feet tall. 'Purple Rain' has smoky purple flowers. 'Endless Love' has violet-blue flowers. Zones 4–8.

Sedum spectabile [Hylotelephium spectabile]

SEDUM, SHOWY STONECROP

Plant Type: Perennial
Hardiness Zones: 3–9
Height: 1–3 feet
Bloom Time: Summer through fall.
Site: Well-drained soil in full sun. Stems tend to topple when grown in too much shade.

This easy-care, clump-forming perennial has large clusters of tiny, starlike flowers that emerge pink, gradually change to deep rose-red, and then turn coppery-rust in autumn, remaining showy through winter. The grayish-green, succulent-like leaves grow in spreading clumps. Flowers are attractive to butterflies. It can be massed or planted in groups or as a specimen. Smaller types are effective edging plants.

Care: Drought- and heat-tolerant, once established. Fertilizer or division rarely required. No pest problems.

Cultivars: 'Autumn Joy' is the old standby with bronze-pink flowers. 'Autumn Fire' is similar but sturdier. 'Bertram Anderson' has small, rounded smoky purple leaves and dusky pink flowers on 6-inch plants. 'Carl' has pinkish stems and rich gray-green leaves. 'Maestro' has blue-green foliage and bright purple stems. 'Ruby Glow' and 'Vera Jameson' have purple leaves and dusky pink flowers on 12-inch plants. 'Xenox' has purple foliage on 18-inch plants.

Related Species: White stonecrop (*S. album*) is a small, spreading groundcover to 6 inches high with clusters of tiny white to pale pink flowers held above the foliage in early summer. Zones 3–9. Variegated orange stonecrop (*S. kamtschasticum* 'Variegatum') has orange-yellow flowers in early summer on 4-inch plants with showy creamy white and pink variegated leaves. Zones 3–8. Two-row stonecrop (*S. spurium*) is a good groundcover in sunny spots, growing 5 to 6 inches tall. 'Dragon's Blood' and 'Ruby Mantle' have good red foliage color. Zones 3–8.

'Harrington's pink' New England aster

'Iron Butterfly' foamflower

Symphyotrichum novae-angliae
NEW ENGLAND ASTER

Plant Type: Perennial
Hardiness Zones: 3–8
Height: 3–8 feet
Bloom Time: Late summer through fall.
Site: Well-drained soil in full sun.

This native perennial has showy flowers with petals ranging from violet to pink to white surrounding yellow centers. Use it in borders to get late summer color. It does well in rain gardens. It is an important late-season pollen source for butterflies.

Care: Tall stems usually need some type of support. Cut plants back to about a foot in spring to promote bushiness. Divide plants in spring every third year to promote vigorous growth. Plants are susceptible to leaf spots, rusts, and mildew, which can leave lower leaves in bad shape by flowering time but usually do no permanent harm. Plants can be cut to ground after flowering if they look too unsightly.

Cultivars: The species is a bit coarse and aggressive, but the many cultivars are good garden choices. 'Alma Potschke' has bright rose-pink flowers on 3- to 4-foot plants. 'Harrington's Pink' has light salmon-pink flowers and grows to 5 feet tall. 'Hella Lacy' grows 3 to 4 feet tall with violet-blue flowers. 'Honeysong Pink' grows about 3½ feet tall and has pink petals with bright yellow disks. 'Purple Dome' is a dense dwarf cultivar (18 to 24 inches) with semi-double, deep purple flowers. 'Red Star' stays about 15 inches tall and has red flowers. 'September Ruby' has deep ruby red flowers on 3- to 5-foot plants. 'Vibrant Dome' has bright pink flowers. 'Wedding Lace' grows 4 feet tall with whitish flowers.

Related Species: Smooth aster (*S. laeve*) grows 4 feet tall and has stunning blue flowers and very nice foliage. Zones 3–8. *S. oblongifolius* 'October Skies' is a compact plant with deep sky blue flowers. Stems typically grow to 18 inches tall. Zones 3–8.

Tiarella cordifolia
FOAMFLOWER

Plant Type: Groundcover
Hardiness Zones: 3–8
Height: 6–12 inches
Bloom Time: Mid-spring
Site: Well-drained, slightly acidic soil in partial to full shade.

This North American native gets its name from the frothy conical clusters of white flowers that are sometimes flushed with pink. They appear in spring. The handsome, bright green, maple-leaf foliage is attractive all summer long, turning a beautiful red in autumn. Plants spread by trailing stolons (horizontal stems), eventually forming a weed-smothering mat of foliage. It is a great groundcover in shade and woodland gardens. Most cultivars are less aggressive and can be used in perennial borders.

Care: Remove unwanted rooted runners at any time to keep plants from spreading too far. Foamflower may need supplemental water during dry periods. No serious pest problems. Deer-resistant.

Cultivars: 'Cygnet' has deeply cut, dark green leaves with dark centers and dense spires of pink flowers that can rise as high as 18 inches. 'Iron Butterfly' has spires of white flowers and deeply cut, dark green leaves with black center blotches and black striping along the mid-veins of the finger-like lobes.

Allium spaercephalon

ORNAMENTAL ONION

Plant Type: Bulb
Hardiness Zones: 4–8
Height: 2–3 feet
Bloom Time: Summer
Site: Well-drained soil in full sun.

This hardy bulb has mauve flowers tightly packed into 1- to 2-inch diamond-shaped clusters. The leaves are fleshy and straplike and have an oniony scent when crushed. Ornamental onions are nice border plants and they make a good cut flowers.

Care: Plant bulbs in fall. Container-grown plants can be planted anytime. Most ornamental onions freely reseed. Remove flower heads after blooming to prevent unwanted seedlings. Divide crowded clumps after flowering. Bulb rot can occur on poorly drained soils. Frost damage may occur on foliage tips, but does not harm the plants.

Related Species: Persian onion (*A. aflatunense*) grows 2 to 3 feet tall with rounded clusters of star-shaped, red-violet flowers. Zones 4–8. Star of Persia (*A. christophii*) stays under 2 feet tall and has round clusters of metallic blue flowers. Giant onion (*A. giganteum*) grows up to 4 feet tall with 6-inch purple flowers. Use it as an accent plant in the border. Zones 5–8. Nodding wild onion (*A. cernuum*) is a hardy native species that grows 12–18 inches tall. It likes full sun and well-drained soil. The nodding flowers are held nicely above the foliage on slightly bent stems. They can be white to pink to lavender and bloom for about a month starting midsummer. Zones 3–8.

Crocus vernus

CROCUS

Plant Type: Bulb
Hardiness Zones: 3–8
Height: 4–6 inches
Bloom Time: Spring
Site: Well-drained soil in full sun

This hardy corm has 1- to 2-inch, upward-facing flowers in shades of purple, white, yellow, lilac, or striped pale or deep blue. The foliage is medium green and grasslike. Plant them in groups of seven or more for best effect. Use them at the front of borders, in rock gardens, or naturalized in the lawn. Plants are long-lived and the clumps will enlarge with time.

Care: Plant corms in early fall, 2 to 4 inches deep and 4 to 6 inches apart. Remember to let the foliage die back naturally. If naturalized in the lawn, do not mow until the foliage matures. Water only if soil is extremely dry. It is not necessary to fertilize. No serious insect or disease problems, but squirrels will dig up newly planted corms.

Cultivars: 'Jeanne d'Arc' is a popular white-flowered cultivar. 'Pickwick' has silver-lilac flowers with darker lilac stripes. 'Purpureus Grandiflorus' has deep velvety purple flowers. 'Remembrance' has violet-purple flowers with a silvery gloss. 'Striped Beauty' has purple and white striped flowers. 'Yellow Giant' is dark gold.

Related Species: Snow crocus (*C. chrysanthus*) blooms several weeks earlier. 'Advance' has flowers that are lemon yellow with purple shading on the outside. 'Blue Bird' has deep violet petals with white margins. 'Blue Pearl' is a delicate blue. Zones 3–8.

Lilies

'Mount Hood' daffodils

Lilium cultivars
LILY
Plant Type: Bulb
Hardiness Zones: 3–8
Height: 2–6 feet
Bloom Time: Summer
Site: Well-drained soil in full sun. Ideally the flowers get full sun but the roots remain cool and shaded.

Lilies grow from true bulbs. Each bulb produces a single stem encircled by glossy leaves. Individual plants are long-lived and become large clumps with time. Garden types include Asiatic, Oriental, Trumpet, or species lilies. Flower colors include shades of pink, red, orange, yellow, and white and can be pendant or upward-facing, spotted, ruffled, or bicolor. Some are fragrant. Plant them in groups of three to five in the gaps between perennials in borders. They are wonderful cut flowers.

Care: Plant bulbs in fall as soon as you purchase them; bulbs dry out quickly. Container-grown plants should be planted in spring. Lilies do not compete well with aggressive, spreading perennials. Fertilize plants in spring to keep them vigorous. They generally do not need supplemental water in summer. Taller types will need staking. You can cut the stem just below the lowest bloom after flowering, but do not cut any lower than this until fall. Aphids can be a problem, often carrying viral diseases. Bulb rot can occur in poorly drained soils. Deer, rabbits, and woodchucks like lilies.

Cultivars: Asiatic hybrids are the easiest to grow and a good place to start. 'Ariadne' has rose-colored flowers. 'Claude Shride' has dark red flowers. 'Connecticut King' has yellow-orange flowers. 'Enchantment' has orange-red flowers with dark spots. 'Iowa Rose' has dark pink flowers. 'Landini' has very dark red flowers. 'Red Velvet' has red flowers.

Related Species: Martagon lily (*L. martagon*) has numerous small turk's cap-type flowers. It prefers light shade. Zones 3–8.

Narcissus species
DAFFODIL
Plant Type: Bulb
Hardiness Zones: 4–8
Height: 6–24 inches
Bloom Time: Spring
Site: Well-drained soil in full sun to light shade.

These long-lived bulbs form nice clumps with time. Flowers bloom for 2 to 3 weeks and come in shades of apricot, orange, gold, yellow, and white and some are bicolor. Flowers can be the familiar trumpet shape, small- or large-cupped, double or single. They are great additions to any border, look great under spring-flowering trees, and some types can be naturalized. Miniature types can be used in rock gardens. All types make great cut flowers.

Care: Plant bulbs in fall, 4 to 8 inches apart and 4 to 8 inches deep, depending on the variety. You can remove spent flowers, but do not cut back foliage until it has died back completely. Plants should be dug and divided after flowering if they start to decline. Daffodils are resistant to pests, including rodent and deer feeding.

Cultivars: 'Actaea' has fragrant flowers with white petals and small, golden yellow cups rimmed with red. 'Ambergate' is a large-cupped variety with copper-orange petals and a deep orange-red cup. 'Aortic Gold' is a trumpet type with yellow flowers. 'Carlton' is a large-cupped type with two-tone yellow flowers. 'Ice Follies' is a large-cupped type with white petals and a flattened ruffled yellow cup that matures to creamy white. 'Lemon Glow' is a trumpet type with yellow and white flowers. 'Mount Hood' is a trumpet type with creamy white flowers. 'Salome' is a long-cupped type with white, pink, and yellow flowers. 'Tete a Tete' is an early bloomer with yellow-orange flowers on 6-inch plants. 'Thalia' has very fragrant, outward-facing, bell-like, pure white flowers with slightly reflexed petals.

Siberian squill

Tulips

Scilla siberica

SIBERIAN SQUILL

Plant Type: Bulb
Hardiness Zones: 2–8
Height: 4–6 inches
Bloom Time: Early spring.
Site: Well-drained soil in full sun; summer shade okay.

This spring bulb has bright blue, star-shaped flowers and narrow, straplike leaves. This delicate plants look best when massed, so plant as many as you can afford. They are beautiful under large shade trees or spring-blooming shrubs and small trees. They blend in well in rock gardens, in woodland gardens, and in perennial borders. They can also be naturalized in lawns. Clumps are long-lived and will slowly expand and reseed.

Care: Plant bulbs in fall, 2 to 3 inches deep and 4 to 5 inches apart. Remember to let the foliage die back naturally. If naturalized in the lawn, do not mow until the foliage matures. Water only if soil is extremely dry. It is not necessary to fertilize. No pest problems and rodents usually leave them alone.

Cultivars: 'Spring Beauty' has a slightly larger, longer-blooming flower in a deeper blue color. 'Alba' has white flowers.

Tulipa cultivars

TULIP

Plant Type: Bulb
Hardiness Zones: 3–8
Height: 12–30 inches
Bloom Time: Spring
Site: Well-drained soil in full sun.

Nothing says spring like a planting of tulips. These cheery bulbs come in almost every color and have a wide range of bloom times. Plant in large masses for best effect. Avoid planting single rows of tulips. Tulips make great cut flowers.

Care: Plant in early fall, making sure the pointed side is up. Plant about five times as deep as the width. The deeper you plant, the later the plants will bloom. Tulips need good drainage. You can snip off spent flower stalks, but allow foliage to brown and yellow before removing it. Rodents can be devastating to tulips, feeding on bulbs and digging them up. Fine, sharp, crushed sand placed around bulbs can deter them. You can cover the entire planting with hardware cloth, but be sure to remove it in spring before foliage emerges. Deer, rabbits, and woodchucks eat plants and flowers.

Cultivars: 'Red Riding Hood' is an early variety with bright scarlet red flowers with a black blotch inside and leaves streaked with brown-purple. 'Stresa' has petals that open out horizontally, giving the flowers a waterlily-like appearance. It blooms very early. Each flower is bright yellow with red stripes and has a yellow interior. The broad, tapered leaves are green but attractively mottled with darker green to brown stripes.

Related Species: Species tulips are longer lived than most hybrids. They are smaller, staying well under a foot in height, and spread slowly to form nice clumps. *T. clusiana* is white with red stripes. *T. tarda* bears several starry white and yellow flowers per stem. These tulips look especially nice in rock gardens. Zones 3–8.

GRASSES

'Karl Foerster' feather reed grass

Blue Fescue

Calamagrostis xacutiflora

FEATHER REED GRASS

Plant Type: Grass
Hardiness Zones: 3–8
Height: 4–5 feet
Bloom Time: Summer
Site: Well-drained soil in full sun. Tolerates a wide range of soil types.

This very showy, upright, clumping grass forms a dense clump that lives for a long time. It is a cool-season grass, so it is up and growing in spring. It has bronzy purple flower heads in early summer that turn an attractive light buff color. It provides a strong vertical accent in borders. Grow as a specimen plant or in groups of three in large gardens. It can be used as a hedge plant.

Care: Cut back in very early spring before any new growth appears. Benefits from division every few years. No pest problems.

Cultivars: 'Karl Foerster' has pinkish flowers in late spring that quickly change to buff-colored seed heads that persist through winter. 'Overdam' is a variegated selection with green and white striped foliage. It grows 3 to 4 feet tall. Flowers are lighter in color. 'Avalanche' is another variegated form with slightly wider leaves and stiff flowers.

Festuca glauca

BLUE FESCUE

Plant Type: Grass
Hardiness Zones: 4–8
Height: 6–10 inches
Bloom Time: Summer
Site: Well-drained soil in full sun. Plants may die out in poorly drained soils. Tolerates light shade, but foliage color is best in full sun.

This cool-season grass forms neat tufts of very fine, blue-gray leaves. The insignificant flowers take a back seat to the foliage, which looks nice from spring until frost. Use it as an edging plant, as a groundcover, in rock gardens, or at the front of borders.

Care: Clumps tend to die out in the center and need to be divided and replanted or replaced every 3 years or so. Cut back foliage in early spring to tidy 3-inch clumps and facilitate emergence of the new leaf blades. Plant 8 to 10 inches apart when planting as a groundcover since clumps do not spread outward very much and weeds may grow between clumps if spaced too far apart. Consider clipping off seed heads to focus attention on foliage. Plants self-sow and can be grown from seeds, but cultivars do not come true. No pest problems.

Cultivars: 'Elijah Blue' has nice powdery-blue leaves and is longer lived than the species. 'Sea Urchin' has very fine blue-green leaves in a dense tuft. 'Solling' is a very fine-textured selection that does not produce flowers. 'Tom Thumb' stays about 5 inches tall.

Japanese forest grass

'Saphirsprudel' blue oat grass

Hakonechloa macra 'Aureola'

JAPANESE FOREST GRASS, HAKONE GRASS

Plant Type: Grass
Hardiness Zones: 5–9
Height: 12–18 inches
Bloom Time: Summer
Site: Does best in a moist, humusy, well-drained soil in partial shade.

This rhizomatous grass grows in dense spreading clumps. It has graceful, arching green leaves that have broad gold stripes. The leaf variegation is affected by the amount of sun it gets. In deeper shade, the striping turns to more of a lime green. Yellow-green flowers appear in loose, nodding panicles. This grass spreads slowly and is usually not a problem for nearby plants. It really brightens up shady mixed borders and woodland gardens. It looks nice draping over paths and walkways. It can also be used as a groundcover, massed, and in containers.

   Care: Trim foliage to the ground in late winter to early spring before the new shoots emerge. Mulch in winter in Zone 5. No serious insect or disease problems and it is not favored by deer. Plants may heave out of the soil in winter and leaves may scorch in hot summers, particularly if consistent moisture is not maintained.

   Cultivars: 'All Gold' is an all-gold selection with a more upright growth habit. 'Stripe It Rich' has long, narrow leaf blades striped in gold and white.

Helictotrichon sempervirens

BLUE OAT GRASS

Plant Type: Grass
Hardiness Zones: 4–8
Height: 2–3 feet
Bloom Time: Summer
Site: Well-drained soil in full sun. Tolerates dry conditions and heavier soils.

This clump-forming, cool-season grass has narrow, spiky, steel blue leaf blades that form a rounded clump. Spikelets of bluish-brown flowers arranged in open, one-sided panicles arching at the tip appear on erect stems rising well above the foliage clump in late spring and turn a golden wheat color by fall. Plants rarely flower in cold climates, however. It is a nice accent plant in borders where the blue foliage offers contrast in a sea of green.

   Care: Easy care; long-lived if given the right conditions. Rust can be a problem in areas of high humidity or moist conditions.

   Cultivars: 'Saphirsprudel' ('Sapphire') has deeper blue foliage and is more resistant to leaf rust. It grows 3 feet tall.

Switchgrass

Little bluestem

Panicum virgatum

SWITCHGRASS

Plant Type: Grass
Hardiness Zones: 3–9
Height: 4–7 feet
Bloom Time: Late summer.
Site: Well-drained soil in full sun. Very drought-tolerant once established.

This native grass is very adaptable, growing on a wide range of soil types. A full-grown clump is a stately sight, especially in fall when the showy seed heads sway above the beautiful golden yellow to deep burgundy leaves. The leaf blades are green, blue-green, or silver. Seeds are produced in open, billowy panicles in late summer. It is great as a specimen or background plant in the mixed border and it can be used as a large-scale groundcover. Birds eat the seeds and use plants for winter cover.

Care: Cut back plants in late winter to 4 to 5 inches. Plants are fairly slow to spread, but division will be needed every 4 years or so to keep plants under control in gardens. Most cultivars to do not produce a lot of seeds but the species will self-sow on open, moist soils. Switchgrass tolerates poor conditions, including poor drainage and occasional flooding. No pest problems. Even deer usually avoid it.

Cultivars: These selections tend to reseed and spread at a much lower rate than the species. Choose a cultivar based on its fall color, the degree of blue in its foliage, its height, or its ability to stay upright. 'Amber Wave' stays less than 4 feet in height. 'Dallas Blues' has broad steel blue to gray-green foliage and huge purple flower panicles. 'Heavy Metal' has metallic blue foliage that turns yellow in fall. 'Northwind' is very sturdy and upright. 'Rotstrahlbusch' has good red fall color. 'Shenandoah' has reddish-purple foliage color by midsummer and a distinct reddish cast to the 3-inch flower heads.

Schizachyrium scoparium

LITTLE BLUESTEM

Plant Type: Grass
Hardiness Zones: 3–9
Height: 2–4 feet
Bloom Time: Late summer into fall.
Site: Well-drained soil in full sun.

This attractive clumping native grass has light green to blue foliage in summer, turning golden to reddish brown in fall and remaining very showy all through winter. Flowering begins in late summer but the thin flower heads really aren't noticeable until they turn to attractive silvery-white seed heads. The fluffy seed heads and crimson-colored foliage are extremely showy in the fall landscape. Little bluestem is among the best native grasses for fall color and its small size makes it easy to use in most gardens. It is good for rain garden use.

Care: Keep in mind this is a warm-season grass and it won't "green up" until late spring. Cut back clumps in late winter. It will reseed. Plants may flop over if the soil is too rich. No pest problems.

Cultivars: 'The Blues' was selected for its good blue-green foliage color. Blue Heaven ('MinnblueA') is noted for its blue-gray foliage, burgundy-red fall color and narrow, upright plant form.

CREATING STRUCTURE

GROWING SHRUBS, VINES, AND SMALL TREES

Most homeowners relegate shrubs and vines to background roles in the landscape—foundation plantings, hedges, screens, and backdrops for showy flowerbeds. And while many of these plants fulfill these roles with style and grace, there are also many that deserve places of prominence in the landscape. Many of these plants have showy flowers, interesting bark, and colorful leaves and fruits, as well as interesting and unusual growth habits.

Before planting any shrub, small tree, or vine, it's essential to know your site and growing conditions, as well as what you want to get from your plant. While a particular plant may look gorgeous in the glossy pages of a nursery catalog, it won't look anywhere near as stunning in your yard if you don't meet its cultural requirements for sunlight, soil moisture, and soil pH. This chapter will help you decide how to use shrubs, vines, and small trees in your gardens, as well as provide information on how to plant and maintain them. You'll also find an extensive list of plants well suited to your area of the country.

Shrubs, small trees, and vines play important roles in gardens, providing structure and form as well as year-round interest.

Many shrubs, such as viburnums, have showy fall foliage and ornamental fruits that persist into winter, greatly extending their landscape value.

SELECTING SHRUBS, VINES & SMALL TREES

A shrub is generally considered to be a woody plant with multiple stems that is usually less than 15 feet tall when mature. It can be deciduous or evergreen. Shrubs are an important design element in gardens. Not only do they provide structure, they also add form and texture and are often relied on to provide a backdrop for showier flowering plants. They often have ornamental characteristics that carry them through more than one season, sometimes throughout the year. Some shrubs are grown for their flowers or fruit, but many are grown for their foliage color and form, which bring structure to a landscape.

Small- to medium-sized shrubs work well in a mixed border, where they complement herbaceous perennials and provide season-long interest. Shrubs with fruits provide winter interest and attract birds and other wildlife. In shade and woodland gardens, shrubs and small trees provide the middle layer that ties together full-sized shade trees and the flowers and groundcovers growing beneath them. Evergreen

Evergreen shrubs are usually planted for the winter color they bring to a garden, but don't overlook their value at other times of the year as well.

shrubs are great for providing year-round interest, either as part of a border, in foundation plantings, or as well-grown specimen plants. Some shrubs can even be used as groundcovers.

Small trees are trees that don't grow over 25 feet tall, or large shrubs that can be easily pruned to a single stem or multiple stems. Small trees are often used as specimen plantings, where the beauty of their flowers, bark, and foliage can really shine. They are good choices for providing shade in small yards, where traditional shade trees grow too big.

Vines are woody plants that have long stems that can be trained to a support structure. Vines often serve a functional role in a garden, screening unsightly views or covering metal fences. They can also be a beautiful part of a garden, bringing color and interest overhead.

EVERGREEN SHRUBS

Evergreens are usually planted to provide interest in the dormant season. While they do excel in this area, they are also valuable for the many other benefits they bring to a landscape. Their evergreen foliage provides a dark backdrop for flowering and fruiting herbaceous plants. They provide year-round screening, and many make good hedges or can be used in foundation plantings, where they offer a certain stability. Evergreen shrubs also offer interest and texture in mixed-shrub borders, provide shelter for birds and other forms of wildlife, or provide food.

Mature evergreens are a real asset when it comes to property value. However, their value goes down quickly if they are diseased or improperly pruned, which is often the case. It is easy to fall in love with cute little "button" or pyramidal evergreens, but keep in mind that they grow into tall or spreading shrubs that aren't easy to keep small with pruning, and they are more susceptible to insect and disease problems when they are growing in a contained space. Most evergreens look best when they are allowed to grow naturally, without a lot of shaping. If you want an evergreen to stay within a certain size range, look for a dwarf or compact cultivar rather than trying to restrict the growth of full-sized species.

A MIXED-SHRUB BORDER

Borders made up of various types of shrubs can be attractive, low-maintenance solutions for many garden situations. They are useful for defining a space or delineating the boundaries of a property. They can be austere, serving as a backdrop

POTENTIAL USES FOR SHRUBS, SMALL TREES, AND VINES

- Accent or specimen plant to stand alone
- Background for other plantings
- Barrier against movement or noise
- Containers
- Creating garden walls
- Directing traffic through your landscape
- Edible fruits
- Foundation plantings
- Groundcovers
- Hedges
- Providing shade
- Providing wildlife habitat
- Screening unsightly views
- Shrub and mixed borders
- Windbreaks

When planted densely, suckering shrubs such as bush honeysuckle (*Diervilla*) make good groundcovers in areas where it's tough to grow lawn grasses, such as in a shady driveway island.

Pruning lower branches helps showcase the showy bark of many small trees, which can be as much of an asset as the flowers and foliage.

QUESTIONS TO ASK WHEN CHOOSING SHRUBS

- Will it survive in your climate?
- How will it be used in your garden?
- What is the mature height and width?
- How much sunlight does it need?
- What type of soil does it require?
- How fast does it grow?
- How much maintenance does it require?
- What is its life expectancy?
- What is the mature form?
- What colors are the flowers and foliage?
- When is the bloom time?
- How long does it bloom?
- Is it fragrant?
- Does it have more than one season of interest?
- Does it have fall color?
- Does it have winter interest?
- Is it tolerant of road salt?
- What are its potential disease and insect problems?
- Do deer or rabbits like to feed on it?

for flowering plants and grasses, or become a brilliant showplace with interest throughout the year.

An effective shrub border is also a way to grow a lot of these interesting plants in an attractive garden rather than scattered throughout the yard. In shrub borders, plants are usually planted a little closer together than their recommended spacing. The idea is to create a solid mass of interesting foliage.

Try to include a variety of foliage and flower colors, but keep in mind scale, balance, and repetition—the principals of design. Include a few small trees to add height and variety. Spring- and summer-flowering shrubs will provide accent color. Deciduous shrubs with attractive bark, persistent fruits, and interesting form, will ensure your shrub border is interesting all year-round. So will evergreens. An underplanting of a shade-tolerant groundcover is all you need to create a low-maintenance shrub garden.

FOUNDATION SHRUBS

Foundation plantings are a part of many homes. But too often they are made up of straggly shrubs that draw attention to the very area they were designed to camouflage. A good foundation planting should not only disguise the foundation, but also lend visual stability, soften corners, and complement the colors of the home. A well-designed planting focuses attention on the front door, which is usually the desired focal point.

Planting dwarf or compact cultivars of shrubs in foundation plantings and other tight spaces reduces your need for excessive pruning. This garden contains compact forms of a spruce and arborvitaes.

SHRUB FORMS

Shrubs come in a wide variety of forms. Here are some terms you may run across when researching what shrubs look like.

- **Arching** shrubs have branches that bend over.
- **Clumping** shrubs have many branches coming up from the base.
- **Columnar** shrubs are tall and narrow.
- **Compact** shrubs have dense foliage.
- **Conical** shrubs are larger at the base than the top.
- **Globular** or **globose** shrubs are globe-shaped.
- **Low-branching** shrubs have branches very close to the ground.
- **Open** shrubs have fewer branches and a sparse look.
- **Prostrate** or **trailing** shrubs run along the ground.
- **Pyramidal** shrubs are dense and upright.
- **Upright** shrubs have rigid branches that grow toward the sky.
- **Vase-shaped** shrubs are tight at the bottom with more-open tops.
- **Weeping** shrubs have branches that bend toward the ground.

It is best to try to keep the natural shape of a shrub, in this case conical, rather than try to severely prune it into an unnatural shape.

Keep foundation shrubs in proportion to the building. Larger homes can handle taller, upright shrubs, but smaller homes require low-growing shrubs with a more horizontal growth pattern. Be sure you know the mature size of the shrub—both height and width—before planting it. Too many houses end up with windows and even doors darkened or completely blocked by shrubs that were tiny and cute when they came home from the nursery. Overgrown shrubs also give intruders an easy place to hide.

Foundation shrubs should be planted in front of the drip line of the eaves so they will receive water when it rains. In snowy climates, keep them in front of the snow line so they won't be crushed when snow slides off the roof. Keep in mind that many foundations are made of limestone or stucco, which can raise the pH of the soil. If this is the case, stay away from acid-loving shrubs.

Shrubs don't have to be limited to foundation plantings and hedges. They work well as part of mixed borders or mixed shrub plantings. This upright columnar evergreen shrub provides a focal point in this mixed border.

Foundation plantings should be carefully thought out to avoid ending up with shrubs that require excessive pruning to keep them away from windows and doorways. These shrubs may look nice, but they will need pruning several times during the growing season.

PLANTING A CONTAINER SHRUB

Shrubs and vines are typically sold in one of three ways: as container plants, balled-and-burlapped, or bare-root. Bare-root shrubs are the most wallet-friendly, but you must plant them before they start growing in spring. Container-grown plants are the most popular and most flexible with regard to planting times. Balled-and-burlapped specimens are large and fill out a garden quicker, but they are also the most expensive. Whenever possible, buy woody plants grown locally. They will have a better chance of surviving in your garden. And they reduce the high costs and fossil fuel inputs associated with transportation.

Container-grown shrubs are the most popular type. They can be planted anytime during the growing season, but the cooler, wetter weather in spring and fall usually gives best results. Bare-root shrubs should only be planted in spring when they are just coming out of their dormancy. Balled-and-burlapped shrubs are usually quite large and challenging to plant. They should be planted in spring or fall as soon as possible after purchase.

Newly planted shrubs should receive an inch of water each week for their entire first growing season. Plan to water if rainfall isn't adequate. Do not fertilize at planting time. Wait a year to fertilizer any newly planted shrubs, and then only if your soil test indicates it or the plant shows signs of a deficiency. Staking is generally not needed for newly planted small trees. They actually grow stronger and are less likely to break if they are grown without support.

1 **DIG A PLANTING HOLE** twice as wide as the root ball, but no deeper. The plant should sit at the same place it was growing in the container or maybe an inch or so above the surrounding soil to allow for settling.

164

2 **PLACE THE CONTAINER** on its side and roll it on the ground while tapping it to loosen the roots. Upend the container and gently pull it off of the plant roots. Do not pull plant by stem.

3 **USE YOUR FINGERS** to loosen any roots that may be matted, gently untangling them. Roots that are tightly coiled should be cut apart and loosened. Gently spread the roots wide so they are pointing outward as much as possible.

4 **SET THE SHRUB** into the hole.

5 **BACKFILL THE HOLE** with the original soil. Mound the soil to create a ridge around the plant to hold water. Water well and cover the soil with organic mulch, keeping it a few inches from the shrub.

CARE OF SHRUBS

Shrubs require all the same basic care that other plants do: adequate water, fertilization when needed, and weed control. These will all vary depending on the individual shrub and where it is grown. In addition, most shrubs also require pruning at some point.

WATERING

In general, water whenever the top 2 inches of the soil is dry. Saturate the soil completely each time you water to encourage deep root systems. Deep watering is especially important during the establishment years. Well-established shrubs usually only need to be watered during dry conditions.

MULCHING

An organic mulch will help conserve soil moisture and reduce weeds. It also keeps the lawnmower and weed-whipper away from stems. Good mulches are shredded bark, pine needles, and wood chips spread 2 to 3 inches deep. Keep the mulch a few inches away from the base of the shrub. Avoid using plastic and stone or weed-barrier fabrics. Very few shrubs grow well in the hot, dry conditions created by the plastic and stone, and weeds eventually grow up into the fabric and it is very difficult to get rid of them.

Azaleas prefer an acidic soil with a pH in the range of 4.0 to 6.0. Iron chlorosis—yellowing of the leaves—often shows up on shrubs that are growing in soil with too high of a pH (alkaline).

FERTILIZING

Most shrubs grow satisfactorily without supplemental fertilizer, but they will benefit from a spring application of 10-10-10 plant food or an organic equivalent sprinkled around the base of plants and watered in well. For some shrubs you may be able to go several years or more before you have to add nutrients. For many native shrubs, an annual application of compost or mulch of shredded leaves is all that's needed to keep them growing well.

Most young evergreens will benefit from a spring application of an acidic fertilizer. Spread a layer of rotted manure or compost around each plant or use a fertilizer such as cottonseed meal, Milorganite, or fish emulsion. If possible, allow needles to fall and decay under plants to return nutrients and acidity to the soil. Keep weeds pulled or smother them with organic mulch. Never cover the roots of these forest trees with plastic or rock.

Plants that lack nitrogen usually have leaves that are a paler shade of green than they should be. The leaves and overall plant size may be smaller than it should be. If you determine your shrub needs fertilizer, the best time to apply it is spring. Avoid fertilizing in the heat of summer or in fall. Fall fertilization can result in new, tender foliage that doesn't have time to harden off before the cold of winter sets in. A slow-release fertilizer with an N-P-K ratio of about 2-1-1 is a good choice for most shrubs. The gradual release of nutrients is less likely to "burn" plant roots.

DEADHEADING FLOWERS

Some flowering shrubs such, as shrub roses, benefit from deadheading to remove the spent blossoms. In some cases it encourages repeat bloom or improves the next season's bloom. It can also make the shrub look nicer. Removing spent flowers is not essential to the health of a shrub, so it is purely optional.

PREVENTING WINTER BURN

Winter burn on evergreens, or browning of needles, is caused by insufficient water during winter. Water deficiency can be due to a sudden drop in temperature, direct sun, desiccating winds, or drought conditions in fall. The sun, reflected from a white snow surface on a still day in February, may cause the temperature in the plants to rise as much as 50 to 60 degrees above air temperature. If the sun goes behind a cloud or building, the temperatures drop suddenly and tissue within the leaves is killed. Plant sensitive evergreens on sites where they will receive some winter shade, and make sure plants receive ample water going into winter.

PRUNING

Pruning is probably the biggest maintenance task with shrubs. You can look at it as a chore, or you can look at as a creative outlet, and one that can often be done in the dormant season when there aren't as many gardening tasks. Many new gardeners don't feel they are up to the task and put it off. But it's much better if you start pruning your shrubs right away when they are young and continue to do minor annual pruning

When cutting a branch back to a bud, make the cut ¼ inch past the bud and angle the cut upward at a 45-degree angle to avoid damaging the bud. If the plant has opposite buds, you can make the cut straight across.

each year rather than let them get overgrown and end up needing major renewal pruning. Regular pruning also helps promote healthier shrubs that produce more blooms.

Start by removing any dead, diseased, or damaged branches. Stand back and take a look. Then decide which branches you should remove to improve the overall shape or size of the shrub. In some cases you will be cutting branches back to a certain point and in some cases you will be removing entire braches at the base of the shrub.

Prune branches back to outward facing buds or to a point where they meet another branch. Avoid leaving stubs of branches, which usually just die back and leave dead sticks on your plant. If your shrub is bushier than you'd like, or if you just want to encourage new growth, remove a few of the oldest branches at ground level. Stand back and take another look and decide if you need to remove a few more branches or not. Remember that once a shrub leafs out, it will appear much larger and shrubbier than when the branches are bare.

PRUNING TOOLS

The three tools that will get you through most pruning jobs are hand-held pruners, loppers, and a small curved saw. Pruning shears are available in two basic designs: bypass and anvil. Bypass shears tend to damage stems less than anvil types and get

THINNING SHRUBS

Shrubs that have numerous stems coming out of the ground can be thinned by cutting some stems all the way to the ground.

Shrubs or small trees with only a few main stems or trunks should be thinned by cutting branches back to a crotch rather than to the ground.

Dogwoods are often grown for their colorful stem color, which is better on younger stems. To encourage continual new stem production, these plants should have some of their older stems removed every year.

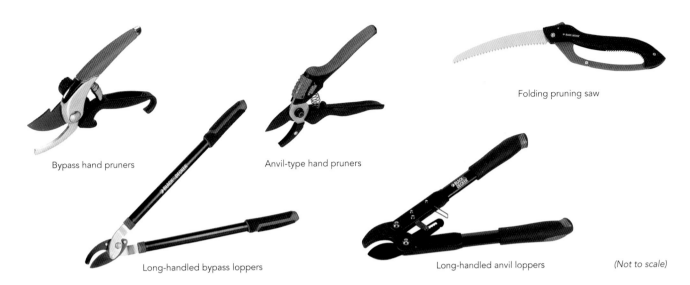

Bypass hand pruners

Anvil-type hand pruners

Folding pruning saw

Long-handled bypass loppers

Long-handled anvil loppers

(Not to scale)

into tighter spots. Anvil shears are more powerful. Loppers are essentially heavy duty bypass or anvil shears with long handles. They can cut branches up to 2 inches thick. A small pruning saw can be used for branches larger than that. Pruning tools are easiest to use and make the healthiest cuts when they are sharp and clean.

WHEN TO PRUNE

Dead, damaged, or diseased wood should be removed as soon as possible to prevent further problems. For the most part, shrubs that bloom on old wood (last season's growth) should be pruned right after they flower and those that bloom on new growth (current season's growth) should be pruned in winter or early spring before growth starts. Pruning cuts made in spring heal quickly and form a callus, preventing moisture loss and dieback. Timing for individual shrubs can be found in the plant section at the end of this chapter.

RENEWAL PRUNING

Shrubs that have gone several years without pruning often end up with all their leaves or flowers at the top of the shrub and bare stems below. These shrubs will benefit from renewal pruning to get rid of some of the older wood and encourage the production of new wood that flowers better. Some shrubs can tolerate having all their branches cut back to a few inches from the ground in spring.

But it is usually best to remove only about one-third of the older, thicker branches at the ground level. If you remember to do the same the next two years, you will end up with a healthy shrub with a new lease on life.

Some shrubs, such at Russian sage, look better when they are treated like herbaceous perennials and cut back hard each year to within a few inches of the ground. This is especially true of shrubs that are marginally hardy and may experience severe dieback each winter.

CREATING A SMALL TREE FROM A SHRUB

There are several large shrubs that can be maintained as attractive small trees with a little regular pruning. You'll have best results with a variety that has a few main branches rather than one with lots of shrubby growth. Pick out a nursery specimen with one strong center stem, or three equally spaced stems if you want a clump form. Remove the unwanted stems at planting time, and each year after that as needed. After a few years, prune off all the lower branches below a certain height, usually about 5 feet off the ground or so, to create a canopy. Maintain the tree form by pruning out any suckers that come up around the base of the trunk.

SHRUBS THAT CAN BE PRUNED AS SMALL TREES

Serviceberry, *Amelanchier ×grandiflora* Zones 3–8

American hornbeam, *Carpinus caroliniana* Zones 3–9

White fringe tree, *Chionanthus virginicus* Zones 4–9

Pagoda dogwood, *Cornus alternifolia* Zones 3–8

Flowering dogwood, *Cornus florida* Zones 5–9

Kousa dogwood, *Cornus kousa* Zones 5–8

Cornelian cherry, *Cornus mas* Zones 5–8

Gray dogwood, *Cornus racemosa* Zones 3–8

Smoke tree, *Cotinus coggygria* Zones 4–8

Dwarf fothergilla, *Fothergilla gardenii* Zones 5–9

Smooth hydrangea, *Hydrangea arborescens* Zones 3–9

Florida anise tree, *Ilicium floridanum* Zones 7–9

Spicebush, *Lindera benzoin* Zones 5–9

Loebner magnolia, *Magnolia ×loebneri* Zones 4–9

Saucer magnolia, *Magnolia ×soulangiana* Zones 5–9

Star magnolia, *Magnolia stellata* Zones 4–8

Holly osmanthus, *Osmanthus heterophyllus* Zones 7–9

Chinese photinia, *Photinia serrulata* Zones 6–9

Carolina cherry laurel, *Prunus caroliniana* Zones 7–10

Hop tree, *Ptelea trifoliata* Zones 4–9

Tiger Eyes® sumac, *Rhus typhina* 'Baitiger' Zones 4–8

Cutleaf staghorn sumac, *Rhus typhina* 'Laciniata' Zones 3–8

Silver buffaloberry, *Shepherdia argentea* Zones 3–9

Nannyberry viburnum, *Viburnum lentago* Zones 3–8

Blackhaw viburnum, *Viburnum prunifolium* Zones 4–8

PRUNING CONIFERS

Most evergreen conifers grow best if allowed to maintain their natural shape, so keep pruning to a minimum. To avoid having an evergreen shrub overgrow its spot, choose a compact or dwarf cultivar in foundation plantings and small gardens.

Many conifers only grow from their tips, so you should make all your pruning cuts in the current season's growth. An annual shaping that only removes new growth back to a bud is best. If you prune too far back behind the foliage, the branch will die. Some evergreens have latent buds all along their branches and can be pruned and shaped quite severely.

The best time to prune most conifers is after the new growth in completed in late spring or early summer. Remove any dead, damaged, or diseased parts of evergreens at any time of year. Give newly pruned plants a good drink of water after pruning to help them get back on their feet.

PRUNING A PINE

Prune pines by pinching the "candles" that appear in late spring. The amount you pinch off depends on how much you want to reduce the plant's size, but try to avoid taking off more than half of the candle in one year.

HEDGES

When shrubs are planted close enough together so that they form a linear row, they are collectively called a hedge. Hedges can be as short as a foot or more than 6 feet tall. A hedge is usually functional in the landscape, marking a property line, providing a backdrop or privacy screen, or blocking prevailing wind.

When the plants are sheared regularly so they have the appearance of almost all one shrub, it is a formal hedge. Formal hedges work best when the shrub used has a naturally dense growth habit and small leaves. Formal hedges usually require trimming several times a year to keep them looking neat.

When shrubs are left more or less in their natural state, they form an informal hedge. They require much less maintenance than formal hedges. How and when they are pruned depends on the species used and when they flower. They are usually pruned once right after flowering and then only again if they require some "touching up." Most shrubs can be used in informal hedges.

With a little annual pruning of suckers that grow from the base, this shrubby serviceberry can become a beautiful multi-trunked small tree.

SHRUBS AND TREES FOR FORMAL HEDGES

Korean boxwood, *Buxus microphylla koreana* Zones 4–9

Common boxwood, *Buxus sempervirens* Zones 5–8

Globe Russian peashrub, *Caragana frutex* 'Globosa' Zones 2–7

Pygmy peashrub, *Caragana pygmaea* Zones 3–7

Red-osier dogwood, *Cornus sericea* Zones 2–7

Hedge cotoneaster, *Cotoneaster lucidus* Zones 3–7

Forsythia, *Forsythia* cultivars Zones 4–8

Dwarf sea buckthorn, *Hippophae rhamnoides* 'Sprite' Zones 4–7

Meserve holly, *Ilex xmeservaea* Zones 5–8

Winterberry, *Ilex verticillata* Zones 3–9

Chinese photinia, *Photinia serrulata* Zones 6–9

Dwarf ninebark, *Physocarpus opulifolius* 'Nanus' Zones 2–7

White spruce, *Picea glauca* Zones 2–6

Alpine currant, *Ribes alpinum* Zones 2–7

Taunton yew, *Taxus xmedia* 'Taunton' Zones 5–7

Techny arborvitae, *Thuja occidentalis* 'Techny' Zones 3–7

Hemlock, *Tsuga canadensis* Zones 3–7

American highbush cranberry, *Viburnum trilobum* 'Compactum', 'Alfredo' Zones 2–7

Formal hedges are an attractive way to provide a barrier or wall, but they require regular shearing to maintain their neat shape.

PLANTING A BARE-ROOT HEDGE

Bare-root plants are good choices for hedging because they are usually less expensive than container or burlapped ball plants. They look scrawny at first, but a healthy, well-grown bare-root plant is easy to plant and often establishes a root system quickly. Healthy bare-root shrubs should have tight buds that haven't leafed out yet, canker-free stems, and roots that are light brown or white, and firm, not slimy.

1 PREPARE THE GROUND thoroughly by digging a trench about 2 feet wide. Amend the soil as needed and return the soil loosely to the trench. Plants should be put in the ground as soon as possible after you get them. If you can, prepare the planting area the previous fall so all you have to do is get the plants in the ground in spring.

2 PLACE EDGING MATERIAL all around the areas where the hedge will be to prevent weeds from moving in. Cover the garden with 2 to 3 inches of shredded bark mulch.

3 HEDGEROW SHRUBS MUST BE SPACED at consistent intervals. Divide the length of your trench by the number of plants you have to determine how far apart to space the shrubs and place the shrubs in their spots. Make sure the spacing is within the guidelines for your shrub type.

4 **PULL BACK THE MULCH** and dig the holes wider and deeper than the largest roots. Make a firm cone of soil in the bottom of each hole.

5 **HOLD THE PLANT UPRIGHT** so the crown is slightly below the soil line, and spread the roots out over the soil cone. Add soil as needed to keep the plant's crown at the correct depth. Make sure to fill in the hole completely with soil to avoid air pockets where the roots may dry out.

6 **WATER WELL** to settle the soil. If the plant drops below the desired level, raise it to the proper level and add more soil beneath the cone. Gently pull the mulch back up around the plant, keeping it a few inches away from the stem itself.

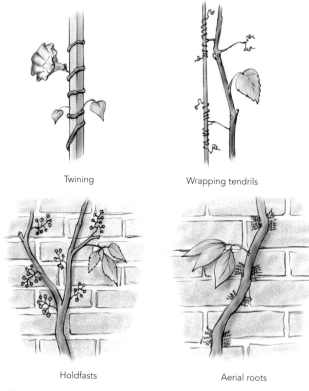

Twining

Wrapping tendrils

Holdfasts

Aerial roots

Vines cling to supports in one of three ways: wrapping tendrils, twining around, or clinging with holdfasts or aerial roots. Be sure you know what type of method a vine needs before you bring it home from the nursery.

VINES

Vines are usually grown up and across a surface. They may or may or may not need support, depending on their growth habits. They can be trained to grow up a trellis, on the side of a building, or allowed to sprawl as a groundcover. Vines are usually called upon to perform a function, such as hiding an unsightly view or creating shade under an arbor. Many have very ornamental traits such as colorful flowers and showy seedpods and are appreciated for the aesthetic value they bring to a garden.

Clinging vines use aerial roots or small sucker pads to attach themselves to their support structure. These vines climb almost anything, including smooth walls, and they can eventually mar the surface of their support.

Twining vines wind their stems around anything they can reach. They will climb on thin, vertical supports such as strings or poles.

Vines with tendrils (modified leaves) coil them around their support structure. These vines need slender supports such as wire or lath, since their tendrils can't usually encircle anything larger than 2 inches in diameter.

Begin training and anchoring vines when they are young. Vines require pruning throughout their life to look good and function properly. They may also need to be pruned to prevent property damage or screening of windows or doors.

Most vines are pruned to keep them from getting out of hand and taking over their support structure. You should also plan to remove dead and damaged stems whenever you see them. And most flowering vines need to be pruned regularly so that the flowers form all along the vine rather than just at the ends. The timing of pruning is similar to shrubs—right after blooming for early-flowering species and early spring for later-flowering species.

When growing a vine against a wall, use a trellis or some other type of spacer to allow for air circulation behind the plant and keep the plant off the house siding. This will make for a healthier plant and simplify home maintenance.

PRUNING CLEMATIS

Clematis are among the most beautiful of vines, with their very showy flowers. They are also very well-behaved. They can be a little tricky to prune, however, mainly because different cultivars bloom at different times. Make sure you know which type of clematis you have before you begin pruning.

Early-flowering clematis bloom on old wood and should be lightly pruned and shaped right after they are finished flowering to avoid losing next year's flowers. *Midseason* types flower from early summer through late summer on the previous year's shoots and then again later on the current year's growth. Prune them in early spring before the new shoots form to avoid losing next year's flowers. By pruning the previous year's stems to slightly different lengths, it's possible to stagger the development of flowers and extend the bloom period. *Late-flowering* clematis flower from midsummer into early fall. Flowers are produced on shoots from the current year's growth, so start pruning before the new shoots form to avoid losing the current year's flowers.

'Victoria' is a large-flowered clematis that has deep pink to mauve flowers in mid- to late summer, so it would be considered a late-flowering type for pruning purposes.

VINES FOR THE MID-ATLANTIC

Hardy kiwi, *Actinidia kolomitka* Zones 4–8

Dutchman's pipe, *Aristolochia macrophylla* Zones 4–8

Crossvine, *Bignonia capreolata* Zones 5–9

Trumpet vine, *Campsis radicans* Zones 4–9

American bittersweet, *Celastrus scandens* Zones 3–8

Clematis, *Clematis* species, hybrids, & cultivars Zones 3–9

Virgin's bower, *Clematis virginiana* Zones 2–9

Carolina jessamine, *Gelsemium sempervirens* Zones 7–10

Climbing hydrangea, *Hydrangea anomela* subsp. *petiolaris* Zones 4–8

Dropmore scarlet honeysuckle, *Lonicera* x*brownii* 'Dropmore Scarlet' Zones 3–8

Trumpet honeysuckle, *Lonicera sempervirens* Zones 4–9

Engelmann ivy, *Parthenocissus quinquefolia* 'Engelmannii' Zones 3–8

Maypop, *Passiflora incarnata* Zones 5–9

William Baffin rose, *Rosa* 'William Baffin' Zones 4–9

Riverbank grape, *Vitis riparia* Zones 3–9

American wisteria, *Wisteria frutescens* Zones 5–9

'Aunt Dee' Kentucky wisteria, *Wisteria macrostachya* Zones 3–9

Climbing roses are often grown as vines but they are not true vines. These plants have long canes, or stems, that must be tied and trained into place to encourage them to grow upward. Use twine or twist ties if stems are light; insulated wire or rubber strips if they are woody.

PLANTS THAT GROW IN PARTIAL TO FULL SHADE

Regent serviceberry, *Amelanchier alnifolia* 'Regent'

Serviceberry, *Amelanchier xgrandiflora*

Carolina allspice, *Calycanthus floridus*

American hornbeam, *Carpinus caroliniana*

White fringe tree, *Chionanthus virginicus*

Virgin's bower, *Clematis virginiana*

Summer sweet, *Clethra alnifolia*

Pagoda dogwood, *Cornus alternifolia*

Flowering dogwood, *Cornus florida*

Mountain laurel, *Kalmia latifolia*

Cornus kousa, *Kousa dogwood*

Dwarf fothergilla, *Fothergilla gardenii*

Large fothergilla, *Fothergilla major*

Climbing hydrangea, *Hydrangea anomala* subsp. *petiolaris*

Oakleaf hydrangea, *Hydrangea quercifolia*

Bigleaf hydrangea, *Hydrangea macrophylla*

Rhododendrons and azaleas, *Rhododendron* species

Yew, *Taxus xmedia*

Arborvitae, *Thuja occidentalis*

Burkwood viburnum, *Viburnum xburkwoodii*

Korean spice viburnum, *Viburnum carlesii*

Arrowwood viburnum, *Viburnum dentatum*

Nannyberry viburnum, *Viburnum lentago*

Blackhaw viburnum, *Viburnum prunifolium*

Sargent viburnum, *Viburnum sargentii*

American cranberry bush viburnum, *Viburnum trilobum*

NORTH AMERICAN NATIVE PLANTS

Serviceberry, *Amelanchier xgrandiflora*

Regent serviceberry, *Amelanchier alnifolia* 'Regent'

Carolina allspice, *Calycanthus floridus*

American hornbeam, *Carpinus caroliniana*

White fringe tree, *Chionanthus virginicus*

Virgin's bower, *Clematis virginiana*

Summer sweet, *Clethra alnifolia*

Pagoda dogwood, *Cornus alternifolia*

Flowering dogwood, *Cornus florida*

Dwarf fothergilla, *Fothergilla gardenii*

Large fothergilla, *Fothergilla major*

Smooth hydrangea, *Hydrangea arborescens*

Oakleaf hydrangea, *Hydrangea quercifolia*

Creeping juniper, *Juniperus horizontalis*

Common juniper, *Juniperus communis*

Mountain laurel, *Kalmia latifolia*

Ninebark, *Physocarpus opulifolius*

Arborvitae, *Thuja occidentalis*

Arrowwood viburnum, *Viburnum dentatum*

Nannyberry viburnum, *Viburnum lentago*

Blackhaw viburnum, *Viburnum prunifolium*

American cranberry bush viburnum, *Viburnum trilobum*

Amelanchier xgrandiflora
SERVICEBERRY

Plant Type: Deciduous shrub or small tree
Hardiness Zones: 3–8
Size: 15–25 feet tall, 20–30 feet wide
Site: Tolerant of wide range of soils, but prefers well-drained, slightly acidic, moist soils in sun to shade.

Serviceberries have cheery white spring flowers and purple-red fruits attractive to birds. Fall color is yellow to rusty red. Its delicate white flowers, attractive purple-red fruits, and silvery-gray bark make apple serviceberry worthy of the mixed border. With a little attention to pruning and shaping, this hybrid makes a striking specimen tree. It is one of a few small trees that is shade tolerant and can be used on the north side of buildings or in the shade of larger trees. It is a good courtyard or patio tree, since birds devour the red fruits before they fall and become messy and the strong wood is resilient in storms.

Care: Regularly remove lower shoots and branches if you want to maintain a small tree. Rust and leaf spot can be cosmetic problems but do not usually affect the overall health of serviceberry.

Cultivars: There are several selections made for showy flowers, good fruiting, and good fall color. Good choices for the Mid-Atlantic are 'Ballerina', 'Autumn Brilliance', 'Robin Hill', and 'Princess Diana'.

Related Species: Regent serviceberry (*A. alnifolia* 'Regent') is a nicely shaped shrub growing 4 to 6 feet tall and wide. It has nice green foliage, large white flowers in spring, and dark purple fruits in late summer. Zones 2–7.

'Princess Diana' serviceberry

Calycanthus floridus

CAROLINA ALLSPICE

Hardiness Zones: 5–9
Plant Type: Deciduous shrub
Size: 6–9 feet tall, 6–12 feet wide
Site: Does best on a deep, moist loam. It grows in shade or sun but does not get as tall in sun.

Place this shrub where you can enjoy the strawberry-like fragrance of the flowers, which is most prevalent in the evening. There is great variation in the fragrance of different plants, so it is a good idea to smell individual plants at the nursery before purchasing. Leaves are dark green in summer and sometimes turn a yellow shade in fall, but it is not a reliable asset from year to year. Flowers are dark reddish brown, maroon to almost red and are up to 2 inches across when fully open. The greatest bloom occurs in June and July. Flowers are borne somewhat inside of the outer layer of foliage so they are often obscured from view. The wrinkly balloon-shaped fruits persist into winter, adding some interest.

Care: Maintain consistently moist soil throughout the growing season, especially during first two years of establishment. A 2- to 4-inch layer of wood chips or shredded bark will help maintain soil moisture and reduce competition from weeds. Prune after flowering as needed to shape plants. No serious pest problems.

Cultivars: 'Athens' has an unusual form growing 6 feet tall with flowers that are yellow and very fragrant. Flowers may be produced after initial late spring flush, often into midsummer. 'Edith Wilder' has reddish-brown, very fragrant flowers. Leaves are more rounded than typical. Fall color is a reasonably good yellow. It grows 10 feet tall. 'Michael Lindsey' has very fragrant red-brown flowers and excellent shiny, dark green foliage and golden yellow fall color.

Carolina allspice

Carpinus caroliniana

AMERICAN HORNBEAM, BLUE BEECH

Plant Type: Deciduous shrub or small tree
Hardiness Zones: 3–9
Size: 20–25 feet tall, 12–18 feet wide
Site: Prefers a moist, fertile, slightly acidic soil in partial shade or sun. Will tolerate full shade and drier conditions.

Blue beech is a bushy native plant with a spreading irregular crown. The beautiful muscle-like bark is bluish gray, smooth, and sometimes marked with dark brown horizontal bands. Slender brownish catkins dangle from branches in early to mid-April. Leaves are dark green in summer, changing to a beautiful orange to red to reddish purple in autumn. The small nutlets hang in clusters and turn brown, adding interest in fall and winter. Plant blue beech where you can enjoy the attractive blue-gray bark in winter. It is good in naturalized plantings and as an understory tree or shrub in woodland gardens. Use it for screening or as a background planting. It can be sheared into a tall hedge or pruned as a single- or multi-stemmed small tree. The early spring catkins are a welcome sight, and the nutlets are food for many birds.

Care: Blue beech is somewhat difficult to transplant. Move balled-and-burlapped or container-grown plants in early spring. Fertilize it lightly when young and shape it with selective pruning to form a single trunk that will showcase the interesting bark. Without pruning, it will send up suckers from the base and become shrubby in appearance. It has no serious insect or disease problems.

American hornbeam

Chionanthus virginicus
WHITE FRINGE TREE

Plant Type: Deciduous shrub or small tree
Hardiness Zones: 4–9
Size: 12–20 feet tall, 12–20 feet wide
Site: Best growth is in deep, fertile soil in sun to partial shade but it is quite adaptable. Flowering is best in full sun.

Fringe tree has one or a few short trunks and a rounded crown. It has dark green glossy leaves that are late to leaf out in spring. Very showy, white, sweetly fragrant blooms appear with the foliage in late spring, cascading downward like the white beard of a wise old man. The fruits, which appear on female plants only, are blue-black and olive-like, held in clusters in late summer. It is a good choice for a small specimen tree or for the back of the shrub border. The flowers are attractive to a variety of insects and fruits are highly desirable to birds. For fruits, plant several of these dioecious shrubs with the hope that at least one will be female. It is tolerant of wind, pollution, and other urban conditions and it can be planted near buildings. Consider it for patio or a courtyard garden. The white flowers look especially stunning at night when illuminated by nearby lights. Keep the mature size in mind. It does become quite wide as it matures.

   Care: Prune right after flowering if shaping is required. No serious pest problems but you may see scale or borers on dry sites. To reduce chances of powdery mildew, prune to open up inside of shrub and increase air circulation.

Clematis cultivars & hybrids
CLEMATIS

Plant Type: Vine
Hardiness Zones: 3–9
Size: 8–10 feet long
Site: Plant clematis in rich, fast-draining soil with a neutral to slightly alkaline pH in full sun or light shade. Roots like to be cool, but the top of the plant requires 6 to 8 hours of sunlight. An eastern exposure is best.

Clematis are among the showiest of vines. Their flowers range from blue to red to white to yellow and many have ornamental seed heads as well. They climb by twisting their leafstalks around their supports. Plant vines next to a trellis, tree trunk, or open framework to provide support.

   Care: Use lime to raise the pH of very acidic soils. The twisting leafstalks may need help climbing up the support. Stems are easily broken so use care when attaching to support. Give plants a complete liquid fertilizer monthly during the growing season. Pruning varies with the type of clematis. Generally, spring-bloomers should be cut back a month after flowering to restrict sprawl, and summer- and fall-blooming types should be cut back in spring to encourage new wood. (See page 175 for pruning information.) South- and west-facing plants must be mulched to keep the soil moist. No serious pest problems.

   Cultivars: There are many. Here are some good choices for the Mid-Atlantic: 'Duchess of Edinburgh' has double white flowers. 'Henryi' has very large white flowers. 'Nelly Moser' has mauve-pink flowers with a deep pink stripe. 'Niobe' has dark red flowers. *C. xjackmanii* is a popular selection with dark purple flowers. All these cultivars bloom in summer and should be pruned in early spring.

   Related Species: Virgin's bower (*C. virginiana*) is a hardy native species with clusters of white flowers followed by showy seed heads. It is a prolific grower that will quickly cover cut stumps or other items that need screening. Grows to 20 feet. Zones 2–8.

White fringe tree

'Jackmanii' clematis

Clethra alnifolia
SUMMER SWEET

Plant Type: Deciduous shrub
Hardiness Zones: 4–9
Size: 4–8 feet tall, 4–6 feet wide
Site: Prefers moist, acidic soil. Avoid hot, dry sites. It does best in dappled shade but tolerates quite a bit of sun if the soil is moist.

This shrub has white to light pink, bottlebrush-like flowers. It blooms mid- to late summer for several weeks when most flowering shrubs are taking a break. Flowers have a deliciously spicy, sweet fragrance that permeates the air. The glossy green foliage is somewhat late to leaf out in spring. Fall color is yellow to golden brown. Showy small fruit capsules turn brown in fall and persist for a year or two, adding winter interest. Use summer sweet as a specimen, in groupings, or in the shrub border. It is multi-stemmed and suckering and can form colonies with time, making it useful for screening. Site it near a deck, patio, or window where the fragrant flowers can be appreciated. Flowers attract butterflies and pollinating insects and fruits attract birds. Smaller types can be used in the perennial border for midsummer color and fragrance. Allow summer sweet to naturalize along a stream or pond where its suckering will help control erosion.

Care: Even old, established plants will require watering during dry spells. Use an acidic fertilizer as needed. Pruning is generally not recommended during the first 3 years to control the size or shape, but you can remove any dead or damaged stems. Older plants can become leggy. Remove a few of the older branches each year over the course of 3 years. Spider mites can be severe on plants in hot, dry locations.

Cultivars: 'Hummingbird' is a dwarf cultivar that is more compact and spreading, growing 3 feet by 3 feet. 'Ruby Spice' has intense deep rose flowers that do not fade in the heat of summer. 'Rosea' has pink flowers that age to white.

Summer sweet

Cornus florida
FLOWERING DOGWOOD

Plant Type: Deciduous small tree
Hardiness Zones: 5–9
Size: 12–30 feet tall, 8–15 feet wide
Site: Prefers a cool, moist, acidic soil that contains organic matter. Full sun promotes the greatest flowering, but tolerates partial shade.

Spring color comes from the four showy bracts that surround the small true flower. They are effective for 10 to 14 days, opening before the leaves. Leaves turn deep burgundy in fall and showy crimson berries appear in clusters on branch tips. This plant is excellent as a specimen, near a patio, at the corner of a house and larger buildings, and in groupings. It is especially effective when planted against dark evergreens or a dark building where the bracts are set off in spring and the branching habit can be seen in winter. It is not tolerant of stresses such as heat, drought, pollution, or road salt, and flower buds can be killed or injured by cold in Zone 5.

Care: Keep roots cool with an organic mulch to avoid leaf and trunk scorch. Lawn mower damage to trunks provides almost certain entry for disease, so mulch is crucial for lawn trees. Dry soil can lead to leaf scorch and susceptibility to diseases. Use an acidifying fertilizer in spring, especially on stressed trees. Prune after flowering only if necessary to shape. Anthracnose (dogwood blight) can be a serious problem, but healthy trees grown in sunny areas with good air circulation and soil moisture are rarely killed. Other problems include dogwood borer, powdery mildew, and crown rot and canker.

Related Species: Pagoda dogwood (*C. alternifolia*) is less showy, but it has the same horizontal branching habit. Zones 3–8. Cornelian cherry (*C. mas*) is shrubbier, typically growing 15 to 20 feet tall with tiny yellow flowers. It can be trained as a small tree. Zones 5–8. Kousa dogwood (*C. kousa*) blooms later and is resistant to many of the pests that plague flowering dogwood. Zones 5–8.

Flowering dogwood

Forsythia xintermedia

FORSYTHIA

Plant Type: Deciduous shrub
Hardiness Zones: 4–8
Size: 8–10 feet tall, 10–12 feet wide
Site: Does best in a well-drained soil in full sun. Tolerates partial shade but flower production is reduced.

This upright, fast-growing, shrub is best known for its cheery yellow flowers in early spring. The rest of the year it is a rather nondescript shrub. Some varieties have fall color ranging from yellow to purple. It can be used as a specimen, in the shrub border, or as an informal hedge. An evergreen background or dark fence will set off the flowers nicely. Plant scillas, dwarf iris, and other spring bulbs under forsythias for additional color. Summer foliage is attractive but not overly interesting, so site plants where perennials or summer-blooming shrubs will offer interest.

Care: Best bloom is on 1-year-old wood. Cut one-third of the oldest stems back to the ground right after blooming to encourage new growth. Severely overgrown untidy plants should be sheared to the ground in spring and allowed to grow back over the next few years. Expect bloom the second year after this drastic pruning. Plants may produce suckers, which can be dug up in early spring and replanted. Extreme winter temperatures or late-spring cold snaps can damage flower buds, reducing spring bloom.

Cultivars: 'Beatrix Farrand' has large, abundant flowers. 'Lynwood' is a vigorous, heavy-blooming selection with somewhat larger-than-usual flowers. 'Meadowlark' is noted for its winter hardiness.

Fothergilla gardenii

DWARF FOTHERGILLA

Plant Type: Deciduous shrub
Hardiness Zones: 5–9
Size: 2–3 feet tall, 2–3 feet wide
Site: Does best in an acidic, well-drained soil in partial shade but can take full sun. It will not tolerate wet or alkaline soils.

Dwarf fothergilla is an attractive shrub for small spaces. It is covered with fragrant white flowers in spring. Fall color is a brilliant yellow to orange to scarlet; often a combination of colors in the same leaf. Use it in foundation plantings, in mixed borders, and in masses where you can enjoy the fragrant spring flowers and fall foliage. It can be mixed with other shrubs in a shrub border; it does especially well with rhododendrons and other acid-loving plants. It can be pruned into a small hedge.

Care: Amend soil before planting to provide the necessary acidic conditions. Water well during dry periods. Fertilize in spring with an acidic fertilizer. Little pruning is needed other than an occasional thinning of the older branches. Plants spread slowly from suckers. No serious pest problems.

Cultivars: 'Blue Mist' is a unique form with leaves that are an attractive blue-green color, especially in light shade. 'Mt. Airy' has dark blue-green foliage and consistent fall color and can grow to 5 feet in height.

Related Species: Large fothergilla (*F. major*) is a larger pyramidal or rounded plant growing to 9 feet in height. Fragrant flowers smell like honey and are very attractive to bees and butterflies. It is a good choice for naturalistic woodland settings. Zones 4–8.

'Northern Sun' forsythia

Dwarf fothergilla

Hydrangea quercifolia
OAKLEAF HYDRANGEA

Plant Type: Deciduous shrub
Hardiness Zones: 5–9
Size: 6–8 feet tall, 6–8 feet wide
Site: Prefers well-drained soil in full sun to partial shade.

This shrub has large oak-like leaves that turn a rich red, bronze, or purple color in fall. The elongated flower clusters start out white in late spring, changing to purplish pink and then brown as the summer progresses. Plants are upright and spreading, with a broad, rounded habit. Long late spring to summer bloom period. Mature stems exfoliate to reveal a rich brown inner bark which is attractive in winter. Mass or group it in a mixed shrub border or allow it to naturalize in a woodland garden. It may also be used for background, accent, or specimen plantings and in foundation plantings or informal hedges.

Care: Young plants may need some winter protection (e.g., burlap wrap) in Zone 5. Little pruning is needed, but can be done any time after flowering. No serious insect or disease problems. Some susceptibility to leaf blight. Heavy flower panicles may droop, particularly wet.

Cultivars: 'Alice' has large flowers and good fall color. Snow Flake ('Brido') has double flowers. 'Pee Wee' and 'Sike's Dwarf' are smaller in size and do not sucker as much.

Related Species: Bigleaf hydrangea (*H. macrophylla*) grows 3 to 10 feet tall and wide. Flower color is based on the availability of aluminum in the soil, which is determined by soil pH. Acidic soils produce blue flowers, and in alkaline soils flowers will be pink. Zones 6–9. Climbing hydrangea (*H. anomala* subsp. *petiolaris*) is a deciduous vine growing 30 to 50 feet tall. It prefers well-drained soil in partial to full shade, but tolerates full sun with moist soil. It clings and climbs by sending out aerial rootlets that grab onto its support. It has flattened clusters of fragrant, white flowers starting in late spring and continuing into early summer. Zones 4–8.

Oakleaf hydrangea

Juniperus horizontalis
CREEPING JUNIPER

Plant Type: Evergreen shrub
Hardiness Zones: 2–8
Size: 2–12 inches tall, 3–6 feet wide
Site: Prefers moist, well-drained soil in full sun, but tolerates dry soils once established. Foliage is sparser in shade. Keep away from road salt. Avoid planting right under drip lines.

This native shrub has long, pendulous stems and bluish-green needles that take on a purplish tint in fall. Many cultivars have been selected for wonderful textures, foliage color, and a variety of shapes and forms. They are suitable for specimens, mass plantings, hedges, foundation plantings, and groundcovers. Junipers are dioecious; only females can produce showy blue cones, or "berries."

Care: Trim early summer to control shape, maintaining the natural growth habit. Bagworms can defoliate plants: remove and destroy all "bags" as soon as you see them. Spider mites can be a problem in hot, dry weather. Juniper blight can show up during wet springs, turning portions of the plant brownish. Snip off diseased parts.

Cultivars: 'Bar Harbor' spreads up to 10 feet and has trailing bluish-green branches that turn purple in fall. 'Blue Chip' is very low growing and has good blue color. 'Hughes', somewhat resistant to juniper blight, has distinct radial branching and silvery-blue leaves and spreads up to 10 feet. 'Wiltonii' is a low form (3 inches tall by 4 feet wide) with intense silvery-blue color.

Related Species: Common juniper (*J. communis*) is an upright native species. Blueberry Delight® ('AmiDak') grows 1 foot tall and 4 feet wide with prolific blue cones when pollinated. 'Depressa Aurea' grows 3 feet tall and 8 feet wide and the new growth is golden yellow. 'Repanda' is a compact form growing 1 foot tall and 6 feet wide and is more resistant to winter burn. Zones 3–6.

'Blue Chip' creeping juniper

Kalmia latifolia

MOUNTAIN LAUREL

Plant Type: broad–leaved evergreen shrub
Hardiness Zones: 5–9
Size: 7–15 feet tall, 7–15 feet wide
Site: Needs an acidic, humusy soil in sun to partial shade. Though often listed as tolerant of heavy shade, plants under those conditions are very thin and open and bloom sparsely. Some exposure to sun is required for proper flower color development of red and pink cultivars.

The showy flowers on this native shrub open in late spring or early summer and last 2 weeks or more. The normal color is pink that fades to nearly white, but breeding has produced red-budded, cinnamon-banded, pure white, and deep pink and red forms. Foliage is dark green and glossy; in full sun it can be yellow-green. Some protection from winter sun and wind is suggested when it is grown in colder areas. Use Mountain laurel in foundation plantings, in partially shaded sites, and for massing and naturalizing.

Care: If necessary, amend soil to increase soil acidity. Avoid windswept sites and heavy, high pH soils. Foliar burn may occur in exposed sites. Use an acidic fertilizer every spring. No pruning is needed but flowers should be removed after they are done blooming. Lace bugs can cause speckling on leaves. Leaf spot can be troublesome on non-resistant cultivars. Avoid damaging plants with sharp gardening tools, as these wounds are common entry points for borers.

Cultivars: 'Bullseye' has white flowers with a purple band. 'Elf' is a dwarf cultivar that stays under 3 feet tall with pink buds opening to pale pink flowers. 'Ostbo Red' has deep, red buds followed by light pink flowers the color of which deepens the longer they are open. 'Raspberry Glow' has burgundy red buds open to pink flowers. 'Sarah' is a compact grower with red flower buds that open to pinkish-red flowers.

Magnolia xsoulangiana

SAUCER MAGNOLIA

Type: Deciduous small tree or shrub
Hardiness Zones: 5–9
Size: 20–30 feet tall, 20–30 feet wide
Site: Acidic, well-drained soil in full sun or light shade.

This hybrid shrub has very showy white flushed with purple flowers in early spring before leaves appear. It is usually used as specimen, but it can be planted in small groups. The roots need ample room to develop. Flower buds are often nipped by last spring frosts. Choose a protected site such as a sheltered courtyard or entryway, especially in northern areas. Plant trees where the flowers will be set off by evergreens or another dark background.

Care: Use an acidic fertilizer in spring. Prune only to shape plants right after flowering in spring. Protect young plants from cold temperatures by surrounding them with a burlap screen filled with leaves. Remove burlap in very early spring just as it starts to warm up. No serious pest problems.

Cultivars: 'Alexandrina' and 'Lennei' have very large purple-pink flowers.

Related Species: Loebner magnolia (*M. xloebneri*), is a group of very showy, hardy hybrids. Star magnolia (*M. stellata*) is the hardiest magnolia, surviving temperatures down to -30 degrees. 'Merrill' can grow up to 30 feet tall and has large, white, starry flowers very early. 'Waterlily' stays under 12 feet tall and has very fragrant, star-like, white flowers that emerge from pink buds and are less floppy. 'Leonard Messel' grows to 20 feet and has fuchsia-pink to purple flowers. Zones 4–8.

Mountain laurel

Saucer magnolia

Physocarpus opulifolius
NINEBARK

Plant Type: Deciduous shrub
Hardiness Zones: 2–7
Size: 5–10 feet tall, 6–10 feet wide
Site: Grows best in full sun and can withstand windy sites once established.

This tough, hardy shrub produces fast-growing shoots that arch out and away from the center. The flowers are clustered in 2-inch heads and are followed by reddish-brown fruits that can be ornamental. Older stems are covered with attractive shaggy bark that sloughs off in long fibrous strips, but the foliage usually covers it. The species makes a good hedge, screen, or windbreak; pruned hedges will have reduced bloom, however. It makes good cover for wildlife. The cultivars are excellent landscape shrubs and can be used in borders, foundation plantings, and as hedges.

Care: Prune to control form and size immediately after flowering. Begin light pruning of hedges the first year after planting. As plants become more vigorous, prune more heavily. Consistent pruning each year will result in a thick, bushy hedge. Overgrown shrubs can be renewed by cutting them all the way back to the ground in early spring. No serious pest problems. Powdery mildew may show up on hedge plants. Snip out infected areas.

Cultivars: 'Center Glow' has bright red foliage. 'Dart's Gold' has yellow foliage growing to 5 feet tall and wide. Diablo® ('Monlo') has leaves that emerge deep purple. It can be pruned harshly each spring to promote vigorous shoots with large, highly-colored leaves. 'Nanus' stays about 5 feet tall and wide. 'Nugget' has deep golden yellow foliage and a dense habit to 6 feet tall and wide. 'Snowfall' is a compact selection with larger flowers. 'Summer Wine® ('Seward') is a compact selection with fine, deeply-cut, dark red leaves and pinkish flowers.

'Nugget' ninebark

Rhododendron 'PJM'
'PJM' RHODODENDRON

Plant Type: Evergreen shrub or small tree
Hardiness Zones: 3–7
Size: 4–5 feet tall, 3–5 feet wide
Site: Needs rich, acidic, well-drained soil high in organic matter. Choose a site in partial shade, ideally on the north or east side of a building to avoid winter sun, which can cause winter burn. Avoid deep shade.

This shrub is covered with masses of magenta flowers in spring. The foliage has nice purple fall color. Rhododendrons are excellent specimen plants, but they also look great as mass plantings and can be used in foundation plantings.

Care: All rhododendrons and azaleas require good soil preparation before planting to ensure a rich soil with a pH in the range of 4.5 to 5.5. Apply an acidic mulch such as pine needles, pine bark, or shredded oak leaves. Fertilize in spring with an acid fertilizer and again right after plants bloom. If the leaves on your plants start to turn yellow between the veins, the soil is probably not acidic enough. Stop watering in mid-September to encourage plants to begin hardening off for winter, but saturate soil in late fall just before the first freeze to make sure plants go into winter with moisture around their roots. Plants require very little pruning. Remove dead or damaged branches at any time of year. To encourage bushier plants, cut back stems on mature plants one-third right after flowering.

Other selections: Northern Lights azaleas are the hardiest deciduous azaleas, all surviving in Zone 4 and some in Zone 3. There are many cultivars, ranging in color from white to yellow to pink to lilac. They all have "Lights" in their name. They require acidic soil and do best with full sun. They cannot survive drought conditions, however, and should be mulched and watered as needed.

'PJM' rhododendron

Rosa cultivars

SHRUB ROSES

Plant Type: Deciduous shrub
Hardiness Zones: 3–8
Size: 4–6 feet tall, 4–6 feet wide
Site: They grow best in slightly acidic soil that has been generously amended with compost, but they will tolerate a wide range of soil conditions. They require full sun to grow and flower best.

Hybrid roses are difficult to grow in the Mid-Atlantic, but there are many beautiful shrub roses that do very well here. These non-native shrubs are generally upright to low-spreading, stiff-caned shrubs, many with thorns or bristles. They bear fragrant, five-petaled flowers for 2 to 4 weeks in early summer. Flower color ranges from white to yellow to pink to red. Many set good quantities of red rose hips that add winter interest and provide food for birds. They are hardier, more adaptable, and more disease- and insect-resistant than hybrid roses. They can be grown as part of mixed borders and in foundations. Most will tolerate saline conditions and drought, making them good for bank covers, street plantings, and other difficult sites.

Care: Prune out any dead canes in late spring and prune as need to shape plant after flowering. These roses can be afflicted with all the same problems as hybrid roses, but usually not to the same extent. Good air circulation goes a long way in reducing disease problems such as black spot and powdery mildew.

Cultivars: There are many shrub roses to choose from. Good choices for low-maintenance are 'Alexander MacKenzie', 'Carefree Beauty', 'Carefree Wonder', 'John Davis', 'Morden Blush', and 'Morden Centennial'. 'William Baffin' and 'John Cabot' are two long-caned roses that can be trained as vines. The Easy Elegance Series roses were bred for disease resistance, hardiness, and long bloom times. Some of the selections in this series include Sunrise, Sunset; Pink Gnome; Little Mischief; and Island Dancer. They are rated hardy in Zones 4–9.

'William Baffin' rose

Spiraea nipponica 'Snowmound'

SNOWMOUND SPIREA

Plant Type: Deciduous shrub
Hardiness Zones: 4–8
Size: 4–7 feet tall, 3–5 feet wide
Site: Performs best in full sun in well-drained soil, but is very tolerant of poor soils, clay soils, heavy soils, and other urban conditions.

This shrub is grown for its arching growth habit, showy white flowers, and attractive blue-green foliage. The small individual flowers appear in clusters in late spring to early summer. Spireas are well-suited to many landscape situations. They can be used in informal hedges and are good candidates for the mixed-shrub border, specimen use, and foundation plantings.

Care: Prune lightly to shape right after flowering. Overgrown plants can be cut to the ground in early spring to control size or rejuvenate plants. No serious pest problems, but aphids may appear on soft new growth at the tips of stems. Avoid overfeeding, which promotes succulent growth attractive to aphids.

Cultivars: 'Halward's Silver' is slightly hardier and more compact, growing 2 to 4 feet tall and wide.

Related Species: Bridal wreath spirea (_S. xvanhouttei_) grows about 7 feet tall and wide. It is an old favorite with arching branches covered with clusters of white flowers mid- to late spring. Foliage is dull bluish green in summer and it occasionally turns reddish in fall. 'Renaissance' is a compact-growing improved selection that exhibits better resistance to leaf diseases. 'Pink Ice' has young foliage splashed with pink and white. It may revert, and the leaves usually mature to a uniform green by summer. 'Snow White' grows compactly to 5 feet and appears less prone to foliar disease. The dead blooms are self-cleaning and the foliage is larger and healthy green. Zones 3–8.

Snowmound spirea

MEYER LILAC
Syringa meyeri 'Palibin'

Plant Type: Deciduous shrub
Hardiness Zones: 3–7
Size: 4–5 feet tall, 5–7 feet wide
Site: Lilacs grow best in full sun, at least 6 hours a day. The main soil requirement is good drainage. Plants will grow and flower best on a fertile loam rich in organic matter, but they tolerate most soils.

Meyer lilac is a small, dense, mounded shrub with a uniform, neat outline. It starts to flower when plants are only about a foot tall. The fragrant, violet-purple flowers are packed in 4-inch-long panicles that cover the plant in spring, and they hold for up to 2 weeks. New leaves have a purplish margin, turning dark green in summer. Flowers usually appear before the leaves are fully developed. Lilacs can be used as specimen plants, in groups, in borders, or in foundation plantings. Plants may sucker very lightly or not at all.

Care: Does not require a lot of pruning, but any shaping should be done right after flowering. Potential problems include scale, stem borers, and powdery mildew, but it is not as susceptible to powdery mildew as other lilacs are.

Related Species: Miss Kim lilac (*S. patula* 'Miss Kim') has a more upright growth habit to 6 feet tall and wide. It blooms later with blue-lavender flowers. Leaves may take on a burgundy color in fall. It is resistant to powdery mildew. Zones 3–7. Tinkerbelle® lilac ('Bailbelle') is part of the Fairytale® Series. It is a compact hybrid growing about 5 feet tall and wide with single pink flowers and good mildew resistance. Zones 3–7. Persian lilac (*S. xpersica*) has a more arching growth habit growing to 6 feet tall and wide. Flowers are pale lilac. It is susceptible to powdery mildew. Zones 4–7.

JAPANESE TREE LILAC
Syringa reticulata

Plant Type: Deciduous small tree
Hardiness Zones: 3–7
Size: 20–30 feet tall, 15–25 feet wide
Site: It will grow best in full sun, at least 6 hours a day. The main soil requirement is good drainage. Plants will grow and flower best on a fertile loam rich in organic matter, but they tolerate most soils.

Japanese tree lilac is an upright, spreading, usually multi-stemmed small tree. It blooms much later than common lilacs. In early summer it is covered with large hydrangea-like clusters of small cream-colored flowers. The flowers have a pleasant honey-like scent less intense than common lilac. The tree also has attractive deep green leaves and dark to reddish-brown bark. It makes an excellent specimen, entry, or street tree, and it is good in the shrub border.

Care: Does not require a lot of pruning, but any shaping should be done right after flowering. Remove suckers at the base of the plant at any time. Removing the flower heads right after blooming will help the plant produce more blooms the next year. Japanese lilac is not as susceptible to the insects and diseases that plague most lilacs. It is resistant to powdery mildew.

Cultivar: 'Ivory Silk' flowers at a young age and is sturdy and compact.

Related Species: Peking lilac (*S. pekinensis*) is another late-bloomer, although not as late as Japanese tree lilac. It is an upright, spreading tree of 15 to 20 feet. It produces clusters of small cream-colored flowers with a mild honey scent. Zones 4–7. Preston lilac (*S. xprestoniae*) blooms later and the scent is not as sweet. Plants grow 8 to 10 feet tall. Plants are resistant to powdery mildew and they sucker lightly or not at all. Zones 2–7.

Meyer lilac

Japanese tree lilac

Taxus xmedia
YEW

Plant Type: Evergreen shrub or small tree
Hardiness Zones: 5–7
Size: 2–20 feet tall, 2–12 feet wide
Site: Well-drained soils in full sun to part shade. Plants have no tolerance for wet conditions; good drainage is essential. Tolerates urban conditions. Best sited in locations protected from cold winter winds.

This group of hybrids was selected for good foliage color and form as well as hardiness. The needle-like, olive to dark green leaves are attractive year-round. Bark is scaly brown. Plants are dioecious (separate male and female plants). Female plants produce red, berry-like fruits instead of cones. Yews are good for foundation plantings, screening, or hedges. They make good groundcovers in shady areas.

Care: Yews are very amenable to pruning and shearing, which is best done in early spring before new growth appears. Plants are susceptible to winter burn, particularly in exposed sites. Twig blight and needle blight are occasional problems. Root rot may occur in poorly-drained soils. Weevils, mealybugs and scale are problems in some areas.

Cultivars: 'Citation' is a tight, upright, columnar cultivar that typically matures to 6 to 10 feet. 'Taunton' is a dwarf spreading selection typically growing 3 to 4 feet tall and spreading to 5 feet or more. 'Wardii' is a very dense, slow-growing, wide-spreading form that may get 6 feet tall.

Thuja occidentalis
ARBORVITAE

Plant Type: Evergreen shrub or small tree
Hardiness Zones: 3–7
Size: 40–60 feet tall, 10–15 feet wide
Site: Plants grow well in full sun, but tolerate partial shade. Deep shade produces open, sparse plants. Arborvitaes thrive in a wide range of soils as long as they drain freely.

This native evergreen has good green color throughout the year. The fragrant foliage consists of many short, scalelike leaves carried in soft, flat sprays. It is used for screening, hedges, foundation plantings, and as accents. Plants can get sun scorch when planted in areas with bright afternoon winter sun and wind, but this is easily pruned out in spring. Avoid planting this shrub under a roofline where snow can drop onto plants and break branches.

Care: Water deeply in fall to help prevent winter burn. Prune in spring just after new growth has emerged, if needed. Formal hedges may be pruned again later in the season, but avoid pruning in fall. Possible problems include bagworm, leaf miner, spider mites, and deer browsing. If deer are a problem in your area, you may need to protect plants with fencing or spray them frequently with repellents.

Cultivars: Many cultivars have been selected for their foliage color, resistance to winter burn, and growth habit, which can include dwarf and globe forms. 'Techny' is a popular cultivar growing only 10 to 15 feet tall, making it a good choice for hedging. It has excellent deep green foliage color and tends to resist winter burning. 'Little Gem' is a good globe form growing to about 3 feet in height and width. 'Hetz Midget' is a globe form that doesn't need any pruning to stay at 2 to 3 feet. 'Woodwardii' is another natural globe that grows 3 to 5 feet. 'Sunkist' has golden yellow foliage when grown in full sun.

Yew

'Techny' arborvitae

Viburnum dentatum
ARROWWOOD VIBURNUM

Plant Type: Deciduous shrub
Hardiness Zones: 3-8
Size: 6-15 feet tall, 6-15 feet wide
Site: Prefers moist, well-drained soil. Will grow in sunny locations but can tolerate moderate amounts of shade and road salt.

This large, multi-stemmed shrub has showy creamy white flowers mid- to late spring. They turn to blue-colored oval fruits in fall. The brightness of the blue color differs from plant to plant, affecting the showiness. The dark green leaves are glossy, smooth, and coarsely toothed with prominent veins. Leaves color fairly early in fall, usually turning a nice yellow, red, or reddish purple before falling. Arrowwood viburnum makes a good hedge or screen. It attracts wildlife, especially birds, which eat the fruits. Since it suckers and spreads, the species is best-suited to a contained space or in naturalized situations. Cultivars are better choices for landscape usage.

Care: Plants may suffer in droughty conditions. Keep the soil evenly moist throughout the growing season, especially the first 2 to 3 years after planting. Some renewal pruning, done right after flowering, is necessary to keep landscape shrubs looking their best. Suckers may need to be pruned to keep plants from getting out of bounds. No serious pests.

Cultivars: Blue Muffin® ('Christom') is a compact selection with exceptional fall fruiting. Autumn Jazz® ('Ralph Senior') and Chicago Lustre® ('Synnestvedt') are upright selections. Northern Burgundy® ('Morton') has good fall color. Cultivars hardy in Zones 4-8.

Related Species: Witherrod (V. cassinoides) grows about 6 feet tall and wide. It is a handsome, compact shrub with creamy white flowers in early summer followed by very showy, multi-colored fruits. Zones 3-8.

Arrowwood viburnum

Viburnum prunifolium
BLACKHAW VIBURNUM

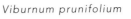

Plant Type: Deciduous shrub or small tree
Hardiness Zones: 4–8
Size: 12–15 feet tall, 8–12 feet wide
Site: It prefers moist, well-drained soils of average fertility in full sun, but is adaptable to a variety of soil conditions, moderate heat, drought, and pollution.

This small tree or shrub is noted for its spring flowers, autumn fruits, fall color, and very dense twigginess, which makes it ideal as a wildlife refuge, as a nonthorny barrier hedge, or in a naturalized group planting. Fall color is variable from dark green, burgundy, red, orange, yellow, or purple, and often a mixture thereof, and can be quite showy, especially when the shrub is sited in full sun. The creamy-white, flat-topped flowers bloom in early May and are effective for 1 to 2 weeks. Fruits are a mixture of green, yellow, and red-pink, changing to blue-black or blue-pink at maturity, often blooming when ripe and attractive to wildlife (especially birds).

Care: Keep the soil evenly moist throughout the growing season, especially the first 2 to 3 years after planting. Feed every spring with a 10-10-10 plant food or an organic equivalent. Remove a few of the older stems each year to keep plants from becoming overgrown and unkempt. No serious pest problems.

Related Species: Nannyberry viburnum (V. lentago) is a large, upright shrub often grown as a single-stemmed tree 20 to 25 feet tall. It does well in partial shade. Zones 2–8. American cranberry bush (V. trilobum) grows 10 to 12 feet tall. It has large, white, lace-cap flowers. Leaves turn beautiful shades of yellow-orange to red in fall. The showy red fruits persist into winter. 'Compactum' and 'Alfredo' are compact selections. 'Hahs' has a neat, rounded growth habit and good flower and fruit display. 'Wentworth' and Redwing™ ('J.N. Select') were selected for heavy fruit production. Zones 2–7.

Blackhaw viburnum

FRAMING AND SHADING

SELECTING AND GROWING TREES

Large trees are valued for their beauty as well as for the shade they provide. But they have a lot more to offer landscapes and gardens. They provide structure with their weight and form. The overhead leafy canopy of a spreading tree frames the elements and the view below it. Trees are home to many types of birds and also provide habitat for butterflies and beneficial insects. Many provide beautiful fall color when their foliage turns shades of red, yellow, and orange. And don't forget the benefits at eye level, especially in the dormant season. Tree bark can have very interesting texture and color.

A tree is a woody plant that grows over 25 feet tall when mature. It is usually a single-trunked plant, but it can have multiple trunks. Some trees retain branches and leaves all the way to the ground, but most develop a canopy that you can walk underneath. Trees may be deciduous or evergreen and they come in various forms: pyramidal, weeping, columnar, roundheaded, vase-shaped, and arching. This chapter will help you in your quest to find the right tree for your needs, and help you care for it and protect it for your use and for future generations.

A mature shade tree is a real asset to a home. Choose the right tree and treat it properly and it will reward you and future generations for many years to come.

CHOOSING THE RIGHT TREE

Planting a tree is a long-term investment, but one that returns a great deal of satisfaction and value. Since most trees are not easily moved once established, you should make sure the tree you select is a good match for your site. Start by finding out what trees are hardy in your climate. You can push the hardiness envelope a little with perennials and even shrubs, which aren't as much of an investment, but with large trees you want to make sure it's going to survive the long haul.

If you don't want to drastically change the soil, you should select a tree based on your soil conditions. It usually makes the most sense to select a species that is native in your area. They are well-adapted to your climate and tend to be more disease- and insect-resistant than exotics. They also provide more habitat for beneficial insects, birds, and butterflies than non-native trees are likely to.

The trees you plant will become major elements in your landscape. Keep the mature size in mind and make sure the tree you select will be in scale with your home. Don't make the mistake of planting a tiny oak seedling 10 feet from your front door or a basswood under a power line. The canopy of a large tree will complement a two-story home, but many shade trees are too large for small lots and one-story homes. There are plenty of trees in the 40-foot-range that provide ample shade and are in better scale with homes. These smaller species are also good choices if you will be planting under an obstruction or near a sidewalk or driveway.

Also consider species diversity. While it isn't usually a good idea to plant a hodgepodge of many different types of trees, you should avoid planting all one species, especially if there are already a lot of this species in your neighborhood. Serious disease and insect problems on trees, which can be devastating to neighborhoods, are often associated with over-planting of a species.

There are some fast-growing trees that will fill in the space quickly. However, almost all of these plants have problems. They are weak-wooded, meaning they will drop lots of branches during windstorms and are more likely to topple over. They tend to drop lots of litter and are prone to pest problems. These trees are better suited to plant as screening and windbreaks than front yard specimens. In general, it is the slower-growing trees that make better long-term investments. If sited correctly, watered appropriately, mulched, and kept pest-free, slow growers may respond with faster-than-typical growth.

Certain trees are more tolerant of urban conditions than others. They're able to handle atmospheric pollutants from industry and cars, as well as compacted soil, poor drainage, night lighting, and salt spray from snow plows. If you will be planting a tree in

Choosing a tree is a big decision, and one that will have long-term ramifications. You can end up with a beautiful specimen that is a real asset to your site, such as this linden. Or you can end up with a weak-wooded tree that litters your yard with debris.

these conditions, look for one that can tolerate these situations. Lastly, some trees can be messy, dropping leaves, flowers, fruits, or twigs. They may be fine for yard trees, but you wouldn't want to plant one over your deck or driveway.

BUYING A TREE AND GETTING IT HOME

Starting with a healthy, nicely shaped seedling will go a long way in improving your long-term success. The tree should have a gentle taper to the trunk, well-spaced branches on all sides, and a single dominant branch, which will be the "leader." You want a single-leadered tree not only because it will look better, but also because it is healthier. Most trees that have a double leader will eventually split because of the weak V-shaped crotch. If you do end up with a double-leadered tree, prune out the weaker leader. It may look funny at first, but the other leader will soon straighten and become the single dominant leader.

The trickiest part of buying a new tree is often getting it home safely. Plan ahead and bring something to protect the interior of your vehicle and to stabilize the tree so it doesn't move around on the ride home. Be sure to only lift the plant by the container or root ball, not the trunk. If the tree is leafed out, wrap it in burlap or plastic to reduce water loss. If you are using an open-bed truck, water the plant before loading to reduce water loss and add weight. Place the plant or plants at the front of the bed and drive slowly to minimize windburn of the foliage.

Don't make the mistake of planting a large tree right next to your house. There are many small- to medium-sized trees, such as redbud, that are in better scale with most homes.

PLANTING FOR ENERGY SAVINGS

All large trees will provide shade, but you'll get the most summer shade and winter sun from a broad-canopied deciduous tree (loses its leaves in winter). The shade of a large tree can reduce the effective temperature up to 10°F, which can be felt inside a house as well. Studies show that a few well-placed shade trees can reduce cooling costs by as much as 35 percent. For maximum cooling, trees should be placed on the southwest or west side of the building to be shaded. Tall evergreens should not be planted on the south side of a building, where they will keep the sun from warming the house in winter.

BENEFITS OF LARGE TREES

Shade and privacy are the two main reasons to plant trees, but there are many other benefits of large trees.

⚜ Framing of views and buildings
⚜ Provide structure for outdoor rooms
⚜ Provide habitat for wildlife
⚜ Summer cooling of homes
⚜ Filtering air pollutants
⚜ Provide seasonal interest
⚜ Protection from wind
⚜ Reduce noise pollution

A large tree not only provides shade, but a focal point and heritage that will last generations.

PLANTING A BALLED-AND-BURLAPPED TREE

Like shrubs, trees are available bare-root, in containers, and balled-and-burlapped. A fourth way to plant a tree is to employ a professional nursery to come in with a tree spade, which gives you a larger tree faster, but it usually is much more expensive.

Bare-root trees must be planted in spring as soon as the soil can be worked. Balled-and-burlapped, container-grown, and tree-spade trees can be planted anytime but the hottest days of summer. Spring is still the best time for planting, however. The fewer or smaller the leaves are, the faster the tree will recover from transplanting. Plant the tree at the same depth at which it was growing in the container or burlap wrap. Bare-root trees should be planted so that the crown is at ground level.

1 DIG A HOLE no deeper than the depth of the root ball but at least twice as wide, preferably three or four times wider.

2 AMEND THE SOIL, if needed, to create a well-drained soil in the correct pH range. To do this, mix the planting soil with organic matter such as well-rotted compost or manure.

3 IF THE WRAPPING IS REAL BURLAP, you simply have to cut and remove the fabric on top of the ball and peel the burlap down the sides so it stays below the soil line. It will eventually decompose. Synthetic burlap must be removed completely. Remove the wire basket that surrounds the root ball and burlap, if present.

4 PLACE THE PLANT IN THE HOLE and adjust the hole depth so that the plant is about 1 inch higher than it was planted in the nursery to allow for settling of soil. Use a shovel handle laid across the hole to help determine the proper depth.

5 SHOVEL IN THE AMENDED SOIL around the root ball, stopping to tamp down the soil when the hole is half full.

6 FILL THE REST OF THE HOLE with loose soil and tamp down again to ensure good contact between the soil and the roots.

7 SOAK THE PLANTING AREA with water. Once the soil has settled, build up a 2- to 3-inch basin around the plant to catch rainfall and irrigation water. However, do not build a basin if your soil is very heavy and doesn't drain well.

8 APPLY 2 TO 3 INCHES OF ORGANIC MULCH such as shredded bark or wood chips, keeping the mulch a few inches away from the trunk.

CARE OF TREES

WATERING

Deep, thorough watering is very important to help young trees get off to a strong start. Place a hose at the base of the tree and let the water trickle out for several hours. Allow the top 2 inches of soil to dry out before watering again. The tree should receive good soakings for the first growing season and possibly the second.

Once established, most trees can tolerate some dry periods, but always water as needed, especially in sandy soils. Saturate the soil thoroughly with each watering to encourage deep rooting.

FERTILIZING

Most soils have enough nutrients for young trees to get off to a good start. Trees 3 to 5 years old may benefit from a spring application of fertilizer. Spread a layer of rotted manure or compost around each tree or use a fertilizer. If possible, allow leaves or needles to fall and decay under trees to return nutrients to the soil.

Staking should only be done if newly-planted trees are located on very windy, exposed sites. This artificial support system encourages tall growth, often at the expense of a supportive trunk and root system. The end result can be a weak tree.

STAKING

In most cases, newly planted trees should not be staked. It is better to allow them a little movement to encourage stronger trunks and healthy root systems. However, trees planted on a very windy, exposed site may benefit from staking for their first season or two, especially if they are top-heavy. String wire through a section of garden hose to protect the bark from injury. The wire should hold the tree firmly without putting undue pressure on the trunk. The staked tree should still be able to sway somewhat in the wind.

POSSIBLE PROBLEMS

Trees are susceptible to insects and diseases—such as oak wilt and Dutch elm disease—that can be fatal. However, most insect and disease problems are purely cosmetic and don't really threaten the tree's life. On large trees, control measures involving fungicides and insecticides are rarely practical.

Some things to watch for on young trees are aphid feeding (spray leaves daily with a strong blast of the hose), iron chlorosis (acidify soil to lower pH), and leaf scorch (water trees well during dry periods and mulch soil). The best defense against insect and disease problems is a vigorously growing tree. By choosing a tree appropriate for your site conditions and providing it with the necessary nutrients and ample water, most pest problems will not become serious. Salt placed on roads and sidewalks in winter can be a problem for some trees, especially evergreens. Avoid planting sensitive trees near roadways.

Bigger problems for trees often come in the form of mechanical damage. Once a tree's bark is girdled by animal feeding or lawn mower or weed-whipper damage, it loses its ability to take up water and it will die. Prevent animal damage by wrapping young trees with cylinders or hardware cloth placed several inches into the soil and extending up to the lowest branch. This hardware cloth can be removed once the tree's bark is hard and corky. An organic mulch around the base of the trunk will keep lawn mowers and weed whippers away.

Frost cracks appear on the south and west sides of thin-barked trees that have been subjected to wide temperature swings during the dormant season. Once they occur, there is nothing you can do to get rid of them and they can be fatal. Prevent the problem by wrapping the trunks or painting them with white latex paint until they are old enough to have corky bark (usually 3 to 5 years). Wrap the trees from the bottom up in autumn and remove the wrap in spring.

PRUNING A TREE

Most landscape trees require regular pruning, not only to keep them looking good but also to keep them healthy. Start training young trees right after planting to encourage strong, healthy mature trees that will stand up to extreme weather. A modest investment of time in the first 5 years will pay off greatly down the road. It costs a lot of money to have a professional arborist come in and trim a large tree that has been neglected.

You should remove any branches that are rubbing against each other because the bark will eventually wear away from one or both of the branches. Remove any suckers that may be growing around the base of the tree. Do not over-prune the tree. Young

TREES THAT CAN BE GROWN AS MULTI-STEMMED CLUMPS

River birch, *Betula nigra*, Zones 3–9
Paper birch, *Betula papyrifera*, Zones 2–6
Katsura tree, *Cercidiphyllum japonicum*, Zones 5–8
Eastern redbud, *Cercis canadensis*, Zones 4–9
Sweet bay magnolia, *Magnolia virginiana*, Zones 5–10
Ironwood, *Ostrya virginiana*, Zones 3–9
Amur chokecherry, *Prunus maackii*, Zones 2–6

Birches are often planted as multi-trunked trees. It is a good way to get an extra dose of the showy, peeling bark.

To protect young trees from rabbits and rodents, place a cylinder of one-quarter-inch mesh hardware cloth around the trunk. The cylinder should extend 18 to 24 inches above the soil and 2 to 3 inches below ground.

Strong older branches develop from young branches with a 45-degree angle between the trunk and the tree; these are the branches you want to retain on your young tree.

trees need plenty of leaves to manufacture the wood they need for strong roots and top growth.

Older trees should be pruned as needed to remove dead, diseased, dying, or dangerous branches and suckers. You should also remove some of the inner branches to thin out the crown. If the tree isn't too large, you can do this yourself. However, pruning of large shade trees is best left to professionals. Never prune the leader of trees or you'll destroy the natural shape, and only remove lower branches if they interfere with the use of the areas under the tree.

If you made proper pruning cuts right above the collar and pruned at the right time of year, you do not need to use a wound dressing. In fact, covering a wound can do more harm than good. The exception is if you need to prune a tree at the wrong time of the year and it is susceptible to attack from a major insect pest, such as oak wilt.

The best time to prune is usually when trees are dormant. You can see their silhouette better, and the chances of disease and insect problems are reduced.

Some trees send up "suckers" at their base. These suckers are easily pruned off at any time to preserve the tree form and keep the tree from becoming shrubby.

PRUNING A TREE

When pruning branches with a saw, make a cut on the underside of the branch first (top) to prevent the branch from tearing the bark as it falls. Finish the cut from above (bottom).

Do not make a flush cut at the trunk. Rather, make a smooth cut at the outside edge of the collar; the swollen area where the branch meets the trunk.

By keeping the collar you will encourage callus tissue to form and heal over the cut, keeping out disease organisms from entering the cut surface.

Branches should also be cut back to a larger branch or to the trunk. Do not leave stubs, which will only die back and provide entry points for insects and diseases.

TREES FOR THE MID-ATLANTIC

TREES SUITABLE FOR STREET USE

Ginkgo, *Ginkgo biloba*

Serbian spruce, *Picea orimika*

Amur chokecherry, *Prunus maackii*

Pin oak, *Quercus palustris*

Northern pin oak, *Quercus ellipsoidalis*

Little-leaf linden, *Tilia cordata*

Japanese zelkova, *Zelkova serrata*

TREES WITH GOOD FALL COLOR

Red maple, *Acer rubrum*

Sugar maple, *Acer saccharum*

River birch, *Betula nigra*

Paper birch, *Betula papyrifera*

Eastern redbud, *Cercis canadensis*

Yellowwood, *Cladastrus kentukea*

Ginkgo, *Ginkgo biloba*

Ironwood, *Ostrya virginiana*

Northern pin oak, *Quercus ellipsoidalis*

Shingle oak, *Quercus imbricaria*

Pin oak, *Quercus palustris*

Shumard oak, *Quercus shumardii*

NORTH AMERICAN NATIVE TREES

Red maple, *Acer rubrum*

Sugar maple, *Acer saccharum*

River birch, *Betula nigra*

Paper birch, *Betula papyrifera*

Eastern redbud, *Cercis canadensis*

Yellowwood, *Cladastrus kentukea*

Ironwood, *Ostrya virginiana*

White spruce, *Picea glauca*

Swamp white oak, *Quercus bicolor*

Northern pin oak, *Quercus ellipsoidalis*

Shingle oak, *Quercus imbricaria*

Pin oak, *Quercus palustris*

Shumard oak, *Quercus shumardii*

Basswood, *Tilia americana*

Acer rubrum

RED MAPLE

Hardiness Zones: 3–9

Size: 40–65 feet tall, 40–50 feet wide

Site: Prefers slightly acidic, well-drained, sandy loam soils in sun to light shade, but tolerates most conditions. Will not grow well in alkaline soils, but will tolerate moderately moist soils.

This medium-sized, native deciduous tree has a broadly rounded symmetrical form, showy red flowers in early spring, and brilliant red, sometimes orange or yellow, color in fall. It is a good shade or lawn tree. All maples have shallow roots and produce deep shade, which can be difficult to grow grass under. It is susceptible to drought and road salt, but tolerant of ozone. Choose northern-grown strains for best success. Fall color can be inconsistent; purchase trees in fall if you want good fall color.

Care: Provide a barrier against lawn mowers and weed whippers, which can seriously damage the thin bark. Leaf scorch can be a problem during dry periods, especially on young trees. Winter wrap all young maple trees to protect them from sunscald. Avoid pruning trees in late winter when sap is flowing. This "bleeding" sap does not harm the tree, but it is messy and unsightly.

Cultivars: 'Autumn Spire' has bright red fall color and a columnar form. 'Northwood' and Red Sunset® have good fall color. Autumn Blaze®, a hybrid with silver maple, is a fast grower with drought tolerance and good fall color.

Other Species: Sugar maple (*A. saccharum*) prefers heavier soils that are moisture retentive, but it will tolerate drier, sandier sites. Avoid compacted, alkaline soils. It grows 50 to 80 feet tall. The brilliant fall color ranges from yellow to orange to scarlet. It is sensitive to salt damage and is susceptible to leaf scorching and tattering when planted on open, exposed sites. 'Legacy' was selected for its good fall color and resistance to leaf tatter. Zones 3–8.

'Autumn Blaze' maple

Betula nigra

RIVER BIRCH

Hardiness Zones: 3–9
Size: 40–70 feet tall, 30–40 feet wide
Site Prefers moist soils and tolerates wet soils, but will do well on upland sites if given supplemental water when young. Needs full sun and a soil pH below 6.5 to prevent chlorosis.

This deciduous native tree has an upright form with an irregularly spreading crown. It is one of the few large trees that can be grown as a multi-trunked tree. Colorful bark is the hallmark of birches. River birch has cinnamon-brown peeling bark that peels away to reveal fresh, smooth underbark. Fall color is also an asset—usually bright or golden yellow. It is the most heat-tolerant of the birches, making it the best choice for most landscape situations. It is usually used as a specimen tree, but its large size prevents it from being suitable in small landscapes. On older trees the bark is darker and corkier.

Care: No pruning needed other than removal of lower branches to enhance appearance of trunk. Select plants from a northern seed source. Acidify soil before planting, if needed. Prune in summer to avoid bleeding. The brittle, twiggy branches break easily in windstorms, and catkins dropping in late spring can be messy, but only for a short period. River birch is highly resistant to bronze birch borer and is rarely troubled by leaf miners; two common pests of birches.

Cultivars: Heritage® ('Cully') is a popular cultivar (perhaps too popular) with lighter-colored bark and larger, glossier, dark green leaves. It grows about 45 feet tall.

Related Species: Paper birch (*B. papyrifera*) grows 50 to 70 feet tall and 30 to 40 feet wide. It is hardier, in Zones 2 to 6, but is susceptible to bronze birch borer, leaf miner, and cankers, especially when grown in sunny landscape situations.

River birch

Cercis canadensis

EASTERN REDBUD

Hardiness Zones: 4–9
Size: 20–30 feet tall, 25–35 feet wide
Site: Prefers moderately moist soils high in organic matter but will grow in drier sites once established. Prefers partial shade, but will tolerate full sun and even full shade.

This native deciduous tree is excellent in shrub or mixed borders, to soften harsh corners, as an understory tree, as a grouping of three in a large lawn, or at the edge of a woodland garden. It is often grown as a clump tree. Pink-purple flowers open in spring before leaves appear. Best flowering occurs on trees at least four years old. The attractive heart-shaped leaves can appear tired and spotted by late summer, but turn a nice yellow in fall. Layered branches give trees architectural form. The zigzag branch pattern and persistent seedpods add winter interest. Zone 4 gardeners should only plant northern-grown strains in sheltered locations to ensure hardiness.

Care: Plants resent being dug from fields as they get larger, so start with smaller trees. Their moderate growth rate will result in a nice specimen in a few years. Redbuds do not do well when stressed. Keep landscape plants mulched and well watered. A spring application of fertilizer may be needed. No major pruning is needed. Canker is the most destructive problem of redbud and it can lead to death of a tree. Protect trunk and bark from damage from lawn mower or weed whipper injury by circling trees with mulch. Redbud is sensitive to road salt.

Cultivars: 'Alba' has pure white flowers. 'Forest Pansy' has scarlet new leaves maturing to maroon. 'Flame' has double pink flowers and seldom sets fruit. 'Silver Cloud' has pink and white variegated leaves and grows 12 feet tall and wide.

Eastern redbud

Cladrastis kentukea
YELLOWWOOD

Hardiness Zones: 4–8
Size: 30–50 feet tall, 40–55 feet wide
Site: Well-drained soil in full sun.

This refined, medium-sized native deciduous tree is good for restricted spaces. It has a short main trunk with major branches starting within 6 feet of the ground. The crown is spreading and rounded. Plant it in the rear corner of the residential backyard landscape or use it as a shade tree on smaller properties. In larger areas it can be planted alongside small trees or larger shrubs to create a woodland setting. The showy, heavily fragrant, white flowers are borne in hanging chains in late spring. They resemble the flowers of wisteria. It doesn't bloom heavily every year, but when it does it is spectacular. Summer leaf color is bright green, almost with a tinge of blue. Fall color can be a clear yellow or sometimes a warm gold-orange. The zigzag branching pattern, seedpods, and smooth gray bark add a lot of winter interest.

Care: Corrective pruning is important when the tree is young to eliminate weak branch forks. Without pruning, the branching structure can be weak, inviting storm damage and ultimately decay. Prune in summer to avoid excessive sap bleeding that occurs in winter and spring. While this bleeding does not harm trees, it is unsightly and messy. Young trees should be wrapped in winter to protect the thin bark from sunscald. No serious pest problems. Trees under stress are susceptible to verticillium wilt, a soil-borne fungal disease.

Cultivars: 'Rosea' ('Perkins Peak') is a very fragrant, pink-flowered form. 'Sweetshade' has abundant white flowers.

Ginkgo biloba
GINKGO

Hardiness Zones: 4–8
Size: 50–80 feet tall, 30–40 feet wide
Site: Prefers sandy, deep, moderately moist soil but grows in almost any full-sun situation.

Ginkgo is a picturesque non-native deciduous tree with a pyramidal to spreading crown at maturity. Grow it for its shade and bold accent in the landscape. It is very adaptable to stressful situations, including poor soils, compacted soils, various soil pH levels, heat, drought, winter salt spray, and air pollution, and is therefore very urban-tolerant. It is sometimes incorrectly used as a street tree due to its extreme urban tolerance, but it is too big for this use. The unique fan-shaped leaves are medium green with a long petiole, causing the foliage to flutter in the slightest breeze. Fall color is usually chartreuse, but may be golden yellow some years. A freeze will cause the leaves to drop almost overnight, even if they are still green. The fleshy covering on the seed is extremely messy and smelly. Plant male trees if you want to avoid this. Trees may not flower (and therefore not fruit) until about 20 years old.

Care: Transplants easily and establishes itself without difficulty. Prune in spring to remove broken branches or to shape, only if necessary. Female trees produce smelly fruits, often in great abundance, which become a mushy mess when they fall in September and October, covering the ground with fleshy, strongly malodorous fruits. Leaf spotting can be seen some years.

Cultivars: 'Autumn Gold' is a male selection with a good spreading habit and bright golden fall color. 'Fastigiata' has a columnar habit. 'Laciniata' has deeply incised leaves. 'Pendula' has weak-growing pendulous branches. 'Princeton Sentry' is a nearly columnar male form.

American yellowwood

Ginkgo

Malus cultivars

FLOWERING CRAB APPLES

Hardiness Zones: 4–8
Size: 8–30 feet tall, 8–25 feet wide
Site: Prefers well-drained, slightly acidic to neutral soils. Full sun is required for best flowering and to reduce the chances of diseases.

These deciduous trees have showy white, pink, red, or purple flowers in spring. They are popular single specimen plants, but they are also effective planted in groups of three or five of the same variety. Dwarf types can be used in borders. Weeping types are especially effective next to water. A background of evergreens will set off the red or yellow fruits that persist into winter on some varieties.

Care: Fruits may present a litter problem when they drop. Prune while trees are dormant to reduce chances of fire blight. Keep the center open to reduce disease problems. Many varieties develop suckers at their base that will need pruning. Protect young trees in winter. Fire blight, cedar apple rust, apple scab, canker, Japanese beetles, scale, and several other pest problems plague these trees. The best defense against diseases is to plant one of the many resistant cultivars. Plant trees at least 500 feet from eastern red cedar, the alternate host of cedar apple rust.

Cultivars: There are hundreds of cultivars of flowering crabapple available. They vary in their flower and fruit colors, growth habit, and resistance to diseases. Here are some that are good choices for the mid-Atlantic: 'Donald Wyman', Red Jewel™, and Sugar Tyme® with white flowers; 'Adams', 'Indian Magic', 'Jewelberry', Centurion®, and 'Prairiefire' with pink to red flowers. 'Red Jade' is a weeping form with a height and spread of 12 feet.

Ostrya virginiana

IRONWOOD, AMERICAN HOP HORNBEAM

Hardiness Zones: 3-9
Size: 25-40 feet tall, 10-18 feet wide
Site: Prefers a cool, moist, well-drained, slightly acidic soil, but adapts to a wide range of landscape situations provided the soil is acidic and not waterlogged. It tolerates full sun, partial shade, and even heavy shade.

This native deciduous tree has birchlike foliage that will provide good summer shade—dense if grown in sun and more open when the tree is grown in light shade. Leaves turn a mild yellow color in fall. The straight trunk and limbs are covered with shaggy gray bark and the wood is very strong and resistant to ice and wind damage. It can be grown as a clump tree. The seeds ripen in flattened, papery pods that are strung together like fish scales or hops to form a little cone and give this tree its common name. These pods turn from light green to gray and are eaten by birds or slowly disintegrate so there is no litter problem. Trees are sensitive to road salt and compacted soil, so it is not a good street tree. Its main drawback for use is its slow growth rate, but this can be somewhat overcome if it is given supplemental water and fertilizer when young.

Care: Somewhat slow to establish after transplanting. Fertilizer young trees if you want faster growth. Water well during dry periods. A mulch of pine needles, shredded oak leaves, or shredded pine bark will keep the soil evenly moist and maintain soil acidity. Sprinkle a granular 10-10-10 plant food around plants in spring and water well to get food down into the root zone. Trees may bleed sap in late winter. No serious insect or disease problems.

'Prairiefire' Flowering crab

Ironwood

Picea omorika

SERBIAN SPRUCE

Hardiness Zones: 4–7
Size: 40–60 feet tall, 15–20 feet wide
Site: Does best in well-drained soil in full sun to part shade. It tolerates both slightly acidic and slightly alkaline soils. It does better in hot, humid weather and air pollution than most spruces.

This evergreen is has a narrow, conical shape. Trees have short, graceful branches that are retained all the way to the ground and scaly, dark brown bark. The stiff needles are dark green on the upper surface, silvery white underneath. The cones start out dark purple and mature to a reddish brown. It makes a nice specimen but also looks nice in small groupings. It can be used as a street tree.

Care: Likes adequate moisture all year and good drainage. No serious pest problems, but trees are susceptible to aphids, spider mites, budworms, and borers.

Cultivars: 'Nana' is a very slow-growing shrub form that stays at 4 to 8 feet in height and width. Zones 4–7.

Related Species: White spruce (*P. glauca*) grows 40 to 60 feet tall and is a lighter shade of green. Black Hills spruce (var. *densata*) seldom grows taller than 40 feet and is denser and more drought tolerant than white spruce, making it a good choice for landscape use. Zones 3–6.

Serbian spruce

Quercus palustris

PIN OAK

Hardiness Zones: 4–8
Size: 60–70 feet tall, 25–40 feet wide
Site: Prefers moist, rich, acidic, well-drained soil but tolerates wet and dry soils.

A well-grown oak is an asset in any landscape, usually greatly increasing property value. These deciduous native trees should be given a prominent place where they can grow to their full potential. Oaks provide food and habitat for a large number of beneficial insects and birds. Do not be put off by oaks' reputation of slow growth or susceptibility to oak wilt, which is not usually a problem in landscape situations. Pin oak has deeply lobed, sharp-pointed, glossy green leaves that turn russet, bronze, or red in fall. It is one of the best oaks for street tree use.

Care: Easier to transplant than other oaks because of its shallow fibrous root system. Acidify soil before planting and as soon as leaves start to yellow. Prune in winter only as needed. Never prune in summer, when oak wilt can be transmitted by beetles attracted to pruning wounds. Oaks are very sensitive to soil compaction, so care should be taken when heavy construction equipment is used around their roots. Iron chlorosis is a problem if soil pH is too high. Several nonserious problems affect oaks, including galls, scale, anthracnose, and lace bug. The most serious problem is oak wilt, which can be fatal.

Related Species: Swamp white oak (*Q. bicolor*) grows 40 to 65 feet tall and is easier to transplant. Zones 3–8. Northern pin oak (*Q. ellipsoidalis*) is less susceptible to iron chlorosis problems and more tolerant of city conditions, but it grows 50 to 80 feet tall. Zones 4–7. Shumard oak (*Q. shumardii*) usually grows 40 to 60 feet tall and requires a more acidic soil. Zones 5–9. Shingle oak (*Q. imbricaria*) grows 40 to 60 feet tall and has good resistance to pests. Zones 5–8.

Chinkapin oak

THE COMPLETE GUIDE TO MID-ATLANTIC GARDENING

Tilia americana

BASSWOOD

Hardiness Zones: 2–8
Size: 60–80 feet tall, 40–60 feet wide
Site: Prefers moist, fertile, well-drained soils but will grow on drier, heavier soils in full sun or part shade.

This native deciduous tree is stately and well-formed with a clean, straight trunk and a broad, rounded crown. The large, heart-shaped leaves are dark green throughout the year fading to pale green or yellow before dropping in autumn. The distinctive straplike leafy bracts support clusters of sweetly fragrant (but not very showy) flowers that are very attractive to bees. The small, gray, round fruit that is produced later persists until midwinter. This tree casts dense shade that is difficult to grow grass under. It needs adequate root space and is not tolerant of soil compaction or air pollution.

Care: Wrap young trees in winter to prevent sunscald. Prune out sprouts that develop at the base of the tree. Few insects or diseases bother it, but you may see Japanese beetles, spider mites, aphids, borers, leaf miners, or scale.

Cultivars Several cultivars do not grow as tall or wide and are better for smaller landscapes. 'Boulevard' grows 60 feet tall and only about 35 feet wide. 'Fastigiata' grows to 50 feet tall and about 35 feet wide. 'Redmond' has a uniform pyramidal habit and grows about 50 feet tall. 'Continental Appeal' has a wide, dense crown supported by narrow, ascending branches. The leaves have attractive silvery undersides, and the tree tolerates poor environmental conditions. Legend™ only grows about 40 feet tall and has a handsome pyramidal form.

Related Species: Little-leaf linden (*T. cordata*) is a non-native species more tolerant of city conditions. It grows to about 65 feet in height. 'Greenspire', the most widely used cultivar, is a vigorous grower that develops a narrow, oval crown with a straight trunk. Zones 3–7.

'Fastigiata' basswood

Zelkova serrata

JAPANESE ZELKOVA

Hardiness Zones: 5–8
Size: 50-80 feet tall, 40-60 feet wide
Site: Prefers well-drained, moist, deep, fertile soil in full sun. Tolerant of drought, wind, and pollution once established.

This deciduous tree has a graceful vase shape that often is compared to the American elm. It branches low, resulting in a short trunk. The toothed leaves are dark green in summer. Fall color varies from yellow-orange to red or reddish purple; on some trees it can be quite showy. Young trees have smooth gray bark that becomes scaly and exfoliates to expose showy inner orange-brown bark on mature trees. Its ease of transplanting and tolerance of urban conditions make it good for along city streets. It is a good shade tree for medium to large yards. The leaves are easy to rake up in fall. Choose a site where it will have room to develop the wide crown.

Care: In colder areas, plant in a protected site to avoid frost damage to young trees. Prune only as needed to shape young trees by thinning out crowded branches. Young trees are subject to frost injury in colder areas; prune out any affected parts in spring. No serious pest problems. It is susceptible to some of the same problems as elms, but to a much lesser degree. It shows fairly good resistance to Dutch elm disease and bacterial canker, but it is not immune. It also has good resistance to elm leaf beetle and Japanese beetle.

Related Species: 'Autumn Glow' has deep purple fall color. 'Green Vase' is strongly vase shaped and has good fall color. 'Green Veil' is more upright and narrow. 'Halka' is a rapid grower with a somewhat loose and open growth habit and yellowish fall color. 'Village Green' is a rapid grower with a smooth, straight trunk and rusty red fall color. 'Illinois Hardy' is more reliably cold hardy than other cultivars.

Japanese zelkova

TAKING CARE

GARDEN MAINTENANCE
AND POSSIBLE PROBLEMS

*There's no getting around the fact that all gardens need some
maintenance. The good news is that if you've prepared your soil correctly
and chosen plants well-suited to your site and climate, the time you spend
on maintenance should be minimal. Keep in mind that growing healthy
plants is the best thing you can do to reduce your overall maintenance
tasks. Well-grown plants are better able to withstand competition from
weeds, survive dry spells, and fight off pests.*

*The key to efficient garden maintenance is to know what needs to
be done and when is the most effective time to do it. There are some
maintenance tasks that you really must do if you want your garden to be
healthy and look good. Weeding is often at the top of this list, followed by
watering as needed and making sure your plants have adequate nutrition.
Then there are other grooming tasks that fall more toward the optional end
of the spectrum, such as mulching, pruning, deadheading, and staking.
These tasks will go a long way in making your gardens look better and your
plants healthier, but they aren't as crucial to overall survival.*

*This chapter focuses on those aspects of garden maintenance that really must
be addressed at some level or another and explains the best times to tackle them.
It also covers some of the most common insect, disease, animal, and cultural
problems you may face and gives suggestions on how to deal with them.*

Try to keep a healthy attitude about maintenance. Look at it as
part of the overall process of gardening. If done correctly and
at the right time, it doesn't have to become overwhelming.
And remember that it provides exercise and goes a long way
in keeping your plants healthy and more productive.

WATERING YOUR GARDEN

Adequate water is crucial to plant growth, but often difficult for the gardener to control. Since you can't always rely on Mother Nature to provide the nice, gentle weekly rainfall most plants like, you will have to be prepared to step in as needed.

Most plants do best with about one inch of water per week. Newly planted plants will need more attention to watering since their roots are shallow. Keep the soil adequately moist until they have a full year of new growth on them. Once fully established, after three to four years, most woody plants should not need supplemental watering. In hot, dry weather, plants may need watering twice a week. If autumn is dry, continue watering until the first hard frost.

Remember that your goal is to water the soil, not the plants. Encourage deep-rooted plants by moistening the soil thoroughly and then allowing it to dry out moderately before watering again. Soaker hoses, drip irrigation, and other watering devices that evenly distribute water over the soil instead of wetting plant foliage are good choices for effective watering. Avoid overhead sprinklers. Not only are they inefficient, but the wet foliage can lead to disease problems on plants.

REDUCE THE NEED TO WATER

- Chose plants based on your soil and rainfall conditions.
- Improve the water-holding capacity of sandy soils by adding organic matter.
- Cover bare soil with organic mulch.

RAIN BARRELS

A rain barrel is one of the simplest, least expensive ways to irrigate a garden. By placing it under a downspout, you can capture runoff and use it on your gardens.

CONTROLLING WEEDS

Excluding unwanted plants is probably the biggest maintenance task in any garden. The most effective way to fight weeds is to do all you can to eliminate them before you put any plants or seeds in the ground. Once a garden or landscape is planted it is important to get the desirable plants established and covering the ground as quickly as possible. A dense planting definitely reduces the potential for invasion by weeds. Mulching is a good way to keep weeds out of your garden. However, mulching is only effective when placed on soil where the existing weeds have been removed.

Weeds are easiest to pull when they are young and the soil is moist. A weekly weed-pulling walk through your garden should be enough to keep most weeds under control. You want to pull them before they go to seed or overtake desirable plants. Be sure to pull out the entire root system, as many weeds can resprout from even a tiny root fragment left behind.

If you have a large area of perennial or woody weeds, you may want to consider using a nonselective herbicide such as Roundup. If you're concerned about the potential hazards of using chemical herbicides, there are alternative herbicides such as those made from potassium salts or fatty acids.

XERISCAPING: WATER-WISE GARDENING

Xeriscaping promotes water conservation by using drought-tolerant, well-adapted plants within a landscape carefully designed for maximum use of rainfall runoff and minimum care. Water-wise landscaping incorporates these seven basic principles:

- Select plants based on their cultural requirements and group plants with similar water needs.

- Determine whether soil improvement is needed for better water absorption and improved water-holding capacity. Mix compost or organic matter into soil before planting to help retain water. Reduce water runoff by building rain gardens, terraces, and retaining walls.

- Use turf grasses as a planned element in the landscape and limit their use. Avoid impractical turf use, such as long, narrow areas, and use it only in areas where it provides functional benefits. Plant groundcovers and add hard-surface areas like patios, decks, and walkways where practical.

- Select plants that have lower water requirements or those that only need water in the first year or so after planting. Native plants are good choices because they are accustomed to local climates.

- Install drip or trickle irrigation systems for those areas that need watering. Install timers and water-control devices to increase their efficiency even more.

- Apply organic mulch to reduce water loss from the soil through evaporation and to increase water penetration during irrigation.

- Properly timed pruning, weeding, pest control, and irrigation all conserve water.

Xeriscaped landscapes are not all drought-tolerant plants and rock. They can be green, cool landscapes full of beautiful plants maintained with water-efficient practices.

TIPS FOR WEEDING

Remove the entire root system or rhizome of a weed, but be careful not to uproot neighboring plants. Use a weeding tool to get leverage if needed.

Weeds in patio blocks can be very difficult to pull by hand. For a nonchemical way to control individual weeds in a patio, sidewalk, or driveway, you can use straight vinegar, boiling water, or a propane torch.

Weeds are not necessarily ugly. Some are quite pretty. But don't be taken in. Weedy flowers such as creeping bellflower (*Campanula rapunculoides*) can quickly spread and overtake a garden, crowding out desirable plants.

KNOW THY ENEMY

An important first step in the war with weeds is to be able to identify which plants are weeds as early in their life cycle as possible. This is challenging, especially for new gardeners who are afraid to pull seedlings because they think they may be desirable plants rather than weeds. Experience will help overcome this fear. Invest in a good weed identification guide that shows weeds at various stages, including the seedling stage, and use it regularly.

Like all plants, weeds come in many forms. It's important to know how your weeds grow to be most effective in your control methods. Once you have identified the weed, learn as much as you can about the growing conditions it prefers. If possible, try to alter the soil and sunlight conditions to reduce the population.

Annual weeds live only one season but they produce many seeds. Control them by pulling before they are done flowering and have gone to seed. Corn gluten meal is an organic herbicide that will prevent seeds from germinating (pre-emergent herbicide). It can be very effective, especially on annual weeds, if used regularly for a couple of years at the recommended amounts (20 pounds per 1,000 square feet). It has the side benefit of adding nutrients to the soil as well.

Examples: lamb's quarters, wild mustard, pigweed, purslane, ragweed, crabgrass, prostrate knotweed, chickweed, shepherd's purse.

Biennial weeds form a leafy rosette their first season and flowers and seeds the next. Control them by removing the rosettes the first season or the second-year plant before it sets seeds.

Examples: mullein, queen's Anne's lace, dandelion, garlic mustard, burdock, prickly lettuce, mallow.

Perennial weeds live from year-to-year and are much usually more difficult to control. Control them by digging the entire plant, including every last bit of root if possible. Keep at it, since many of these plants also set seeds and have persistent creeping stems that will continue to plague you for years. Learn to spot perennial weeds in their seedling stage so you can get them out while they are young and easy to pull and definitely before they go to seed.

If you have persistent perennial weeds in an established garden and hand pulling has not been

Prostrate knotweed is an annual weed that thrives in dense, packed soil. Improving the soil often helps reduce the population of this weed.

Garlic mustard is a biennial weed that can wreak havoc in shaded areas. Seeds remain viable in the soil five years or more, so effective control requires a long-term commitment.

effective, you may want to consider spot treatments with a nonselective systemic herbicide such as Roundup. To apply it without harming yourself or nearby desirable plants, choose a calm day; protect yourself with long sleeves, safety glasses, and gloves; and carefully but thoroughly spot-spray individual weeds. Perennial weeds in sidewalks and driveways can also be controlled with flame torches. However this can be dangerous and should only be used where there is no risk of fire.

Examples: quackgrass, creeping Charlie, plantain, Canada thistle, canary reed grass.

Woody weeds are at least usually easier to distinguish than herbaceous weeds. The smaller they are, the easier they are to pull, so keep an eye out and try not to let them grow for more than a year before pulling. It only takes one growing season for most woody plants to become hard to eradicate by hand pulling.

Creeping Charlie, also known as creeping Jenny and ground ivy, is a low-growing perennial that prefers shady, moist spots but will grow well in sunny, dry soil as well.

Larger plants may require the use of a nonselective systemic herbicide applied directly to the plant. Cut the woody trunk low to the ground and use a disposable foam paintbrush to immediately apply a glyphosate- or triclopyr-based herbicide labeled for woody plants (such as poison ivy) on the fresh cut. The herbicide will work its way into the trunk, destroying the plants and any plants that grow from the same root system. If you are careful and selective about using these herbicides and do not use them near water, they can effectively control weeds in the garden while causing little harm to the environment.

Examples: buckthorn, poison ivy, multiflora roses, English ivy, kudzu vine.

Poison ivy and English ivy are both woody plants that can become weedy and are difficult to control once established.

WHAT'S GOOD ABOUT MULCHING

There are so many good things about mulching, it's hard to know where to start. Here's a list of the benefits:

- Keeps down weeds and makes it easier to pull weeds that do appear.
- Holds water in the soil so soil stays more evenly moist and requires less watering.
- Organic mulch improves fertility as it breaks down, adding nutrients at a slow and steady pace. Reduces soil erosion and compaction.
- Softens the impact of pelting rain.
- Helps keep nutrients from washing away during hard rains.
- Moderates soil temperatures, protecting plant roots and beneficial soil organisms from drastic swings.
- Keeps dirt from splashing up on plants. This not only makes them more attractive, but also reduces the chances of soil-borne diseases infecting your plants.
- Keeps the lawnmower and weed-whipper away from tree trunks.

The one maintenance activity that will give you the most bang for your buck is mulching. Mulching not only helps keeps the weeds down, it also helps maintain soil moisture and fertility and prevents erosion of the soil. And, a well-chosen mulch sets plants off nicer than nondescript bare soil.

MULCHING

A mulch is a protective layer of material spread on the surface of the soil. There are several good organic mulches. Select one based on your plants and garden type and what's available in your area.

WHAT TO USE

Shredded leaves make a good mulch in almost any situation, but they are not always available. Shredded bark or wood chips are good in shrub borders or woodland gardens, but they can be too coarse for flower beds. Chopped straw is good in flower beds but it's not as attractive as other mulches. Pine needles are a good choice for acid-loving plants, since they lower soil pH as they decompose. Bark nuggets or cocoa-bean hulls provide the most decorative look but they are the most expensive. Several layers of newspapers can be used to smother weeds in paths of vegetables gardens. They can be allowed to decompose naturally without harming plants. You can cover the newspaper with some other type of mulch to make it more attractive.

There are a few materials that do not do well as mulch. Grass clippings are not very attractive and they mat down and become smelly if they are not completely dry. Plus, decomposing clippings are a source of excess nutrients that can flow into a storm drain system and be harmful to wetlands. It is better to compost them before using them on your gardens. Peat moss tends to form a nonpermeable crust that makes it difficult for water to penetrate the soil. Avoid black plastic and rock mulch, which are not a good choice for any garden plant. Black plastic alone can be used in vegetable gardens, however, to warm the soil in spring. And gravel alone works well in hot, dry climates and rock gardens.

WHEN TO APPLY

Mulch is most effective when placed on soil where the existing weeds have been removed. Do everything you can to rid a new garden of weeds and weed seeds before laying down mulch. If you are mulching around existing plants, leave a 1- to 2-inch space between the mulch and the plant stem. Mulch smothering the base

Bulk mulch is usually sold by the cubic yard. To determine how much mulch to buy, keep in mind that a cubic yard of mulch will cover approximately 100 square feet when spread 3 inches deep. A 10 by 20 foot garden (200 square feet) will require about 2 cubic yards of mulch. If you only want to spread your mulch 2 inches deep, the same garden will only require 1⅓ cubic yards of mulch.

WHEN NOT TO MULCH

Snails and slugs love moist, dark places—the conditions found under mulch. If you have a problem with either of these, you may want to avoid using wood-chip mulches.

Keep mulch a few inches away from the base of trees to discourage mice from hiding there in winter.

of a plant increases the chance of disease and pest problems. Most organic mulches will need to be replenished every year or two.

You'll find that most gardening references recommend mulching your new garden after planting. This certainly is an option. However, putting the mulch down before you plant is easier and reduces the chances you will harm your tender new plants in the process of spreading it. It will also reduce the soil compaction that can result from walking around on bare soil.

FERTILIZING YOUR PLANTS

Plants get the nutrients they need from the soil, water, and air around them. Of these, the most critical for gardeners is soil, since the nutrients that plants derive from the soil may not always be in adequate supply and plants are continually using these nutrients. Chapter 1 covered the basics of soil fertility. If your soil is low in fertility or the nutrients are unavailable to your plants for some reason, you will need to supplement their diet by adding fertilizer.

Side-dressing is the process of applying granular fertilizer to an established plant. Sprinkle the granules around the plant being, careful not to get granules on plants leaves; it can burn them. Then gently scratch them into the soil, being careful not to damage roots, and water well.

HOW MUCH?

Using your soil test results, you can calculate how much fertilizer to add to get to recommended levels for your plants. If the test recommends 2 pounds of actual nitrogen per 1,000 square feet and you are using a 5-10-10 fertilizer, here is your calculation:

- 2 pounds divided by .05 = 40 pounds.
- For every 1,000 square feet of garden, it will take 40 pounds of a 5-10-10 fertilizer to supply 2 pounds of nitrogen.
- If you didn't have a soil test done, follow the directions on the package, starting with the lowest recommended amount. Be careful not to over-fertilize, which can be harmful to plants.

FERTILIZER TYPES

Fertilizers come in many different forms. They can be organic or inorganic, natural or synthetic. Natural fertilizers include composted manure, bone meal, fish meal, and blood meal. They are available to plants over a longer time, are generally safer to use because they do not burn plants readily, and are less likely to leach from the soil into surrounding waterways. Synthetic fertilizers provide more nutrients to plants quickly, but they have the risk of burning plants if applied too heavily and they do readily leach from the soil. Additionally, the manufacture of synthetic fertilizers requires a great deal of fossil-fuel input and does not reuse nutrients from other living sources like organic fertilizers do.

Synthetic fertilizers are available in several forms, including granular, tablets or spikes, water-soluble powders, and liquids. They can also be slow-release, which allow you to apply a greater amount of fertilizer all at once with reduced risk of burn. Slow-release fertilizers are more expensive, but they only need to be applied once during the growing season. They are good for container gardening, where plants would otherwise require regular applications of water-soluble fertilizer.

Choose a type of fertilizer based on your garden conditions or plants. Granular fertilizers are good for covering large areas and for side-dressing. Tablets and spikes are meant to be buried in the soil and are usually used for large trees and shrubs. Powders and liquid fertilizers are easy to use and provide almost instant nutrients to your plants. They can be expensive to use in large gardens, however.

Strong, healthy, beautiful plants grow in healthy soil rich in nutrients. The best approach to making sure your plants have all the nutrients they need is to build a healthy soil using organic fertilizers and soil amendments. A regular application of compost, rotted manure, or other organic fertilizers should keep your soil's fertility at adequate levels. If you find that certain elements are lacking, you may need to supplement some plants with quicker-acting synthetic fertilizers on an as-needed basis. With all fertilizer applications, be sure to carefully follow the manufacturer's directions to avoid over fertilizing or leaching into nearby water features.

UNDERSTANDING THE LABEL

As you learned in chapter 1, plants require about fifteen different elements to grow well, the most important of these being nitrogen, phosphorous, and potassium. These three nutrients are the main ingredients in most commercial fertilizers. Their amounts are indicated by numbers such as 10-5-5 on packaging. Nitrogen is often higher than the other two elements since it is used in larger quantities by most plants. Some fertilizers contain only one or two of these elements. Superphosphate, for example, is sold as 0-20-0.

In addition to these three main nutrients, fertilizers will have filler material and some may have secondary nutrients such as sulfur (S), calcium (C), or magnesium (Mg) in them. Some may also have elements that can raise or lower soil pH. If you are growing acid-loving plants such as azaleas or blueberries, you may want to look for an "acid fertilizer."

If you prefer to use organic products instead of inorganic fertilizers, there are several options. To improve your overall soil fertility, add compost, well-rotted manure, fish emulsion, or Milorganite. Improve soil nitrogen content by adding soybean meal, alfalfa meal, or compost. Soil phosphorus content can be increased by adding bone meal or rock phosphate, and potassium comes from granite dust, greensand, seaweed, or wood ashes. Be sure to follow your soil test recommendations carefully to avoid adding excess nutrients to your garden.

As a general rule, use a fertilizer lower in nitrogen and higher in phosphorus (e.g. 5-10-5) for flowering and fruiting plants and one higher in nitrogen (e.g. 20-10-10) for foliage plants. Too much nitrogen will encourage lush leafy growth and fewer flowers and fruits. It is best to try not to add ingredients other than what is recommended in your soil test. The unneeded ingredients can do more harm than good. Along the same lines, you should really only apply a secondary nutrient if you are sure a plant is deficient; because amounts that are too high can lead to toxicity, which is just as bad. A soil test is the best way to indicate if a trace element is lacking.

WHEN?

The best time to fertilizer most plants is spring, when they are putting on their most active growth. Annuals and vegetables will probably require additional fertilizer during the growing season. Don't fertilize in late summer or fall. Plants need to start winding down for winter dormancy and you don't want to encourage new growth at this time. It can lead to problems with winter survival.

The first number on a fertilizer package represents the percent by weight of nitrogen, the second phosphorous, and the third potassium.

COMPOSTING

Composting is essential to successful gardening. Compost not only adds valuable nutrients to the soil at a slow pace, it improves soil texture—both in sandy soils and in clay soils—and makes a great mulch. It also provides a way for you to recycle your yard waste into a useful product. It's no wonder many gardeners refer to it as "black gold."

Compost is created by mixing high-carbon and high-nitrogen materials proportionately with air and moisture. High-carbon materials include straw, hay, leaves, sawdust, shredded newspaper, and pine needles. High-nitrogen materials are generally succulent green plant parts such as grass clippings, weeds, perennial prunings, and vegetables. Kitchen scraps such as eggshells, vegetables and fruits, and coffee grounds can also be added to the compost pile. Do not add meat scraps, bones, or grease, which attract rodents and other pests. There is debate about whether or not you should add diseased plants or weeds with seed heads to the compost pile. Some experts feel the heat of a properly working compost pile will be enough to kill off the diseases and seeds. Others don't think it's worth the risk. To be on the safe side, you should probably avoid both.

Composting can be a challenge for small-space and city gardeners, but it is worth it. An ideal location for a compost bin is one hidden from view but close enough for you to easily bring stuff to it and haul the finished compost away. It is also nice to have the compost pile near a water source so you can add water during dry spells, but it's not necessary. Some type of creative screening is usually necessary.

1 **YOU WILL NEED SOME WAY** to contain your compost. You can simply pile up the debris, but it is more effective to build or purchase some type of bin.

2 **BUILD YOUR COMPOST PILE** as materials become available, layering carbon materials alternatively with nitrogen materials. If you have an abundance of carbon materials, put some of them on the side until more nitrogen materials become available. Too many green grass clippings can mat down and prohibit the composting process. Mix them with looser materials such as straw or dried leaves or allow them to dry in the sun before adding them to the pile.

3 **IT'S A GOOD IDEA** to add thin layers of topsoil or finished compost to a new pile to introduce the decay organisms that create compost. Add water as needed to keep the pile moist but not soggy.

4 **TURN YOUR COMPOST REGULARLY**—once a week if possible—to get air into the pile. If you don't turn your pile, you'll still get compost, but it will take a lot longer. If you want to speed up the composting process, turn the pile more often, add more nitrogen-rich materials, and shred or chop the carbon materials before adding them to the pile so they break down more quickly. Ideally, you will have several piles going at the same time so you will always have some finished compost available. You'll know your compost is ready for the garden when it is dark, crumbly, and most of the plant parts are decomposed.

MAKING AN ACCURATE DIAGNOSIS

Do not jump to conclusions. The insect or disease symptoms you see first may not be the cause of the problem.

Find the "root" of the problem. Many problems that show up on the above-ground plant parts are actually symptoms of root problems.

Examine all plant parts. Look under leaves and, when possible, at the roots.

Know what the plant is supposed to look like when it's healthy and how long it's supposed to live.

Many pests are plant-specific. If more than one plant is affected, there is a good chance it may be due to cultural or environmental problems.

NONCHEMICAL CONTROL STRATEGIES

Grow disease- and insect-resistant varieties of plants.

Get rid of damaged plant parts as soon as you see them. Do not put in compost pile.

Clean up your garden in fall to remove overwintering sites for pests. (But remember you will also be removing overwintering sites for beneficial insects.)

Spray sturdy plants with a strong water stream from a hose to dislodge some insect pests.

Hand-pick larger insects and egg masses and put them in a jar of soapy water.

Identify and encourage beneficial insects.

Install barriers such as floating row covers and cut worm collars whenever possible.

If possible, rotate annual crops so they are not always growing in the same soil each year.

Sow vegetable and annual seeds earlier or later to avoid certain stages of a pest's life cycle.

WHAT CAN GO WRONG

The key to managing garden pests and problems is to really get to know your garden and the plants in them. Early detection, accurate diagnosis, and understanding how pesticides work are essential for pest management. It is much easier to control a problem before it reaches epidemic proportions. Monitor your garden carefully and often. If you spot a problem, identify it correctly, find out what is causing it, and decide if it is serious enough to warrant attention. To make an accurate diagnosis, consult a reliable reference or website or have the plant examined by an expert at your local university or garden center.

Keep in mind that most pest problems are purely cosmetic. And most healthy plants can tolerate loosing up to 30 percent of their leaves without suffering long-term damage. You have to decide what your level of tolerance is and determine whether you want to take action or live with the problem. Your goal should be to attack any problem with the least toxic method and avoid using pesticides of any type whenever possible.

Many problems are due to cultural conditions, such as poorly drained soil, incorrect soil pH, insufficient sunlight, or improper planting, rather than insects or diseases. And often by the time you identify the problem it is too late to effectively control it this season. Make notes about your observations and plan to take preventative measures next growing season.

STEPS TOWARD A HEALTHY GARDEN

- Choose the right plant for the site.
- Improve the soil before planting.
- Provide adequate water.
- Mulch.
- Remove diseased and insect-eaten plant parts are soon as you notice them.
- Keep the garden free of weeds.
- Clean up plant debris in fall.
- Grow a wide variety of plants.
- Maintain adequate spacing between plants.
- Encourage beneficial insects.
- Rotate crops in a vegetable garden.

CULTURAL AND ENVIRONMENTAL PROBLEMS

The majority of plant problems usually aren't caused by insects or diseases but rather by inappropriate growing conditions, environmental conditions, and mechanical damage. Growing conditions (soil texture and pH, sunlight, fertilization, and plant spacing) and plant selection are usually within the gardener's control, as well as avoiding most types of mechanical damage. But environmental conditions, such as hail and wind storms, are usually outside the gardener's control.

Some plant problems are easy to diagnose, and some are a little more complicated because they can be caused by a number of things. Here are some common plant problems and the cultural, environmental, and mechanical conditions that can cause them. Some solutions are easy and within your control; others are more difficult to adjust and may require a better plant for the site. If you don't have any of the conditions listed, then move on to possible insect or disease problems.

Make an accurate diagnosis of a problem by careful observation and consultation of a reliable reference. A timely and proper diagnosis may prevent the need for toxic chemical use or the replacement of the plant.

TROUBLESHOOTING GUIDE

FEW OR NO FLOWERS

Condition: Dead flowers are prohibiting new flower production.
Solution: Remove spent flowers before they go to seed (deadhead).

Condition: Flower buds pruned off before plants bloom.
Solution: Prune plants at the appropriate time, usually right after blooming.

Condition: Plants are getting too much nitrogen.
Solution: Cut back on fertilization and wait a year or two for the plants to respond.

Condition: Plants aren't getting enough sunlight.
Solution: Move plants to a sunnier location and replace with shade-tolerant plants.

In years with a late frost, early-blooming magnolia flowers may turn brown and refuse to open.

Wilting is caused by the plant's inability to take up water.

Condition: Plants are overcrowded.
Solution: Thin out some plants.

Condition: Plants are too young. Century plant, crab apples, and flowering cherry all need to reach a certain age before they flower.
Solution: Be patient.

Condition: Inadequate winter cooling. (Plants that require a period of cold temperatures to flower include spring bulbs, crab apples, and lilacs.)
Solution: Choose another plant that does not require a certain number of days of cold temperatures to flower.

Condition: Plants aren't receiving the necessary day length. For example, glossy abelia and weigelas both require long days to set flower buds while chrysanthemums and gardenias require short days.
Solution: Replace with plants that don't have day-length requirements.

Condition: Frost or cold temperature damage caused flower buds to turn brown and not open.
Solution: Hope for better conditions next winter or replace plant with something hardier.

Condition: Alternate blooming. Some plants, flowering dogwoods and flowering crab apples included, are biennial bloomers, having heavy flower production every other year and very light flower production on alternate years.
Solution: Choose a plant that doesn't exhibit this trait.

WILTING

Condition: Plant is receiving insufficient water.
Solution: Increase watering or replace with plant better suited to the site.

Condition: Plant is receiving too much water.
Solution: Improve soil drainage to increase air spaces around roots or replace with plant better suited to the site.

Condition: Fertilizer burn.
Solution: Water plants thoroughly to flush away excess fertilizer and avoid overfertilizing in the future.

Condition: Intense heat or wind.
Solution: Water for short term, but choose a better plant for the site for long term.

Condition: Transplant shock.
Solution: Make sure a newly planted plant has adequate water and protection from the sun.

Condition: Mechanical damage to roots.
Solution: Avoid cultivating too deeply around plant roots.

POOR OVERALL GROWTH OR DISTORTED GROWTH

Condition: Lack of sunlight.
Solution: Replace with a plant better suited to the available light conditions.

Condition: Unseasonable weather.
Solution: Protect plants with cloches and season extenders, if possible, until weather improves. Replace dead plants.

Condition: Natural dormancy. Some plants drastically slow down their growth and even disappear if conditions are unsuitable.
Solution: Surround plants with other interesting plants that will fill in when plants go dormant.

Dried, brown spots or edges on leaves, called leaf scorch, occurs when a shade plant such as hosta receives too much direct sun.

Condition: Nutrient deficiencies.
Solution: Have the soil tested and apply recommended soil nutrients.

Condition: Damage from insecticide, herbicide, or fungicide sprays.
Solution: Only apply pesticides on calm days and follow directions carefully. Prune off injured plant parts and rinse plants well with water.

Condition: Air pollution.
Solution: Rule out all other problems, including insects and diseases. Check with neighbors to see if they are experiencing similar problems on the same plants. There is nothing that can be done about the effects of air pollution.

LEAF BROWNING, BLEACHING, OR SCORCHING

Condition: Lack of water.
Solution: Increase watering or replace with plant better suited to the site.

Condition: High winds dry out plants.
Solution: Water well during hot weather and provide protection from wind if possible.

Condition: Sunburn from too much light.
Solution: Shade young plants until they are established. On older plants, move to a shadier spot.

Condition: Road salt damage.
Solution: Leach salts from soil with heavy watering. Improve soil drainage. Avoid salting in winter, if possible. Prune out damaged branches. Replace with salt-tolerant plants.

Condition: Winter injury.
Solution: Prune out dead branches. Water plants well all season long and in fall up until the ground freezes. Apply a winter mulch once plants are dormant.

YELLOWING LEAVES

Condition: Lack of nitrogen causes general yellowing of leaves, including the veins.
Solution: Increase nitrogen by applying fertilizer.

Condition: Iron chlorosis causes yellowing between the veins of leaves.
Solution: Lower soil pH by adding sulfur and maintain soil acidity by using acidic fertilizers and mulches. Or replace plant with one more tolerant of alkaline soil.

Condition: Overwatering.
Solution: Allow soil to dry out, if possible. Consider improving soil drainage or moving plant to a new location.

Yellow leaves caused by soil pH that is too high.

NEEDLE BROWNING ON EVERGREENS

Condition: Normal browning and dropping of older needles nearest the trunk.
Solution: None needed.

Condition: Road salt toxicity.
Solution: Flush soil with water to try to wash out salts. Replace plants with something more tolerant of road salt.

Needle browning; evergreens, such as pines, regularly lose inner needles as new needles are produced along the ends of branches.

BARK DAMAGE

Condition: Lawn mower or weed-whipper has cut through bark.
Solution: Protect trees by installing mulch around them or covering the lower trunk with a protective ring. Fertilize and water trees showing minor damage; they often recover with proper care if the trunk isn't completely girdled.

Condition: Mice or rabbits have chewed through bark.
Solution: Protect young plants by wrapping hardware cloth around them in winter until they have a layer of corky, hard bark. Fertilize and water trees showing minor damage; they often recover with proper care.

Condition: Sunscald and frost crack.
Solution: Wrap young trees in winter to prevent scalding and splitting of the trunk. Fertilize and water trees showing damage; they often recover with proper care.

Frost cracks occur on thin-barked trees such as maples and honey locusts. The condition can kill trees by cutting off the uptake of water and nutrients through the bark.

DISEASES

Most diseases are caused by fungi or bacteria that thrive on cool, moist conditions. They can be spread by wind or splashing water or live in the soil. Signs that your plant may have a disease problem include leaf spots, water-soaked areas, discolored stems and roots, cankers, or powdery areas. Prevention in the form of good site selection and proper planting distance is the best way to avoid disease problems. If disease problems become severe you'll need to pull up the infected plants and choose another plant for that spot.

ORGANIC CHEMICAL CONTROLS

Fungicides and bactericides can be both synthetic and organic, but all can be dangerous and should only be considered when absolutely necessary for the health of the plant. Here are some organic chemicals used to prevent diseases:

Bordeaux mix is effective against both fungi and bacteria. It is composed of copper sulfate and can be quite toxic to humans and animals at high levels.

Copper is a component in several organic fungicides. They can be effective in controlling diseases, but can also be quite hazardous to the environment and human health if misapplied.

Baking soda-based fungicides are relatively safe and are good for minor infections but are not always effective on severe outbreaks.

Sulfur is a relatively safe fungicide that's quite effective but it must be used regularly. It can also build up in the soil and eventually lower the soil pH.

Most chemicals provide a protective barrier on the leaf blade surface. To be effective, they must be applied before the spore lands on the leaf, so timing is important. The chemical must also be renewed periodically as it wears off. Once symptoms are well developed, it's usually too late to spray for the current season. The following spring, treat with an appropriate chemical before symptoms appear. Always read the label carefully before applying any chemical controls.

PRACTICES TO HELP DETER DISEASES

Many fungal diseases require water on plant leaves to develop. Avoid wetting leaves when watering by using methods that water the soil, not the plants. Water in the early morning so plants have time to dry off well before cooler evening temperatures set in.

Diseases often develop on plants that are stressed, so keep your plants as healthy as possible.

Once a disease has infected a plant, prune off diseased tissue as soon as possible and destroy it to get rid of the pathogen.

To reduce infection from soil-borne diseases, improve drainage and water less frequently so the soil has a chance to dry out between watering cycles.

Thin out some plants to increase air circulation and speed up drying of foliage.

Many diseases look worse than they are. Tar spot is a fungal disease that affects maples. It is rarely serious enough to threaten the health of trees, but heavy infestations make for unsightly trees and early leaf drop. It is not worth the expense and effort to treat a tree with fungicides. The most effective treatment is to rake and destroy leaves in fall to reduce the number of overwintering spots where spores can be produced the next spring.

VIRUSES

Viruses are microscopic organisms that act somewhat like diseases. They disrupt normal cellular processes, reproducing and spreading readily by insects and by wind. They are also spread by gardeners' hands and tools. Symptoms of virus infection include dead spots, abnormal dark green and light green mosaic and mottling of leaves, growth distortion, stunting, and ring patterns or bumps on plant foliage. Plants do not always die from viral infections, but there is no practical cure for infected plants. It is best to dig up the infected plants and find something else better suited to the location. There are some plant varieties that are more resistant than others.

Aster yellows is caused by a viral-like organism that is spread by leafhopper feeding. Plants become discolored and have irregular, stunted growth and often flowers do not open and leaves turn yellow. Aster yellows can affect over 300 plants, including both ornamentals and vegetables. It is difficult to control and infected plants should be destroyed to reduce chances of infecting nearby plants. Floating row covers can help protect vegetables from the insects that spread this virus. Controlling weeds around gardens can also help, since many weeds harbor the virus.

COMMON PLANT DISEASES

BLACK KNOT

Black knot

PLANTS AFFECTED: *PRUNUS SPECIES (PLUMS AND CHERRIES, INCLUDING ORNAMENTAL TYPES)*

Description & Symptoms: This fungal disease first shows up as greenish knots or elongated swollen areas on twigs and branches. Fungal spores form during wet weather in spring and the knots appear six months to a year after infection. They develop into black, corky, cylindrical masses that slowly enlarge and elongate. They can range in size from ½ to 1½ inches in diameter and up to 12 inches in length. The knots eventually cut off the flow of water and nutrients to the branches, causing stunting, wilting, and dieback.

   Prevention & Control: Prune and destroy infected branches during fall and winter. Cut at least 4 inches below visible signs of infection. On the trunk or large limbs cut out knots down to the wood and at least ½ inch outward past the diseased tissues. You can use a copper-based preventative fungicide in spring on highly valued trees. There are resistant varieties of many trees and shrubs available.

CANKERS

Canker on tree trunk

PLANTS AFFECTED: *MAINLY FOUND ON WOODY PLANTS*

Description & Symptoms: Cankers are localized areas on a stem, trunk, or branch that are sunken or raised and are usually dry, dead, and often discolored. Cankers may ooze or bleed. Infected branches will die back and trunk cankers may girdle and kill entire trees. Canker-causing organisms can be spread by wind, splashing water, and contaminated tools.

   Prevention & Control: Cankers generally infect weakened or unhealthy trees and shrubs. Do everything you can to keep your plants growing well—including providing proper fertilization and water—and free from insects and other disease problems. Avoid wounding or severe pruning of plants. Prune out and destroy any branches infected with cankers. Disinfect pruning tools between pruning cuts with a mild bleach solution. There are no practical chemical controls for cankers.

CROWN AND ROOT ROTS

Shriveled stems and foliage are often symptoms of fungal rot disease.

PLANTS AFFECTED: *ALL PLANT TYPES BUT MAINLY HERBACEOUS PLANTS*

Description & Symptoms: Crown and root rots (often called "blights") are caused by soil-borne fungi, bacteria, and nematodes. They thrive in wet, poorly drained soils, but can survive in any type of soil. They may or may not require wounds to enter plants. Crown rots generally occur at the soil line. The infected tissue may turn brown to black and may migrate upward and downward around the outside of the tissue from the point of infection. When the pathogen has almost completely encircled the stem, the plant will begin to show wilting and dieback symptoms. Symptoms of root rots typically do not show up until late in the infestation when the disease has progressed beyond control. Leaves appear drought stressed and may turn color. They eventually die and fall off. Perennial plants may survive several years before the disease becomes fatal.

   Prevention & Control: Improve soil drainage and avoid overwatering on heavy soils. Allow soil to dry out before watering. Plant trees and shrubs at the proper depth. Look for resistant varieties or less-susceptible plants if your soil is heavy or you've had problems in the past. Remove and destroy infested plants, if possible. Practice crop rotation in the vegetable garden. Chemicals are not generally effective in controlling root rots.

DAMPING OFF

PLANTS AFFECTED: *SEEDLINGS OF ALL PLANT TYPES*

Damping off is a soil fungus that causes new seedlings to collapse and die.

Description & Symptoms: The fungi that cause this disease are prevalent in all soils and are the cause of death of seeds and seedlings. The fungi can even attack seeds before they germinate. Seedlings are attacked just at or below the soil level, causing them to fall over. Older seedlings are more resistant, but can still be infected. They show dark lesions on the lower stems and roots that stunt and weaken plants.

Prevention & Control: Damping off is worse in soil that is rich in nitrogen, is constantly wet, or is too warm or too cold for good seedling growth. Prevention is the key. If starting seeds indoors, use clean equipment, a sterile planting medium rather than garden soil, and good quality seeds. Avoid high temperatures, excess moisture, and poor light conditions. Cover newly planted seeds with a thin layer ($\frac{1}{6}$ to $\frac{1}{4}$ inch) of milled sphagnum moss. For outdoor sowing, improve soil drainage if needed. Don't add nitrogen fertilizer until seedlings have produced at least one pair or true leaves. Don't plant seeds until soil is warm enough.

FIREBLIGHT

PLANTS AFFECTED: *ALL MEMBERS OF THE ROSE FAMILY, WHICH INCLUDES APPLES, FIRETHORN, MOUNTAIN ASH, AND PEARS*

Fire blight causes leaves and branches to look as if they have been burned by fire.

Description & Symptoms: This bacterial disease spends the winter in infected bark and oozes out in spring to attract the insects that will spread it. It spreads especially rapidly in warm weather (65°F or warmer). Infected plant parts suddenly wilt and turn dark brown or black, looking like they have been scorched by fire. Severe cases can girdle and kill major branches or whole trees.

Prevention & Control: The main way to prevent this devastating disease is to only prune susceptible plants while they are dormant. Prune out infected branches 12 to 15 inches below an visible discoloration and destroy the debris. Disinfect pruning shears in between cuts. A preventative spray of copper sulfate before bud break in spring can help prevent infection. It must be repeated at 5- to 7-day intervals until the end of bloom so it is only worth it on high-value trees. Avoid overfertilizing; young, tender growth is more susceptible to infection. There are resistant trees and shrubs.

LEAF SPOT

PLANTS AFFECTED: *ALL PLANT TYPES*

Rudbeckia species (especially the popular cultivar 'Goldsturm') can be afflicted with several leaf spot diseases, especially when they are grown where overhead watering is used and the disease organisms are easily splashed from plant to plant.

Description & Symptoms: Leaf spots are the result of a number of diseases, most caused by fungi, but some are bacterial. Spots vary in size and color and can be small, distinct areas or coalesce to form large, irregular shapes. Spots often have concentric rings or dark margins. Leaves may turn yellow and drop. While these diseases can make foliage quite unsightly, they rarely kill plants. Established plants can tolerate quite a bit of leaf spotting and defoliation, especially if it happens late in the growing season. Newly planted shrubs and trees are at higher risk, and defoliation of a young plant three years in a row can be fatal. Moisture is required for infection and most damage occurs during wet weather in spring.

Prevention & Control: Keep foliage as dry as possible. Avoid overhead watering and water early in the day so plants have plenty of time to dry off before cooler temperatures set in. Do not touch plants while they are wet; this can spread the disease. Increase air circulation by pruning inside branches and removing some nearby plants. Grow resistant varieties when possible. Prune out and destroy diseased tissue. Get rid of dead leaves and stems in fall to remove next year's inoculum. Avoid overfertilizing; young, tender growth is more susceptible to infection. Fungicides will only prevent leaf spots, not cure infected leaves, and must be applied in early spring and repeated every two weeks or so. It may be best to replace plants that are continually plagued by leaf spot diseases.

POWDERY MILDEW AND OTHER MILDEWS

PLANTS AFFECTED: *ALL PLANT TYPES*

Monarda is often afflicted with powdery mildew.

Description & Symptoms: Mildews are caused by fungi and appear as whitish powdery patches on leaf surfaces. As the disease progresses, black spots may appear in the powder and leaves, flowers, and fruits may be misshapen. The fungi thrive on warm days and cool nights so mildews often show up in fall and spring. They are more unsightly than harmful to plants, and plants rarely die from mildew infections.

Prevention & Control: Increase air circulation by pruning inside branches and removing some nearby plants. Avoid overhead watering and water early in the day so plants have plenty of time to dry off before cooler temperatures set in. Do not touch plants while they are wet; this can spread the disease. Grow resistant varieties when possible. Prune out and destroy diseased tissue. Get rid of dead leaves and stems in fall to remove next year's inoculum. If you want to make the effort to prevent this disease on landscape plantings without using synthetic fungicides, Cornell University has developed a baking-soda-based spray: Mix 1 tablespoon baking soda and 1 tablespoon horticultural oil with 1 gallon of water. Spray each plant completely about once a week, starting before infections appear. It's a good idea to test the spray on a few leaves before spraying the entire plant to make sure the spray won't do more damage than the disease. All fungicides must be applied as a preventive treatment.

RUSTS

PLANTS AFFECTED: *ALL PLANT TYPES*

Rust on hollyhock

Description & Symptoms: These fungi are apply named. Yellow, orange, or brown spots usually appear first on the undersides of leaves and stems. Plants are usually weak and stunted and have yellow leaves that wither and drop early; severely infected plants may die. Some rusts, such as cedar apple rust, alternate between two plant hosts and you need both plants present within a certain distance for the disease to occur.

Prevention & Control: Many rust fungi can't infect their host plants unless the foliage remains wet for at least 6 hours. Water early in the morning so foliage dries quickly and avoid overhead watering. Give plants ample spacing for good air circulation. Clean up plant debris in fall. Remove and destroy any infected plant parts as well as severely infected plants. Plant resistant varieties when available.

Japanese beetles are among the most frustrating and difficult pests to control. Plants that are especially susceptible to feeding include roses, Rose of Sharon, mountain ash, grey birch, Japanese and Norway maples, crab apples, elms, lindens, Prunus species, sassafras, and black walnut. Plants that show some resistance to Japanese beetles include ashes, dogwoods, hollies, red and silver maples, oaks, pears, sweet gums, tulip trees, and lilacs. You can set commercially available pheromone traps a week before expected emergence in your area; make sure that traps are no closer than 50 feet from vulnerable crops and are hung 5 feet off the ground. Handpick any stragglers. Japanese beetles prefer roses over almost any other plant. If you have roses, try to kill as many Japanese beetles as you can when they first appear. This may help save your other plants from severe infection.

HAND PICKING

If insect populations are low, they can be picked off affected plants by hand. Wear gloves if this makes you squeamish. Drop the insects into soapy water to kill them. All can be harmful to beneficial insects.

INSECTS

The first thing to keep in mind when talking about insects in a garden is that most are not only harmless but are vital to the health of a garden or landscape. In fact, only about 1 percent of all the insect species on earth cause problems for humans. The rest are important as pollinators, decomposers, predators on other insects, and other activities vital to the cycle of life. So, some insect damage is a good thing. It shows that your garden is a biodiverse habitat providing important food sources for the native insects that are the basis of our entire food chain.

Consequently, the first thing you need to do with insects is accurately identify them as friend or foe. Some of the well-known "good guys" are predators such as lady beetles, walking sticks, wasps, and praying mantis. Spiders are also beneficial predators. But the list of insects that should be also considered beneficial based on their importance as bird food includes unlikely candidates such as grasshoppers and locusts, plant bugs, lacewings, leafhoppers, and spiders. Dragonflies are important mosquito-eaters, and remember that those hungry caterpillars turn into beautiful butterflies and moths. Ants do not damage plants; if you see them they are probably there feeding on honeydew that has been excreted by some other insect or on sap excreted by the flower itself, as in the case of peonies.

Keep in mind that most plants can tolerate quite a bit of insect feeding before they are actually harmed by it. Even if you do have a large population of Japanese beetles or another devastating feeder, it's still never worth it to use insecticides. Not only are they toxic to you and your garden guests, they destroy too many beneficial insects. If an insect problem becomes so bad that the health of your plant is questionable, you should consider replacing the plant with something better suited to the conditions. It's cruel to lure birds and butterflies to your landscape and then use herbicides, insecticides, and other pesticides that can poison and destroy them.

The best way to confirm an insect problem is to catch the critter in the act or to find evidence of them from their shed skins, droppings (or "frass"), webbing, honeydew (a sticky substance secreted by some insects), sooty mold, pitch, galls, or slime trails. There are other clues to help in your diagnosis. Insect damage is caused by chewing, piercing-sucking, or rasping. Examine the plant to help determine what

Lacewings may look dainty, but their larvae are voracious eaters, consuming a wide variety of insects pests, including aphids, scale, spider mites, and thrips.

type of insect is doing the damage. Chewing damage can be the entire leaf, holes, skeletonization, and leaf mining. Piercing-sucking damage results in spittle on plants, leaf spotting and stippling, galls, and distorted leaves. Rasping damage shows up as strips of discoloration.

ORGANIC AND BOTANICAL INSECTICIDES

Organic insecticides are derived from natural substances, often bacteria. Botanical insecticides are naturally occurring chemicals found in plants. Don't be fooled by the names, however. These products are not necessarily less toxic than synthetic insecticides; in some cases they can be just as harmful. Most have a short residue period, however, so they tend to break down more quickly in the soil and air than synthetic pesticides. If you do use any of these products, every precaution should be taken to protect yourself and the environment. Wear protective clothing, spray on a calm day, and only treat severely infected plants that are worth the risk and effort.

Bacillus thuringiensis (Bt) is one of the safest and most effective organic insecticides. It is very target-specific bacteria, usually used for caterpillars or flies, so it is among the least toxic to beneficial insects. It needs to be eaten by the insect pest, so good coverage of the plant is required.

Diatomaceous earth is the skeletons of long-dead microscopic organisms. It is quite effective in killing any crawling insects that travel over its rough edges. It is only harmful to humans if it is inhaled.

Horticultural oils surround and suffocate insects and are often used to treat scale. They are often called organic, but many are synthetically produced. Heavier dormant oils are usually applied in the dormant season because they can be dangerous to leaves. Summer oils are lighter and less harmful to leaves.

Insecticidal soaps work by removing the waxy cuticle layer on insects, which causes them to dry up and die. Soaps work slowly, but they can be quite effective, especially against soft-bodied insects such as aphids. They are safe for humans, but some plants may be damaged by soaps. Test spray a small part of your plant before spraying the whole thing.

Pyrethrum is a fast-acting contact poison extracted from pyrethrum daisy. It is effective on most insects, including beneficials, but does not control mites.

Rotenone is a botanical insecticide mainly used to control leaf-eating caterpillars and beetles. It is quite toxic to animals, including humans, and really shouldn't be used.

Sabadilla is a contact poison most effective against true bugs with little residual toxicity. It is, however, very toxic to honey bees.

GALLS

Galls are examples of plant problems that look much more serious than they are. These abnormal growths or swellings are found on leaves, twigs, or branches and may be simple lumps or complicated structures, plain brown or brightly colored. Galls are usually caused by insect and mite feeding or egg laying. They may also develop as a response to infections by several kinds of fungi, bacteria, and viruses. In most cases, galls are unsightly but will not damage the plant and chemical control is not effective.

Galls are common sites on some plants and are often confused with normal features such as seed-bearing parts.

COMMON INSECTS PESTS

Aphids feeding on flower buds

APHIDS

PLANTS AFFECTED: *ALL*

Description & Symptoms: Aphids are small (up to ¼ inch), somewhat pear-shaped, soft-bodied insects. They can be orange, green, black, or white. There can be many generations in one growing season. They suck the juices from leaves and stems, causing foliage to be pale or have yellow spots. Whole leaves may turn yellow or brown, or may be curled, puckered, or stunted. Flower buds may be seriously damaged and the blossoms distorted. A sticky honeydew residue is another sign of aphid feeding. Check for clusters of these common pests on the underside of leaves or clustered on new buds, tender stems, and young leaves. Some aphids carry plant viruses and diseases.

    Prevention & Control: In most cases aphids are not life-threatening, but they will make your plants unsightly. They tend to be a bigger problem during hot, dry spells. Give infested plants daily blasts of water with your garden hose to dislodge the insects before they become too numerous. Be sure to spray the undersides of the leaves. Heavy infestations can be treated with insecticidal soap. Many beneficial insects feed on aphids, including lacewings, ladybugs, aphid midges, and braconid wasps. These are all available commercially. Clean up your gardens in fall to eliminate aphid eggs that may overwinter.

Bark borers

BARK BORERS

PLANTS AFFECTED: *WOODY PLANTS*

Description & Symptoms: Bark borers are among the most devastating of insect pests. They are the larvae of various insects, but mainly beetles. They tunnel and feed under the bark, causing branch dieback, structural weakness, overall decline, and often death. Infestation sites also provide entry points for plant diseases. Because the insects are commonly concealed beneath the bark or in the wood, it can be difficult to detect and control them. Borer damage often shows up in the upper branches of tree crowns first and progresses downwards as the tree weakens. Common symptoms include sudden wilting and discoloration of foliage in the tree tops and branch die-back. Infested trees will probably also exhibit D-shaped emergence holes and sinuous or zigzag patterns in their bark. Major borer pests include bronze birch borer, emerald ash borer, rose cane borer, and lesser peach tree borer.

    Prevention & Control: Borers usually attack weakened plants, so healthy trees and shrubs are your best defense against these pests. Select the right plant for the conditions, prevent injury to plants, water during dry spells, and practice proper pruning techniques and timing. Woodpeckers are known to consume borers in large quantities, so if you see them on your trees, that may be a sign of borers. Cut and destroy infested wood by chipping or burning. You may need to consider use of chemical insecticides to protect particularly valuable plants. On large trees, this will probably require professional help.

Colorado potato beetle

BEETLES

PLANTS AFFECTED: *ALL TYPES*

Description & Symptoms: There are many beetles that damage garden plants, both in their larval and adult stages. They damage plants by eating leaves, stalks, flowers, and sometimes plant roots as well as boring into stems, flower buds, and fruit. Their damage can appear as chewing damage, holes, and skeletonizing. Some of the most common beetle pests found on ornamental plants include Asiatic garden beetles, black blister beetles, tiny jumping flea beetles, metallic green and copper-colored Japanese beetles, and rose chafers, also known as rose bugs or rose beetles. Vegetable beetle pests include the asparagus beetle, carrot weevil, Colorado potato beetle, Cucumber beetle, flea beetle, harlequin bugs, Japanese beetles, and Mexican bean beetle.

Prevention & Control: Light infestations can be controlled by handpicking, sometimes two to three times a day during their heaviest feeding. You can crush them or drop them in a pail of soapy water. A spray of pyrethrum and isopropyl alcohol, mixed at the rate of one tablespoon of alcohol per pint of diluted pyrethrum mixture can be applied every 3 to 5 days for 2 weeks, or until the problem is corrected. To prevent future problems, cultivate your garden soil late in the fall and again in the spring to expose beetle eggs, larvae, and pupae to the weather and to predatory birds. An application of a heavy organic mulch around vulnerable plants may prevent emergence of beetles from the soil.

CATERPILLARS AND CANKERWORMS
PLANTS AFFECTED: *ALL*

Holes in leaves are usually caused by chewing insects such as caterpillars.

Forest tent caterpillar

Description & Symptoms: Moths and butterflies are welcome in most gardens, where they drink nectar from flowers and help pollinate flowers. However, their larvae—caterpillars—can be devastating to garden plants. Caterpillars come in many shapes and sizes but all have mouthparts adapted to chewing plant tissue, preferably tissue that is soft and succulent. They can feed as leafminers between the upper and lower surfaces of the leaves or as skeletonizers, eating only the leaf surface. Cankerworms, also known as inchworms, are small caterpillars with legs only at the front and back. They "inch" their way along stems and leaves of trees and shrubs, feeding as they go. The two most destructive types are spring and fall cankerworms

Prevention & Control: Inspect plants regularly for these insects, which are usually easy to see. Pick them off by hand whenever practical. Search for and destroy leaves with egg masses or branches that have large populations of caterpillars on them. The bacterial insecticide *Bacillus thuringiensis* (Bt) is effective against many types of caterpillars and cankerworms. Cankerworms can be prevented from climbing trees by placing a barrier of sticky material around the trunk in spring and again in fall to trap the cankerworms as they crawl up the trunks. Remember that most caterpillars are choice bird food and many turn into beautiful butterflies so light infestations should be tolerated whenever possible.

CUTWORMS
PLANTS AFFECTED: *VEGETABLES AND FLOWERS, SOMETIMES VINES AND TREES*

Cutworm feeding on grass blade

Description & Symptoms: Cutworms are large, fleshy caterpillars that curl up when disturbed. Surface cutworms feed on the succulent tissue of newly transplanted or emerging plants. One insect can destroy many plants in just one night. They chew or cut off the plant at or just below the soil surface, leaving most of the plant toppled over on its side. Climbing cutworms feed on any above-ground plant part, but especially like tender young shoots and buds. Both surface and climbing cutworms are nocturnal, hiding under dirt clods or soil during the day. Subterranean cutworms live in the soil, feeding day and night on roots and underground stems, causing plants to wilt and die. Confirm their presence by digging in the soil.

Prevention & Control: Surface cutworms are easily controlled by placing cutworm collars around young plants. Cut paper towel tubes into 3-inch lengths and place a section around each transplant when you plant. Push it at least a half inch into the ground. By the time the tubes start to disintegrate, your plants will be large enough to sustain damage from cutworms. Inspect your plants at night with a flashlight and pick off and destroy any cutworms you find. Cultivate the soil thoroughly in late summer and fall to expose and destroy larvae and pupae.

LEAFHOPPERS

PLANTS AFFECTED: *ALL TYPES*

Leafhopper

Description & Symptoms: Leafhoppers are small insects that hop or fly away when disturbed. Both the nymph and adult stages feed on plants, causing leaf stippling, stunting, and distortion of leaves and stems. This feeding weakens plants and they may spread viral diseases. Plants are often covered in honeydew, which encourages sooty black mold.

Prevention & Control: Leafhoppers are difficult to control. Use floating row covers to exclude leafhoppers from vulnerable vegetable crops. To control serious infestations, use insecticidal soap laced with isopropyl alcohol. Alternately, spray pyrethrum on all surfaces, particularly the undersides of leaves, at 3- to 4-day intervals. Clean up and destroy infected plants before winter and keep nearby weeds down. Anything you can do to attract chickadees, purple finches, sparrows, swallows, titmice and wrens to your yard with the appropriate food and shelter will help reduce your leafhopper population.

LEAF MINERS

PLANTS AFFECTED: *ALL TYPES*

Leaf miner damage on columbine

Description & Symptoms: Leafminers are the larvae of flies, moths, or beetles that lay eggs on the undersides of leaves. Upon emerging, the larvae tunnel into the leaves between the upper and lower surfaces, feeding on the inner part. Affected leaves have light green to brown serpentine mines or tunnels and dark specks of excrement or tiny maggots may also be visible. Affected leaves may turn completely brown or yellow, look blistered or curled, or collapse. Leafminers can also damage stems below the soil and carry black leg and soft rot diseases.

Prevention & Control: Regularly check the undersides of the leaves of vulnerable plants for telltale rows of small, chalky white eggs, then scrape them off and destroy them. Pick off and destroy all infested leaves, pruning back stems to healthy areas. If leafminers are a recurring problem, consider covering vulnerable plants in the spring with floating row covers. Leafminers overwinter in the soil; their chances of survival are reduced with a thorough fall cleanup. Remove weeds, especially lamb's-quarters. Cultivate soil in the late fall to expose these insects to birds and other predators. Do not add soil or plant material that may be infested to the compost pile.

PLANT BUGS

PLANTS AFFECTED: *ALL TYPES*

Four-lined plant bug damage

Description & Symptoms: There are several plant bugs that can harm garden plants, the most common being chinch bugs, harlequin bugs, squash bugs, stink bugs, and tarnished plant bugs. Both the nymphs and adults damage plants by sucking juices. Damage often shows up as white and yellow blotches on leaves and results in leaf wilt and drop. Large discolored areas on leaves can develop, and affected leaves may wilt, curl, and turn brown. Two of the biggest problems for gardeners are the tarnished bug and the four-lined plant bug. The tarnished plant bug injects poison into young shoots, flowering buds, and fruit while it punctures cells to suck juices. It also carries fire blight disease. Damage includes black spots; pitting on stem tips, buds, and fruit; deformed roots; blackened terminal shoots, and ruined flowers. Four-lined plant bug damage shows up as small discolored areas on leaves. Injured areas will turn black or become translucent and after several weeks the dead tissue may drop out, leaving small holes. The adults feed on the upper surfaces of leaves and are voracious feeders. The topmost leaves will generally be the first to be injured.

Prevention & Control: Most of the damage from plant bugs is cosmetic, so try to live with it whenever possible. Handpicking is effective for some plant bugs, especially if you manage to get rid of the very first adults and their eggs as they appear. Weed control helps deter some plant bugs. Clean up leaf litter in fall to reduce overwintering sites. Prevent damage to vulnerable crops with floating row covers.

SCALES

PLANTS AFFECTED: *ALL TYPES*

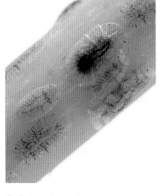

Scale insects on stem

Description & Symptoms: Scales are sucking insects with hard or soft scale coverings. After hatching, the young scales wander over the plant searching for a spot in which to settle and begin producing their distinctive shell coverings. Adults are sedentary. The most common symptoms are yellow leaves or dropping leaves. Plants may also be stunted and covered with sticky honeydew that attracts ants. You will need a hand lens to detect the tiny young scales; they will resemble minute, animated pancakes.

Prevention & Control: Minor infestations can be scraped off plant surfaces with a dull knife or your fingernail or treated with a cotton swab dipped in rubbing alcohol, making sure the alcohol contacts the scale insects. Spray more seriously infested plants with a mixture of 1 cup isopropyl alcohol, 1 tablespoon insecticidal soap, and 1 quart of water; repeat applications every three days for two weeks. Since the young scales are unprotected by the waxy covering that renders mature scales difficult to kill, sprays timed to coincide with the crawler stage are most effective.

SLUGS AND SNAILS

PLANTS AFFECTED: *HERBACEOUS PLANTS, ESPECIALLY THOSE GROWN IN MOIST, SHADY SPOTS*

Slug damage on hostas

Description & Symptoms: Slugs are not true insects, but rather soft-bodied, soil-dwelling creatures. They are ½ to 3 inches long and can be gray, black, or brown. Slugs have rasping mouth parts and produce holes in leaves, stems, flowers, and fruits. The succulent tissue of young seedlings and bulbs are especially susceptible to slug damage. Sometimes whole leaves may be sheared off by slugs. Because slugs are soft-bodied and require cool, moist conditions to survive, they avoid the sun during the day and hide under leaves, rocks, boards, and overturned pots in the garden. They are nocturnal and can be found feeding on plants at night or in the early morning. Most overwinter in the soil as eggs. The eggs hatch in spring and the young begin to feed. The young look like the adult and increase in size as the summer progresses. Eggs are laid in the ground in fall in protected locations.

Prevention & Control: Hand-pick slugs in the evening or early morning. Trap slugs by placing boards around plants to act as collection sites. Collect and dispose of the slugs that are escaping the midday sun on the undersides of the boards. Sink shallow pans of beer into the ground so the lip is at ground level to attract slugs. Empty the pans at least twice a week. Place a 5-inch grit barrier such as diatomaceous earth, sharp or builder's sand, ground gritty nut hulls, or ground eggshells around plants. The sharp edges lacerate the bodies of slugs, causing them to dehydrate and die. Copper strips or copper wire placed around the base of plants or pots makes an effective barrier or deterrent.

SPIDER MITES

PLANTS AFFECTED: *ALL TYPES*

Description & Symptoms: Spider mites suck juices from plants, causing them to look stippled, dull, and unhealthy. Leaves become bronzed, curled, and completely enveloped in webbing when infestations are severe. Leaves may drop and plants may suffer from overall reduction in vitality. When a leaf or branch is tapped over a white sheet of paper, the mites appear as small specks of pepper that move. As many as 10 generations may occur each year. Reproduction of the two-spotted spider mite is favored by hot, dry conditions, so serious damage is likely to occur in mid-July to September.

   Prevention & Control: Regularly spray all sides of the plant—including leaf undersides—with a strong stream of water to dislodge spider mites. Remove and destroy severely infected plant parts. Adult female spider mites overwinter under loose bark, in cracks in the soil, in leaf litter, and in other protected places. There are several natural predators that feed on spider mites. Insecticidal soaps are effective if used frequently until the problem is under control. A summer application of horticultural oil can be very effective in controlling spider mites. Follow label directions to avoid damage to some plants that may be sensitive.

Spider mites and their damage

SQUASH VINE BORER

PLANTS AFFECTED: *SQUASHES, PUMPKINS, GOURDS, CUCUMBERS, MELONS*

Description & Symptoms: This fat white caterpillar with a brown head tunnels into the main stem of vining plants near the base to feed. The most obvious symptom of damage is the sudden wilting of all or part of a vine. You may also see moist, sawdust-like debris (frass) piled outside of small holes. If you cut such a vine lengthwise, you will probably find one or two caterpillars.

   Prevention & Control: Your best defense is to try to prevent these pests. Clean up all weeds. Cut and destroy any plant stalks that may harbor overwintering eggs or pupae. Rotate the location of vulnerable plants. Protect crops with floating row covers, but remove them when plants begin to flower. Pull up crops vulnerable to squash vine borer as soon as they finish bearing and put them in a large, preferably clear, plastic bag. Tie the bag and leave it in the direct sun for a week or so, and you will destroy a major source of next year's borer population. Bt (*Bacillus thuringiensis*) is useful if applied early in the season just as the borers are entering the plants and then re-applied at weekly intervals. An effective if somewhat tedious mechanical control method involves slitting affected stems lengthwise in the area of the borer hole, removing the insect, and binding the stem together with green twine. You can also handpick the easily visible eggs from the main stems near the base of the plants; they are brown to reddish-brown and disk-shaped.

Squash vine borer damage

ANIMAL PESTS

Insects and diseases aren't the only pests you'll find in your garden. Deer and rabbits are often more serious and difficult to control. Moles, voles, and groundhogs can present serious problems as well.

DEER

If deer are a problem in your area, you are not alone! Many gardeners are plagued by deer feeding. Deer tend to leave torn leaves or stalks with ragged edges as they tear or jerk plants when feeding. Their damage tends to appear higher up on trees and shrubs than rabbit damage. Male deer can also injure plants when they rub their antlers on trees; saplings are especially vulnerable. Signs are vertical scrapes and shredded bark on saplings, exposing the wood.

RABBITS

A few rabbits nibbling here and there is usually not a big problem, but when their populations are high their feeding can be devastating. They can be especially troublesome in spring, when young, tender plant material becomes widely available.

A 2- to 3-foot wire mesh fence around the garden is the best rabbit deterrent. The bottom of the fence must be secured to the ground or buried 3 inches in the ground so rabbits can't burrow under it. The wire mesh should be 1-inch or smaller so the rabbits can't squeeze through. You can also protect individual plants with wire cylinders which can be removed after plants have matured and are no longer appealing.

Several types of odor and taste repellents are available. Most are water soluble and need to be applied after every rain, making them labor intensive. In addition to commercially available products, you can also try blood meal, ground hot pepper, chili powder, talcum powder, or human hair placed around plants.

Rabbits thrive when they have suitable habitat adjacent to sources of food. Eliminate all brush and brush piles, stone piles, and weed patches near plantings, and establish plantings as far away as possible from the edges of thickets and woods and from areas where rabbits are known to be.

TIPS FOR DETERRING DEER

- Owning a large dog can be effective in deterring deer.
- The best long-term solution for a serious deer problem is to install some type of fencing, which must be at least 8 feet tall to be effective and often isn't very attractive.
- You can also make plant choices based on deer feeding. For starters, plant a wide variety of plants so an entire section of your landscape won't be eliminated in one meal. Although no plant can really be considered "deer proof" under all conditions, deer generally avoid plants with thorns, aromatic plants, and plants with leathery, fuzzy, or hairy foliage.
- Once deciduous trees reach about 6 feet in height and their bark has become corky, they are out of reach of deer browsing. Young trees can be protected with a wire cage.
- Planting patterns can deter deer as well. Deer do not like to cross hedges or solid fences where they can't see what's on the other side. They do not like to force their way through dense shrubs or shrubs with thorns and firm branches. By massing plants, you will discourage deer from feeding in the center of the planting, where you can plant more-susceptible plants.
- There are many repellents available. However, all of them are temporary solutions and they require a lot of time and effort to be effective.

A plant's resistance to deer feeding is affected by fluctuations in deer populations, availability of alternative food, the time of year, environmental factors, and even individual animal preference. This arborvitae shows severe deer feeding.

A dog can be a good deterrent. Any other scare devices should be considered temporary; a rabbit may run, but will return when the immediate threat is gone and it learns that the device is not harmful. Complete eradication is difficult because rabbits often are mobile and numerous enough to fill any empty niche created when other rabbits are removed.

Live traps are especially effective in winter. Use apple slices, corn (on cobs), dried apples, or rabbit droppings as bait. Rabbits can be very hard to catch—use a cover over the trap to simulate a hiding place and position it in feeding spots. Check traps at least twice a day so that any rabbits caught can be released immediately, as well as other animals or birds. It is inhumane in the extreme to allow an animal to remain in a trap without food or water for any length of time.

MOLES, VOLES, AND MICE

Moles are insectivores, eating mainly grubs and worms, so for the most part, they are beneficial in keeping insect populations in check. It is their shallow feeding tunnels that cause distress for gardeners. They often uproot plants as they tunnel along.

Voles also build elaborate surface runway systems, 1 to 2 inches wide, with many burrows. Their runways and tunnels can also cause roots to dry out, creating problems for many shrubs. Voles can cause extensive damage to woody landscape plants in winter when they girdle the bark from the lower trunks. Voles and mice, both of which are plant eaters, often use mole tunnels for access to seeds, bulbs, and roots.

Trapping is the most successful and practical method for controlling moles. Use several traps set in the most recently constructed tunnels. To determine the best place to put a trap, press down portions of the tunnel. The next day, observe which areas have been raised. Where the soil has been raised is considered an active tunnel and the trap should be placed there. If the trap fails to catch the mole after two days, the mole has probably changed habits or the runway was disturbed too much while setting the trap and the mole detected it. In either case, the trap must be re-set.

Moles can be flushed out of their tunnels with water. Open the molehill, poke a garden hose into the hole, and turn the water on for 10 to 15 minutes. Watch for the animal to emerge and then dispose of it.

Buried fencing of small mesh or tightly woven hardware cloth controls moles, voles, and mice in small gardens. The fence should be slightly above the soil surface and extend 18 to 24 inches below ground. The underground portion should be bent outward (away from the protected area) in an L shape.

Signs of rabbits include distinct round droppings around plants, gnawing on stems of older woody plants, clean-cut clipping of young stems and leaves, and in winter, tracks.

Moles, voles, and gophers are all underground rodents that can wreak havoc on a garden by pushing up soil mounds and uprooting plants.

Control voles using snap-type mouse traps baited with apples placed in the surface runaways or burrows. Eliminate weeds, groundcover and litter in and around crops and cultivated areas to reduce the capacity of these areas to support voles. Mow lawns regularly. Small piles of pea gravel placed around the base of fruit trees prevent voles from girdling the lower trunk in winter.

There are no commercially available repellants for these pests, but castor bean plants growing around a garden have shown to repel moles.

GROUNDHOGS

Groundhogs can be especially troublesome for vegetable and flower gardeners. They eat almost any plant material and are especially fond of tomatoes. They may also burrow under garden sheds or other outdoor structures.

The best way to keep groundhogs from damaging your garden is to prevent their access with a strong 4-foot fence buried 12 inches in the ground. An electric fence wire placed 4 to 5 inches off the ground and the same distance outside the fence should be used to prevent the groundhog from climbing over the fence. They can also be live-trapped with fresh fruit or vegetables used as bait. Pre-bait, but don't set the trap for several days until the groundhog is accustomed to using it as a feeding station. Place traps near the burrow entrance just before daylight and remove before it gets dark outside. Do not relocate the trapped animal. Some states require that the animal be turned over to animal control to be humanely destroyed. This is to prevent the spread of rabies and the creation of problems at the new location.

RESOURCES LIST

STATE EXTENSION WEBSITES

Delaware
http://ag.udel.edu/extension

Rhode Island
http://cels.uri.edu/ce

Maryland
www.umd.edu/outreach

Connecticut
http://www.extension.uconn.edu

New Jersey
http://njaes.rutgers.edu/extension

Pennsylvania
http://extension.psu.edu

New York
www.cornell.edu/outreach

Massachusetts
www.umassextension.org

SOURCES OF PLANTS

http://plantinfo.umn.edu

NATIVE PLANTS

**Lady Bird Johnson Wildflower
Center.** www.wildflower.org/explore.
Information on individual species,
including garden and landscape use.
Native plant lists by state.

Plant Native. www.plantnative.org.
Native plant lists by state and lists of
native plant suppliers in each state.

USDA Plants Database. http://plants.
usda.gov. Information on individual
species.

PHOTO CREDITS

INDEX

COMMON PLANT NAMES

Also available from
CREATIVE PUBLISHING
international
Where Homeowners Go for Expert Answers

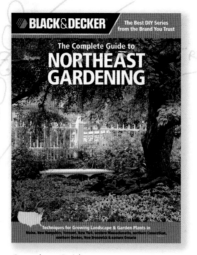

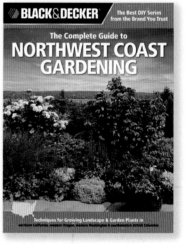